Targeting the Computer

KENNETH FLAMM

Targeting the Computer

Government Support and International Competition

THE BROOKINGS INSTITUTION
Washington, D.C.

Library of Congress Cataloging-in-Publication data:

Flamm, Kenneth, 1951–
  Targeting the computer.

  Includes index.
  1. Computer industry—Government policy—United
States.   2. Computers—Research—Government policy—
United States.   3. Computer industry—United States—
Technological innovations.   4. Competition, International.
I. Title.
HD9696.C63U516466   1987   338.4'7004'0973   87-11706
ISBN 0-8157-2852-2
ISBN 0-8157-2851-4 (pbk.)

9 8 7 6 5 4 3 2 1

THE BROOKINGS INSTITUTION is an independent organization devoted to nonpartisan research, education, and publication in economics, government, foreign policy, and the social sciences generally. Its principal purposes are to aid in the development of sound public policies and to promote public understanding of issues of national importance.

The Institution was founded on December 8, 1927, to merge the activities of the Institute for Government Research, founded in 1916, the Institute of Economics, founded in 1922, and the Robert Brookings Graduate School of Economics and Government, founded in 1924.

The Board of Trustees is responsible for the general administration of the Institution, while the immediate direction of the policies, program, and staff is vested in the President, assisted by an advisory committee of the officers and staff. The by-laws of the Institution state: "It is the function of the Trustees to make possible the conduct of scientific research, and publication, under the most favorable conditions, and to safeguard the independence of the research staff in the pursuit of their studies and in the publication of the results of such studies. It is not a part of their function to determine, control, or influence the conduct of particular investigations or the conclusions reached."

The President bears final responsibility for the decision to publish a manuscript as a Brookings book. In reaching his judgment on the competence, accuracy, and objectivity of each study, the President is advised by the director of the appropriate research program and weighs the views of a panel of expert outside readers who report to him in confidence on the quality of the work. Publication of a work signifies that it is deemed a competent treatment worthy of public consideration but does not imply endorsement of conclusions or recommendations.

The Institution maintains its position of neutrality on issues of public policy in order to safeguard the intellectual freedom of the staff. Hence interpretations or conclusions in Brookings publications should be understood to be solely those of the authors and should not be attributed to the Institution, to its trustees, officers, or other staff members, or to the organizations that support its research.

*To Esther and Jerry
and Dianne*

Foreword

PUBLIC policies that foster research and development of new technology are frequently justified on both economic and national security grounds. In the United States, national security has been the primary justification for government policies supporting innovation in technology-intensive industries. But in recent years accelerating international competition has made the economic consequences of national policies that affect such industries a central issue for debate.

In this book Kenneth Flamm, a research associate in the Brookings Foreign Policy Studies program, analyzes the role of government in the development of computers—a technology and industry that have become symbols of rapid innovation. The economic importance of this industry over the last forty years spurred government involvement even when no obvious military motive was evident. Flamm traces the roots of government support for computer technology in the United States, Western Europe, and Japan, and outlines how those policies evolved over time in response to changes in both economic and security concerns. He concludes that the ways in which investments in computer technology have been organized, as well as the amount of funding, are important in explaining the industry's course of development. In the future the economic arguments for public efforts to stimulate investment in computer technology are likely to become even more compelling and may well lead to policies different from those dictated by military requirements.

The author is grateful to John A. Alic, Nestor E. Terleckyj, and Larry Westphal for providing many useful comments on a long first draft of the manuscript. He also received helpful suggestions on some or all parts of the manuscript from Charles Bashe, Ramon Barquin, Robert Costrell, Bob O. Evans, Peter Evans, Joseph Fennell, Sidney Fernbach, Harry

vii

G. Hedges, Robert Z. Lawrence, Richard R. Nelson, Almarin Phillips, William B. Quandt, F. M. Scherer, John D. Steinbruner, Shigeru Takahashi, Akio Tojo, Richard Thomas, Jack E. Triplett, Victor Vyssotsky, and Clifford M. Winston.

In addition, the author would like to thank Glen Bacon, Eric Bloch, Arnold Cohen, Fernando Corbató, Kent Curtis, Michael Dertouzos, Robert M. Fano, Daniel L. Flamm, David S. Flamm, Craig Fields, A. G. Fraser, Kazuhiro Fuchi, Katsuya Hakozaki, Robert E. Kahn, J. C. R. Licklider, Robert Lucky, John McCarthy, William C. Norris, Jack Osborne, Emerson W. Pugh, Sidney Rubens, T. Saito, Paul B. Schneck, Robert Spinrad, Kenneth G. Stevens, Jr., James Thornton, Gordon Welchman, Terry Winograd, Lowell Wood, and Cliff A. Warren for giving generously of their time in personal interviews and conversations that contributed much to this volume.

Jeff Marzilli and Daniel A. Lindley III provided research assistance, and Paul Morawski and Carole Newman helped to extract needed data from computer tapes. Barbara de Boinville and Caroline Lalire edited the manuscript, and Daniel A. Lindley III and Margaret A. Siliciano verified its factual content. Florence Robinson prepared the index. Ann M. Ziegler, Virginia Riddell, Kathryn Ann Ho, and Maxine Hill provided secretarial support.

Funding for this study was provided in part by grants from the Ford Foundation, the German Marshall Fund of the United States, and the John D. and Catherine T. MacArthur Foundation. The author and Brookings are grateful for that support.

The views expressed in this book are those of the author and should not be ascribed to those persons or organizations whose assistance is acknowledged or to the trustees, officers, or other staff members of the Brookings Institution.

BRUCE K. MACLAURY
President

April 1987
Washington, D.C.

Contents

1. Introduction   1
   The Computer as a High-Tech Product *4*
   The Military Link *6*
   A Fast-Growing Industry *8*
   An International Industry *10*
   The Nature of Commercial Competition *12*
   The Issues *14*
   Summary *18*

2. The Economic Impact of Computer Technology   19
   A Bird's-Eye View of Computers *19*
   Measuring Improvements in Performance *21*
   Declining Costs *25*
   Elasticity of Demand *29*
   Social Benefits *32*
   The Rate of Return on Investments *35*
   Summary *40*

3. Federal Support for Computer Technology   42
   A Brief History *42*
   The Legacy of the Fifties *43*
   Funding Research and Development *44*
   The Defense Department *47*
   The Atomic Energy Commission *78*
   The National Aeronautics and Space Administration *84*
   The National Science Foundation *85*
   The National Institutes of Health *90*
   Summary *91*

4. Government Policy and the American Computer Industry · 93

Research and Development *93*
Procurement *107*
Fiscal Assistance *110*
Market Structure *113*
Software *121*
Summary *123*

5. Government and Computers in Japan and Europe · 125

Technology Policy in Japan *125*
Technology Policy in Europe *153*
Summary *168*

6. National Technology Policy: Past, Present, and Future · 173

The Past: A Summary *173*
The Present: Probing the Technological Frontier *185*
The Future: New Technology for American Industry *196*

Appendixes

A. Modeling the Cost of Information Processing Capacity *207*
B. Social and Private Rates of Return on Investment in Computer Technology *223*
C. U.S. Government Expenditure on Computer Research and Development *240*
D. Information Technology R&D in Japan and Europe *248*

Index · 256

Text Tables

1-1. Ranking in High Technology as Assessed by Chief Executives of More Than 200 European Firms · 4
1-2. Research Intensity of Selected American Industries · 5
1-3. U.S. Expenditures on Research and Development by Source of Funds, Selected Years, 1930–61 · 7
1-4. The Worldwide Operations of U.S. Computer Firms, 1977, 1982 · 11
2-1. The Declining Cost of Computer Hardware, 1957–78 · 27
2-2. Computer Production in Relation to Gross National Product, 1958–85 · 29
2-3. Estimated Rates of Return on Investments in Computer R&D · 38
3-1. Federal Funding of Mathematics and Computer Science Research, Fiscal Years 1967–86 · 46

3-2. Federal Funding of Mathematics and Computer Science Research in Universities and Colleges, Fiscal Years 1973–86   47

3-3. IPTO Funding for Computer Research, Fiscal Years 1974–84   53

3-4. IPTO Funding as Percent of Defense Department Support for Computer Science Research, Fiscal Years 1976–84   54

3-5. Federal Expenditures in Advanced Computer Research by Subject Area, Fiscal Years 1983–85   62

3-6. National Science Foundation Grants for Computer Facilities, Fiscal Years 1956–70   86

3-7. Major Computing-Related Programs of Three Civilian Federal Agencies, Fiscal Years 1984–87   92

4-1. Government and Private Funding of Research and Development at Selected Companies, Fiscal Years 1949–59   96

4-2. Government and Private Funding of Research and Development at Selected Companies, with DOD, NASA, and AEC Share, Fiscal Year 1963   97

4-3. Federal Share of Research and Development Funds in the Office, Computing, and Accounting Machines Industry, 1972–84   99

4-4. Federal Support in Relation to Computer R&D, by Industry, Universities, and FFRDCs, Fiscal Years 1972–84   102

4-5. The Federal Role in Computer-Related Research, Fiscal Years 1967–84   104

4-6. IBM's R&D in Relation to the U.S. Computer Industry, 1972–84   106

4-7. IBM Sales of Special Products and Services to U.S. Government Agencies, Selected Years, 1956–73   108

4-8. Distribution of Federal Computers by User Agency, Selected Years, 1966–81   109

4-9. Federal Computers as a Percentage of U.S. Computer Installations, 1972–80   110

5-1. Major MITI Research Programs and Cooperative Research Associations since 1962   132

5-2. Percent Distribution of Industrial R&D by Product Field and Social Objective, Japan 1983   135

5-3. Information Technology R&D in Japan, 1970–84   138

5-4. Types of Research and Development Performed, by Sector, Fiscal Year 1983   142

5-5. Selected Tax Measures Favoring the Japanese Computer Industry   148

5-6. Fiscal Measures Benefiting the Japanese Computer Industry, 1972–81   150

5-7. Government Subsidies to Computer and Microelectronics Development, Three European Countries, 1967–80   155

5-8. Business Expenditure on Research and Development in the Office and Computing Machines Industry, Three European Countries, Selected Years, 1965–81   161

5-9. Average Annual Expenditure on Computer and Microelectronics
Programs in France, West Germany, and the United Kingdom,
1967–80   162

5-10. International Comparison of Industrial R&D in Computers,
Selected Years, 1965–83   169

Appendix Tables

A-1. Average Price of Computer System Components, 1955–78   215

A-2. Measures of Component Performance, 1955–78   216

A-3. Price (Adjusted for Performance) per Unit Bandwidth, System
Components, 1955–78   218

A-4. Value of Major Components as Share of Computer System Cost,
1955–78   220

A-5. Fisher "Ideal" Price Indexes for Computer Systems, 1957–78   221

A-6. Unweighted Average Rates of Change, Real Computer Price,
1958–85   222

B-1. Internal Social Rate of Return on Investment in Computer
Technology   226

B-2. Impact of Key Parameters on Social and Private Return   233

B-3. Rates of Return on Computer R&D with Normal Foreign Sales   234

B-4. Rates of Return on Computer R&D with No Foreign Sales   236

B-5. Social Rates of Return and Private Pricing Behavior with
Minimum Sustainable Profits   239

C-1. R&D Expenditure by Computer Producers in the Early 1950s   241

C-2. NSF Data on R&D Funds in the Office, Computing, and
Accounting Machines Industry, 1972–84   242

C-3. Federal- and Company-Funded R&D in the Office, Computing,
and Accounting Machines Industry, 1981–84   243

C-4. Support for Computer-Related Research, 1967–86   245

C-5. Estimated Funding and Performance of Basic Computer Research,
1979, 1981, 1983   246

D-1. Expenditures on Information Technology R&D in Japan, 1970–84   249

D-2. Selected MITI Support for Computer Technology, 1970–85   250

D-3. Role of Japan Electronic Computer Corporation in Japanese
Computer Demand, 1960–81   252

D-4. Liberalization of the Japanese Computer Industry   254

D-5. Japan's Tariff Rates on Computer Hardware and Integrated
Circuits   255

Text Figures

1-1. U.S. Trade Balance in High-Technology and Other Manufactured
Products, 1970–84   2

1-2. National Shares of Total World Exports in Selected Technology-
Intensive Products, 1984   3

1-3. Constant-Dollar Shipments of U.S. Computer Industry, 1958–85   10

2-1. Basic Elements of a Computer 20
2-2. Effect of Declining Memory Cost on Computer System Design, 1955–78 23
2-3. Real Price Indexes for Major System Components, 1957–78 24
2-4. Real Price Indexes for Other System Components, 1957–78 26
2-5. Rates of Change in Computer System Cost, 1958–78 28
2-6. Quantity of U.S. Computer Systems Capacity Installed per Unit Output, 1957–78 30
2-7. Social Benefits from the Decline in Computer Cost 33
4-1. Defense Share of Defense- and Company-Funded R&D, Selected Companies, 1956–85 98
5-1. Public Support for Information Technology R&D in Japan, 1970–84 140
5-2. Computer Purchases and Assets of the Japan Electronic Computer Corporation, Fiscal Years 1961–81 146
6-1. Public versus Private Investments in Technology 182

Appendix Figure

B-1. Benefits from Advances in Computer Technology 228

CHAPTER ONE

Introduction

THERE are important links between advancing technology and a high standard of living. Technology-intensive products raise incomes directly by increasing productivity and the quality of the goods and services produced. More indirectly, when the innovator can collect some of the benefits as a technological "rent," further investment in developing new technology is stimulated. The United States is an "inventor" country, and rents that it collects by selling its superior technology abroad directly benefit the domestic economy. U.S. industry sells technology-intensive manufactures to the world and imports, on the whole, simpler goods (see figure 1-1).[1]

Advanced products are responsible for much of the dramatic postwar increase in foreign operations by U.S.-based companies. Superior knowledge or technology gives American firms a competitive edge in overseas markets that more than compensates for the costly disadvantages of operating in a foreign country.[2] The commanding lead that the United States once enjoyed in many technology-intensive products, however, has shrunk in the past decade (see figure 1-2). The United States still dominates trade in aircraft, computers, engines, and agricultural chemicals, but Japan shows great strengths in consumer electronics, instruments, and communications equipment. Europe is strong in drugs, plastics, and chemicals.

1. National Science Foundation, National Science Board, *Science Indicators, 1982* (Government Printing Office, 1983), pp. 20–23.
2. The theory and evidence that support this view are summarized in John H. Dunning and Alan M. Rugman, "The Influence of Hymer's Dissertation on the Theory of Foreign Direct Investment," *American Economic Review*, vol. 75 (May 1985), pp. 228–29; and Richard E. Caves, *Multinational Enterprise and Economic Analysis* (Cambridge: Cambridge University Press, 1982), chaps. 1, 7.

Figure 1-1. *U.S. Trade Balance in High-Technology and Other Manufactured Products, 1970–84*

Billions of 1972 dollars

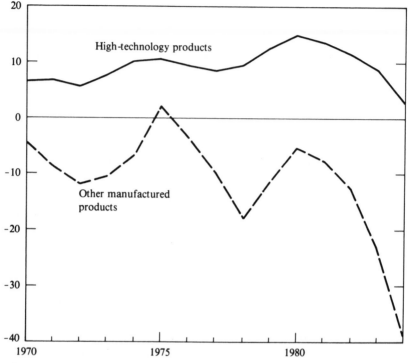

Source: National Science Foundation, National Science Board, *Science Indicators: The 1985 Report* (Government Printing Office, 1985), pp. 11, 198.

Other industrialized countries, particularly Japan, trail close behind in many applications that were pioneered in America. Indeed, they have reached or exceeded U.S. technology in a spectrum of products. Evaluations of technological strengths are always subjective to some degree since they necessarily involve qualitative assessments of nonquantifiable factors. But knowledgeable and disinterested third parties regard commercial Japanese technology as being on a par with that of the United States in much of electronics and manufacturing and ahead of the United States in areas of robotics and certain advanced materials, such as high-performance ceramics and semiconductor wafers (see table 1-1).

This may not be particularly surprising; it is cheaper after all to catch up than to lead. But it does mean the engine of technological advance has been installed in vehicles other than our own, and the track is no

Figure 1-2. *National Shares of Total World Exports in Selected*
Technology-Intensive Products, 1984

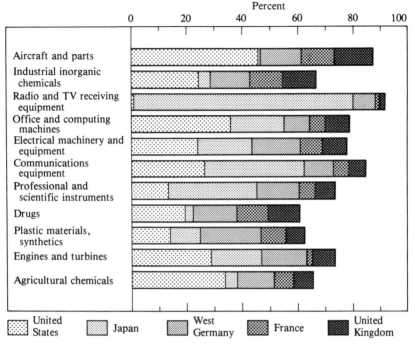

Source: Unpublished data from the National Science Foundation.

longer exclusively ours to travel. Economic competition from abroad
has generated a broad array of new proposals in the United States,
including increased incentives for U.S. firms to form cooperative research ventures, tax breaks to stimulate industrial research, even the
formation of new government agencies dedicated to maintaining America's commercial technology base. At the very least, considerable
technological rents received by American producers—and increasingly
paid out by American consumers—are at stake in the new competitive
international environment. At worst, disputes over the rules of the game
for investment and trade in these products may seriously disrupt the
international system.

This book explores the relationship between government policies and
the growth of high-technology industries around the world. To make this
vast theme more concrete, a single industry—computers—is analyzed.
This industry is in many ways the epitome of high technology. Numerous

Table 1-1. *Ranking in High Technology as Assessed by Chief Executives of More Than 200 European Firms*

Industry	United States	Japan	West Germany	Scandinavia	United Kingdom	France
Computing	1	2	3	4–5	6	4–5
Electronics	1–2	1–2	3	4	6–7	6–7
Telecommunications	1	2	3	4	5–6	5–6
Biotechnology	1	2	3	4	5	n.a.
Chemicals	1	2	3	4	5	6–7
Metals/Alloys	2	1	3	4	5–6	5–6
Engineering	1	2	3	4	5	6
Manufacturing	1–2	1–2	3	4	5	6
Robotics	2	1	3	4	6	5
Mean rank	1.3	1.7	3.0	4.2	5.4	5.8

Source: *Management and Technology—A Survey of European Chief Executives, 1984*, sponsored jointly by *Wall Street Journal/Europe* and Booz-Allen and Hamilton. Reprinted in John Marcum, "High Technology and the Economy," *OECD Observer*, no. 131 (November 1984), p. 5.

n.a. Not available.

issues raised in computer research and development are "generic," common to most high-tech industries.

The book has three objectives: to explain as precisely as possible the quantitative dimensions of government support for the development of computer technology at home and abroad; to examine the organization and overall impact of such government support on the computer industries of the United States, Western Europe, and Japan; and to assess the effectiveness of the different national policies in stimulating a competitive, commercial industry.

The Computer as a High-Tech Product

A high-tech product is one in which research and development (R&D) costs, or other measures of science and engineering inputs, are a significantly greater portion of output or value added than is true for industry in general. A narrow definition of high technology in the U.S. economy would generally include the pharmaceutical, computer, communications equipment, electronic components, and aerospace industries.[3] Computers were near the top of the list in 1980 with 12 percent of

3. Richard W. Riche, Daniel E. Hecker, and John U. Burgan, "High Technology Today and Tomorrow: A Small Slice of the Employment Pie," *Monthly Labor Review*, vol. 106 (November 1983), pp. 50–58.

Table 1-2. *Research Intensity of Selected American Industries*

Industry	R&D as percent of net sales in R&D-performing firms, 1980	R&D scientists and engineers per 1,000 employees, 1982
Total	3.0	32
Food	0.4	6
Textiles and apparel	0.4	3
Wood	0.8	n.a.
Paper	1.0	16
Chemicals	3.6	50
Industrial	3.3	43
Drugs	6.2	76
Other	1.9	35
Petroleum refining	0.6	22
Rubber	2.2	n.a.
Stone, clay, glass	1.4	14
Primary metals	0.7	9
Ferrous	0.7	8
Nonferrous	0.7	15
Fabricated metals	1.4	15
Machinery	5.0	40
Office, computing, accounting machines	12.0	69
Other nonelectrical machines	2.3	23
Electrical equipment	6.6	52
Radio and TV receivers	4.3	n.a.
Communications	9.1	61
Electronic components	7.9	66
Other	4.9	n.a.
Motor vehicles and equipment	4.9	32
Other transport equipment	0.6	8
Aircraft and missiles	13.7	102
Scientific instruments	7.5	n.a.
Scientific and measuring	8.4	n.a.
Optical, surgical, other	6.9	n.a.
Other manufacturing	0.4	8
Nonmanufacturing	n.a.	15

Source: National Science Foundation, *Research and Development in Industry, 1982* (Government Printing Oﬁce, 1984), pp. 23, 38.
n.a. Not available.

sales, on average, accounted for by R&D (see table 1-2). Only aircraft and missiles at 13.7 percent have a higher research content, and communications equipment at 9.1 percent trails as a reasonably distant third. Among products dominated by commercial sales, computers are arguably the most technology-intensive product produced by American industry. Using research scientists and engineers as a fraction of 1982 employment, a similar ranking of technology intensity is produced. Again, only aircraft and missiles lead computers in relative use of technical inputs.

Computers, communications equipment, and electronic components are becoming increasingly integrated into one industrial complex, spurred on by the continuing, rapid advances in electronics technology. Today an entire electronic product can be manufactured on the surface of a single integrated circuit. In that chip, computing and communications functions may be joined. Therefore, traditional industrial boundaries are losing their meaning. Even the more parochial insights gained from studying the computer industry now have relevance far beyond the nominal boundaries of this sector.

The Military Link

The growth of high-technology industry in the United States is directly linked to World War II. The degree to which scientists and engineers were mobilized in support of the Allied war effort and the scale of their activities were unprecedented.[4] Table 1-3 clearly shows the greatly expanded government role in supporting wartime technology development in the United States. During the war scientific manpower, largely siphoned off from other pursuits, was organized in a vast government R&D project.

After the war that support for research continued. From 1941 to 1945 an average of $600 million a year was spent, almost entirely on military applications. In 1947, long after the hostilities had ceased, the U.S. military spent perhaps $500 million (out of $625 million in federal research funds) on R&D, with 80 percent going to industrial and university laboratories on contract.[5] Whereas before the war the government had paid for 15 percent to 20 percent of U.S. research, after the war it funded more than half of a vastly expanded national effort and almost two-thirds of American R&D by the early 1960s.

4. For example, in 1935 less than 4 percent of Bell Telephone Laboratories personnel were working on military projects; in 1943 roughly three-quarters of its staff and over 80 percent of its budget went to defense activities. See Bell Telephone Laboratories, *A History of Engineering and Science in the Bell System: National Service in War and Peace (1925–1975)* (Murray Hill, N.J.: Bell Telephone Laboratories, 1978), pp. 11, 356.

5. The President's Scientific Research Board, *Science and Public Policy*, vol. 1: *A Program for the Nation* (GPO, 1947), p. 12.

Table 1-3. *U.S. Expenditures on Research and Development
by Source of Funds, Selected Years, 1930–61*[a]
Funds in millions of dollars

Year	All funds	Federal funds	Percent by source		
			Federal	Industry	Other[b]
1930	166	23	14	70	16
1932	191	39	20	63	17
1934	172	21	12	73	15
1936	218	33	15	70	15
1938	264	48	18	67	15
1940	345	67	19	68	13
1941–45 average	600	500	83	13	4
1947	1160	625	54	39	7
1953	5207	2759	53	43	4
1955	6279	3509	56	40	4
1957	9912	6119	62	35	3
1959	12540	8059	64	32	3
1961	14552	9264	64	33	4

Sources: For 1930–47, President's Scientific Research Board, John R. Steelman, chairman, *Science and Public Policy*, vol. 1: *A Program for the Nation* (GPO, 1947), pp. 10, 12; figures exclude research on atomic energy. For 1953–61, U.S. Bureau of the Census, *Historical Statistics of the United States: Colonial Times to 1970*, bicentennial edition, pt. 2 (GPO, 1975), p. 965. Figures are rounded.

a. Statistics for 1930–47 are not strictly comparable with later years because of changes in methodology and coverage.

b. "Other" includes universities, colleges, and nonprofit institutions.

New technologies—the atomic bomb, the proximity fuze, radar, battlefield medicine, fire control systems—had profoundly changed the face of warfare.[6] Extraordinary advances were made in many areas of science, and the postwar boom in the fields of materials science; aerospace, electrical, and nuclear engineering; physics; and operations research reflected much of the return on wartime research and development investments. The critical role of technological success stories to the war effort guaranteed continued military and strategic interest in maintaining the accelerated pace of technology development in the tense postwar years.

The development of the computer was one of these wartime successes. Its use in breaking enemy codes was, until recently, a highly secret but absolutely essential piece of the Allied victory.[7]

In the early postwar years the centerpiece of military and political strategy was to continue this steady stream of significant innovations.

6. James Phinney Baxter III, *Scientists against Time* (Cambridge: MIT Press, 1968).

7. The wartime origins of computing technology are discussed extensively in Kenneth Flamm, *Creating the Computer: Government, Industry, and High Technology* (Brookings, forthcoming).

It became evident that these technological changes were having wide-spread economic consequences. And interest developed in managing a large-scale program of research and development efficiently. Modern economic analysis of research and development is built on a series of pioneering studies by American economists in the 1950s and early 1960s.[8]

The economic returns from these new technologies were an unanticipated benefit of U.S. investments in R&D. Eventually, as the economic benefits of these projects began to be appreciated, a political constituency for government's role in priming the pump of technological progress developed. But the formulation of U.S. policy was made more difficult by the original and continuing link between technology and strategic advantage. The two objectives—economic and military—clearly were intertwined, and the precise rationale guiding policies was, therefore, easily confused. In computers, as in electronics, communications, advanced materials, and aerospace, this greatly complicated matters when the objectives and payoffs of technological investments were being weighed.

A Fast-Growing Industry

The rate of technological advance in the computer industry appears to have far exceeded that experienced in any other industry over a

8. One military-sponsored focus for this research was the Rand Corporation. See Charles Hitch, "The Character of Research and Development in a Competitive Economy" (Santa Monica, Calif.: Rand, 1958); Charles J. Hitch and Roland N. McKean, *The Economics of Defense in the Nuclear Age* (Rand, 1960); A. A. Alchian, K. J. Arrow, and W. M. Capron, *An Economic Analysis of the Market for Scientists and Engineers* (Rand, 1958); Richard R. Nelson, "The Simple Economics of Basic Scientific Research," *Journal of Political Economy,* vol. 67 (June 1959), pp. 297–306; and Kenneth J. Arrow, "Economic Welfare and the Allocation of Resources for Invention," Jora R. Minasian, "The Economics of Research and Development," A. W. Marshall and W. H. Meckling, "Predictability of the Costs, Time, and Success of Development," and Burton H. Klein, "The Decision Making Problem in Development," in National Bureau of Economic Research, *The Rate and Direction of Inventive Activity: Economic and Social Factors* (Princeton University Press, 1962). Research on defense procurement at the Harvard University Business School was another significant early force in introducing economists to the problems of R&D. See Merton J. Peck and Frederic M. Scherer, *The Weapons Acquisition Process: An Economic Analysis* (Harvard University Press, 1962); and Robert Schlaifer and S. D. Heron, *Development of Aircraft Engines and Fuels* (Boston, Mass.: Harvard University, Graduate School of Business Administration, 1950).

sustained period. Historically, the performance of computer systems has improved faster than the already rapid progress in the electronic components from which they are constructed, largely because of advances in organization and architecture. During the past few decades, the hardware cost of processing information has dropped by perhaps 28 percent per year in real terms—without a doubt one of the steepest sustained declines in an important price in the history of industrial society. From 1780 to 1815, the peak of the first industrial revolution, the real cost of cotton cloth, the commodity most affected by contemporary advances in mechanical energy production and engineering, dropped at a rate of 3.4 percent per annum.[9]

The production and use of computers, like other high-technology products, have also grown at an extraordinary rate. This, of course, is intimately related to the declines in cost attributable to technological progress.

Figure 1-3 charts the growth of the market for computer systems in terms of constant-dollar shipments (in 1982 dollars) by U.S. producers. Census Bureau statisticians included computers with calculating and accounting machines until the early 1960s, then lumped them with calculators, and finally gave them their own distinctive category in 1967.

Despite these counting problems, a clear picture of roughly exponential expansion emerges. During periods of economic recession, however, the more or less continuous growth stalled, and sales actually declined. The slowdowns of 1962 and 1967 decreased growth rates, and the recessions of 1970 and 1975 were accompanied by declines in production. But demand in the late 1970s was so robust that the mild recessions of 1979 and 1981 had little impact on continued growth. The sensitivity of computer sales to business cycle fluctuations is typical of demand for electronic capital goods and inputs.

In the early history of the industry, particular leaps in demand are notable. In 1959 and 1960 there was a sharp jump in sales, as many firms invested in a new generation of business-oriented computers. This trend,

9. D. N. McCloskey, "The Industrial Revolution, 1780–1860: A Survey," in Roderick Floud and Donald McCloskey, eds., *The Economic History of Britain since 1700,* vol. 1: *1700–1860* (Cambridge: Cambridge University Press, 1981), tables 6.1, 6.2. Replacing animal, water, and wind power with steam power (perhaps the single most significant of the many incremental changes associated with advances in textile production) roughly halved the marginal cost of the power required for producing the output of England's mills in 1800. See G. N. von Tunzelmann, *Steam Power and British Industrialization to 1860* (Oxford: Clarendon Press, 1978), pp. 150–56.

Figure 1-3. *Constant-Dollar Shipments of U.S. Computer Industry, 1958–85*[a]

Millions of 1982 dollars

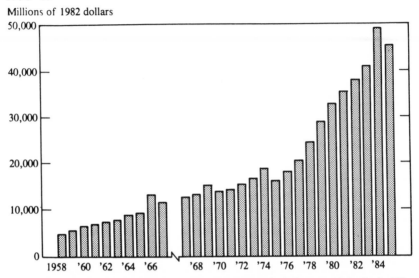

Sources: For 1958–67, unpublished data from the Bureau of Labor Statistics for input-output industries; for 1967–82, U.S. Bureau of the Census, *1982 Census of Manufacturers, Industry Series: Office, Computing, and Accounting Machines* (GPO, 1985), p. 35 F-S; for 1983–85, partial (but almost complete) shipments data in Bureau of the Census, *Current Industrial Reports: Computers and Office and Accounting Machines, 1985* (GPO, 1986), p. 1, expanded under the assumption that the ratio between partial shipments and total shipments would remain the same in 1983–85 as found in the 1982 overlap.

a. Shipments are standard industrial classification (SIC) industries 3573 and 3574, deflated to 1982 dollars using the GNP implicit price deflator from *Economic Report of the President, February 1985*, p. 236.

noted at the time,[10] shows up in these figures. There is also a noticeable jump in the mid-1960s that coincided with the first large-scale deliveries of IBM's important System 360.[11] Concepts introduced by IBM in this family of compatible computers profoundly affected the economics of the industry, and the statistical blip affirms the importance of the 360.

An International Industry

The U.S. computer industry from the start looked for a global market. In recent years American computer firms have typically made 40 percent

10. N. Nisenoff, "Hardware for Information Processing Systems: Today and in the Future," *Proceedings of the IEEE* [Institute of Electrical and Electronic Engineers], vol. 54 (December 1966), p. 1822.

11. The significance of System 360 is discussed in Flamm, *Creating the Computer*, chap. 4.

Table 1-4. *The Worldwide Operations of U.S. Computer Firms,
1977, 1982*[a]

Billions of dollars unless otherwise specified

Firms and structure	1977	1982
Parent firms		
1. Domestic sales	20.5	43.6
2. Net royalties and fees received from unaffiliated sources	0.02	0.02
3. Export sales to unaffiliated customers	0.6	1.2
4. R&D performed for self	2.2[b]	4.6
5. R&D performed for U.S. government	n.a.	0.9
Majority-owned affiliates		
6. Sales to unaffiliated customers	16.4	27.2
7. Net royalties and fees received from unaffiliated sources	n.a.	0
8. R&D performed by affiliates	n.a.	0.6
Structure of operations		
Foreign sales as percent of worldwide sales $[(3 + 6)/(1 + 3 + 6)]$	45.4	39.5
Foreign R&D as percent of worldwide R&D $[8/(4 + 5 + 8)]$	n.a.	9.8
Parent R&D for self as percent of parent sales $[4/(1 + 3)]$	9.2[b]	9.0
All Parent R&D as percent of parent sales $[(4 + 5)/[(1 + 3)]$	n.a.	10.8
Worldwide R&D as percent of worldwide sales $[(4 + 5 + 8)/[(1 + 3 + 6)]$	n.a.	8.5

Sources: U.S. Department of Commerce, Bureau of Economic Analysis, *U.S. Direct Investment Abroad, 1977* (GPO, 1981), pp. 289, 326, 380, 391, 395, 400, and *U.S. Direct Investment Abroad: 1982 Benchmark Survey Data* (GPO, 1985), pp. 222, 230, 296, 306, 315–16, 338–39.

n.a. Not available.

a. Data refer to nonbank U.S. parent firms in the office, computing, and accounting machines industry and their majority-owned nonbank affiliates.

b. R&D expenditures for parent's own benefit whether or not performed by parent.

to 50 percent of their worldwide sales in foreign markets. Table 1-4 charts the broad contours of the U.S. computer industry's international scope. In 1977 more than 45 percent of sales were racked up abroad; and in 1982, in spite of a painfully overvalued dollar, 40 percent of the dollar volume of industry sales probably came from overseas markets.[12]

The internationalization of this industry has been achieved mainly through the establishment of a worldwide network of marketing, service, and manufacturing affiliates and not, for the most part, through direct

12. Data in table 1-4 refer only to the operations of majority-owned foreign affiliates and exclude income and sales from affiliates with a minority interest. Foreign sales and income are therefore understated to a small extent.

exports from the United States. Computer technology is guarded within the boundaries of the firm, sold in products but rarely sold outright. Royalties and fees from the sale of technology to outsiders are virtually nil.

In addition, the search for talent and ideas has been global. Roughly 10 percent of the industry's R&D in 1982 was performed in the foreign laboratories of U.S. firms. This international focus is a characteristic of other high-technology industries. Many studies have linked the relative importance of foreign investment and trade to the degree of research intensity of an industry.[13]

The Nature of Commercial Competition

Industrial competition in computers, as in other technology-intensive products, has evolved in directions quite different from the standard accounts in economics texts of perfectly competitive markets. The powerful paradigm of efficient, competitive markets producing a socially optimal allocation of resources rests on the assumption of a mature, widely diffused technology used to produce a standardized commodity. This scenario falls wide of the mark when a technology-intensive product like computers is considered. Instead, a realistic model of competition in a high-tech industry must include elements such as continuous investments in creating a superior, closely held technology; advanced, differentiated products over which an innovator holds a monopoly (albeit temporarily); and the significant monopoly rents received by an innovator justifying and financing continued investments in research and development.

As early as the 1940s, economist Joseph Schumpeter noted the contradictions between conventional accounts of competitive markets and the dynamics of economies in which technological innovation was the central driving force.[14] Only through some degree of monopoly,

13. See, for example, C. Fred Bergsten, Thomas Horst, and Theodore H. Moran, *American Multinationals and American Interests* (Brookings, 1978), pp. 242–45; Edwin Mansfield, Anthony Romeo, and Samuel Wagner, "Foreign Trade and U.S. Research and Development," *Review of Economics and Statistics,* vol. 61 (February 1979), pp. 49–57; and Kirsty S. Hughes, "Exports and Innovation: A Simultaneous Model," *European Economic Review,* vol. 30 (April 1986), pp. 383–99.

14. Joseph A. Schumpeter, *Capitalism, Socialism and Democracy,* 3d ed. (Harper and Row, 1950), chap. 8.

argued Schumpeter, could the economic benefits of superior technology be captured by an innovating firm in a market economy. Some inefficiency in the allocation of resources, due to monopoly power, is tolerated in exchange for dynamic gains from creating new technology. This "Schumpeterian" view has played a central role in economic analysis of innovation since then.

The picture is further complicated by the fixed, "sunk cost" nature of expenditures on research and development. Because the costs of developing a new product are, for the most part, unaffected by the scale on which that product is later produced (there are economies of scale in the use of newly created technology), volume of sales and size of market can greatly affect the average cost of producing a technology-intensive product. Given a particular new product, the largest producer may have the lowest production costs.

The advantages of size, however, are far from permanent. New technology has a way of leaking out over time to competitors, who may then produce without incurring the costly initial investments in developing the technology. The correct view of competition in such products, then, may be to think of continuous investments in technology creating a sequence of temporary monopolies on new products, with rents earned on current products financing the investments in the next round of innovation.

Furthermore, it is by no means obvious that the advantages of size lead an innovator to pioneer the next round of innovation. If new products compete in existing markets for technology-intensive products, then a new firm with no existing product lines at stake may have a greater incentive to hasten the development of the next round of advanced products than has the current market leader.[15]

Very different policies may foster the development of technology-intensive industries. For example, the advantages of size in reducing the

15. This argument, now called "the Arrow effect," was first set out by economist Kenneth J. Arrow in "Economic Welfare and the Allocation of Resources for Invention." Jennifer Reinganum, "Innovation and Industry Evolution," *Quarterly Journal of Economics,* vol. 100 (February 1985), pp. 81–99, has extended this argument to a highly simplified model of an idealized economy with a sequence of innovations over time. She shows that with a particular set of assumptions, an incumbent, dominant firm has less of an incentive to invest in further innovation than challenger firms, purely as a consequence of the rents it enjoys from its existing technological advantage. A similar result is derived in other circumstances by John Vickers, "The Evolution of Market Structure When There Is a Sequence of Innovations," *Journal of Industrial Economics,* vol. 35 (September 1986), pp. 1–12.

average development cost of a new product may encourage policymakers to merge existing firms into a single "national champion" and to reserve national markets for this champion to further increase sales volume. Such "rationalization" policies may hurt smaller start-up firms likely to pioneer the next round of innovative products and remove the incentive for the state-appointed firm to introduce new products in a timely fashion. They also may dampen the cost-reducing discipline that competition imposes. Thus a realistic understanding of the dynamics of competition is essential in the formulation of public policies to address the special requirements of technology-intensive industries.

The Issues

The exceedingly brisk pace of progress in computer technology brings into sharp focus issues that may be less obviously important in other technology-intensive industries. This section examines three of these issues: the military origins of technology policy, the economic basis for government support, and international competition in high-tech products.

Military Origins of Technology Policy

As noted earlier, the early successes of many technology-intensive sectors of the U.S. economy—electronics, computers, radio communications, aerospace—largely were the result of applications funded by and developed for military users.[16] This may have been partially a reflection of political realities. The postwar history of science policy in the United States is a study in counterbalanced tensions.[17] The prevailing economic culture strongly pulls the United States toward a decentralized system reliant on market forces, yet is tempered by pragmatic government action when imperfections in market outcomes hinder important social and economic objectives. The military budget is largely immune from the philosophical and ideological passions raised by arguments

16. Richard R. Nelson, ed., *Government and Technical Progress: A Cross-Industry Analysis* (Pergamon Press, 1982), gives a useful cross-industry view of many of these developments.

17. Much of this history is traced in James L. Penick, Jr., and others, eds., *The Politics of American Science, 1939 to the Present*, rev. ed. (MIT Press, 1972).

about the role of government in the economy. One recurring phenomenon has been the sheltering of research programs under the protective wings of the military services.

Much technology of industrial interest ultimately winds up in products of military utility, and vice versa. (One is hard pressed to name a class of high-tech products that has absolutely no military significance, particularly when the underlying industrial base is linked to the capacity to fight a prolonged war.) Thus virtually any important technology can be justified in either economic or military terms.

One of the consequences, therefore, of the military origins of technology policy in the United States is a certain muddying of the waters when the justifications for research programs are considered. Programs central to the future economic performance of U.S. industry can be funded on strategic grounds, and a competitive assessment of alternative investments, which might influence the formulation of a program aimed explicitly at improving the future economic performance of U.S. industry, forgone.

Furthermore, the nature and objectives of research programs may be affected by their sponsorship. The products designed for military ends are not necessarily the most commercially successful. Restrictions on the transfer and dissemination of technology, a natural outcome when military products are being developed, can slow the application of technologies of more general commercial interest. Given the growing importance of advanced technology to U.S. economic performance and the still dominant role of military support in many fields of applied research, the extent to which commercial application of new technologies is affected by military sponsorship of research is a significant issue.

The Economics of Technology Policy

The economic arguments for government support of technology are diverse and complex. Essential features inherent in technology (and more generally information) are economies of scale in its use, difficulties in the private appropriation of benefits flowing from the development of new technology, and special problems for private capital markets posed by very large and risky projects.

It is possible to construct models in which R&D is the battlefield on which struggles for market power are fought, and excessive R&D, or rates of expenditure on R&D, are the outcome, as firms struggle to gain a monopoly position through innovation.

Wasteful spending on research and development is another possible outcome of competition for market power through R&D. Firms can spend money on "patenting around" established inventions, duplicating results already obtained by others, or even tying up competitors in legal knots. In all of these cases incentives can be created that lead to excessive research, in expectation of private gains that surpass social returns.

Thus theoretical models of innovation in a market economy lead to the conclusion that private returns greater or smaller than the social return to innovation can exist; the only consensus seems to be that there is no reason to expect the theoretically optimal amount and type of R&D to be undertaken. The empirical literature, on the other hand, argues that there is a general tendency to underinvest in research.[18] Economists of all stripes generally support some degree of government involvement in encouraging research, particularly basic research (arguably the most difficult to appropriate for private use). Opinions diverge widely when more applied projects, directly relevant to commercial needs, are proposed.

Additional strategic considerations are critical ingredients in government attitudes toward technology. As is true for other high-tech sectors, computers are a key intermediate input to other products. Everything from autos to bathroom scales now use computers in their underlying mechanisms. If current price trends prevail, this use of computers can be expected to maintain its dramatic growth.

Thus computers are an economically strategic good, an essential input to a broad and growing list of industrial products. Having access to the best available technology is a prerequisite for economic competitiveness in all of these sectors, and excessive dependence on foreign technology, it might be argued, is as potentially debilitating as is dependence on a commodity import like oil. American producers may complain of being sent to the back of the queue in sales of economically strategic products such as high-performance computer chips and semiconductor production equipment, where foreign manufacturers sometimes now sell the most advanced technology commercially available. Lack of access to important inputs may cripple "downstream" industries that otherwise might

18. See, for example, Edwin Mansfield and others, "Social and Private Rates of Return from Industrial Innovations," *Quarterly Journal of Economics,* vol. 91 (May 1977), pp. 221–40.

be competitive in world markets.[19] For these economic reasons, as well as the strong link to military advantage, governments have been key actors in helping national firms develop and maintain a strong computer technology base.

International Markets

International markets are a key to industrial competition in high technology. Because of the fixed cost nature of R&D investments, a significant foreign market can greatly increase the rate of return on investments in technology. And foreign markets are essential in the business strategies of American computer firms.

Trade conflict over government involvement in high technology is no longer a matter of distant concern. All over the world trade battles are now being waged, and it is technology policy that guides this struggle. In the United States, for example, the "targeting" of high-tech industries by foreign governments has recently emerged as a highly visible trade complaint, the subject of concerted lobbying efforts as well as government investigations. And a mushrooming list of trade complaints alleging infringement of patent and other intellectual property rights is being placed before the U.S. International Trade Commission, a fundamentally political body, instead of appearing in the less politically supercharged forum of the patent and legal system.

Finding constructive ways to channel competition in government-funded research in high-tech products is a formidable challenge. Any package of policies must consider all forms of subsidy, not just in R&D. But of all the issues research and development is the most complex and difficult, perhaps because of the historical and economically justifiable role of government in supplying these public goods.

The quest for technological rents drives the entire process of innovation, and governments have a legitimate interest in creating the infrastructure that national firms require to compete effectively. Yet there are clear gains to be had from establishing common standards for

---

19. When there is monopoly control over a specific input to production (such as a technology-intensive good), the monopolist can generally increase monopoly profit by integrating forward into the user industry and eliminating the firms that otherwise might be customers. See John M. Vernon and Daniel A. Graham, "Profitability of Monopolization by Vertical Integration," *Journal of Political Economy,* vol. 79 (July–August 1971), pp. 924–25.

acceptable practices in fostering technology. The long-term interests of a world increasingly reliant on the benefits from continued technological progress may ultimately be served by policies that eliminate wasteful duplication of basic research, establish trade rules that encourage the widest possible market for technology-intensive goods, and protect the rights of innovators to collect a fair return on their R&D investments in order to stimulate further research and development.

Summary

Early research and development of the most radically new concepts in computer technology—as opposed to refinements, improvements, and incremental advances built on current practice—have with continuing high frequency been bound up with government support. The natural question—whether, in the absence of government support, private, commercial interests would have stepped in over the near term with efforts of approximately the same intensity—may be answered with a fairly clear "no."[20]

The major objectives of this book are instead to document the scale and manner of public support for technology in the computer industry and to try to explain why some national policies are more effective than others. Before examining the national policies that have fostered the development of the computer, it is useful to understand why governments have taken such an interest in the pace of technological advance in computers. The next two chapters explore the economic impact of computer technology and trace the history of federal support for computer research. Chapters 4 and 5 examine in detail government policies affecting the development of computer technology in the United States, Western Europe, and Japan and evaluate their aggregate impact on the technology and the commercial industry. The final chapter assesses the role governments have played in the development of advanced computer technology and identifies those issues that are likely to grow in importance as technology becomes *the* major arena for international economic and political competition.

20. The true skeptic will want to read Flamm, *Creating the Computer,* which explores in detail how the history of the industry was linked to government investments in particular technologies.

CHAPTER TWO

The Economic Impact
of Computer Technology

TECHNOLOGICAL progress in the computer industry has significantly benefited the entire U.S. economy. During the past three decades, the cost of information processing systems declined sharply. Research and development of computer technology has been highly productive, even when compared with R&D investments in other fields.

The social return from computer technology investments is mainly reaped by domestic consumers who pay less for information processing services; of lesser importance are technological rents earned by producers in foreign and domestic markets. Quite the opposite is true, however, when private return is considered. Cost declines that are not immediately passed on to consumers create a technological rent that can be collected by an innovating firm, and foreign markets pay a significant share of the rents that are received by American computer firms. At the margin, foreign markets can be a crucial factor when private technology investments are considered by these companies.

Governments' interest in computer technology has historically been based on both economic and strategic factors, but today strategic reasons are not needed to justify these investments. The economic benefits alone warrant society's continued willingness to plow resources into the development of computer technology.

A Bird's-Eye View of Computers

Simply put, every computer has a central processor, a memory, and input-output peripheral equipment (see figure 2-1). Its function is to manipulate data. The input-output subsystem connects the machine to

Figure 2-1. *Basic Elements of a Computer*

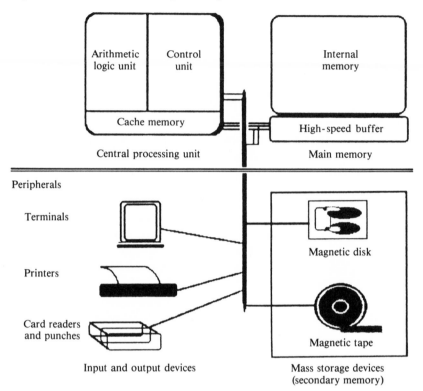

the external world, which feeds it data (punched cards, human keystrokes from a terminal, digitized images, frequency samples from sound signals, electrical voltage levels from an industrial control sensor) and to which data are eventually returned. The central processor performs a variety of operations on the data. The memory permits the machine to be programmed, that is, instructed to perform a sequence of operations, and to remember the results of those operations. With only a small vocabulary of logical operations, the simplest of processors, along with the simplest of memories, can accomplish virtually any symbolic or arithmetic task that can be precisely defined.

The basic computer design invented during World War II called for data to be read into the processor, where it would be operated on by the processor, and then written out. This *serial design,* so-called because a single processor would execute its programmed instructions one after another sequentially over time in a sequence determined by the program, is also known as the Von Neumann design, after the scientist whose name appeared on the first report describing it in detail.[1] The great improvements in computer hardware over the past twenty years are of two kinds: improvements in the basic physical components with which the system is actually built and improvements in the computer's "architecture," the way in which the parts of the system (its central processor, the hierarchy of storage areas that make up its memory, and its mechanisms for moving data to and from the external world) are designed, connected, and controlled. Of a roughly five order of magnitude (that is, 10^5) improvement in computer processing speeds since the 1950s, three orders of magnitude are due to better components, the remainder to improvements in architecture.[2]

Measuring Improvements in Performance

How, then, have these technological advances in components and architecture affected the cost of computing power? Before this question can be answered, it is necessary to somehow measure what computers do.[3] Unfortunately, the performance of even the simplest, stylized computer system can be quite difficult to measure. Like any complex system, the effective rate at which it can work is limited by the speed of its parts, as well as by its organization. Computers vary on both accounts, and speed in any given task will depend on the specifics of the task being performed. Furthermore, significant design trade-offs exist. Improving one component can sometimes compensate for deficiencies in another. For example, in problems that mainly involve computation, a slow input-

1. The Von Neumann design is now commonly referred to as a single instruction stream, single data stream (SISD) computer. Such a computer executes an order taken from a single sequence of instructions (a "program"). The operation performed by the processor acts on an operand selected from a single sequence of data items. See Michael J. Flynn, "Very High-Speed Computing Systems," *Proceedings of the IEEE* [Institute of Electrical and Electronics Engineers], vol. 54 (December 1966), pp. 1901–09.

2. See R. W. Hockney and C. R. Jesshope, *Parallel Computers: Architecture, Programming and Algorithms* (Bristol, U.K.: Adam Hilger, 1981), p. 3.

3. Some have even argued that not correcting for improvements in computer performance introduced significant errors into the U.S. system of national income accounts. See Jane Seaberry, "U.S. Weighs Computer Price Shift," *Washington Post,* May 2, 1985. Seaberry cited a Council of Economic Advisers staff paper that claimed that a 10 percent annual decline in computer prices would have added a full percentage point to real GNP growth in each of the three previous years.

output subsystem can be finessed by a memory controller constantly reading data into fast memory while the central processor is busy calculating, thus keeping the limitations on input and output from slowing down the job. The technological history of computers makes amply clear that shifts in the relative prices of computer components have greatly affected the way that a computer system is put together.[4] Sharp declines in the cost of internal memory have coincided with large increases in the amount of internal memory configured into the average computer system (see figure 2-2).

The only sure way of getting an accurate reading on how much work a machine does is to pick a specific job, run it on a lot of machines, and see how much time it takes. The relative productivity of the machines, unfortunately, varies considerably by the job.[5] Furthermore, since new applications are constantly being introduced, the mix of jobs being run on machines, in the aggregate, is constantly changing. In the early days of computers, no one was concerned enough about recording performance for posterity to define a standard job, and now alas it is too late.

A second way to measure performance is to select certain characteristics of machines related to their performance on a particular type of job, assume some "typical" set of weights, and construct an index.[6] Obviously, deciding what problems are typical, and at what time they are typical, is a perilous task. Worse yet, as component prices have changed, the mix of components and therefore the impact of performance changes in these components have also changed.

A third approach is to hypothesize that computer prices are related in a stable way to some set of measurable characteristics contained within the computer. This so-called "hedonic" function, relating prices to

4. For an interesting discussion of current trade-offs in computer system design, see Leonard Kleinrock, "Distributed Systems," *Communications of the ACM,* vol. 28 (November 1985), pp. 1200–13.

5. For some comparisons of this sort, see Daniel P. Siewiorek, C. Gordon Bell, and Allen Newell, *Computer Structures: Principles and Examples* (McGraw-Hill, 1982), pp. 47–61; and C. Gordon Bell, J. Craig Mudge, and John E. McNamara, *Computer Engineering: A DEC View of Hardware Systems Design* (Bedford, Mass.: Digital Press, 1978), pp. 541–52.

6. Examples of this approach may be found in Kenneth E. Knight, "Changes in Computer Performance," *Datamation,* vol. 12 (September 1966), pp. 40–54; R. P. Cerveny and K. E. Knight, "Performance of Computers," in Anthony Ralston, ed., *Encyclopedia of Computer Science and Engineering,* 2d ed. (Van Nostrand Reinhold, 1983), pp. 1127–31; and Theodore J. Gordon and T. R. Munson, "Research into Technology Output Measures" (report prepared for the National Science Foundation, November 1980).

Figure 2-2. *Effect of Declining Memory Cost on Computer System Design, 1955–78*[a]

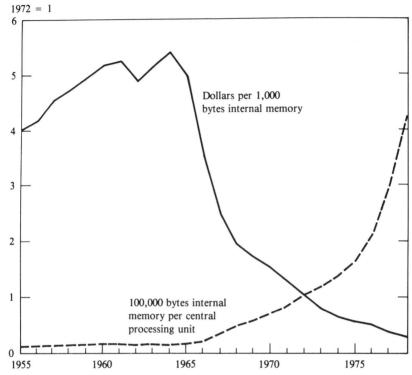

1972 = 1

Dollars per 1,000
bytes internal memory

100,000 bytes internal
memory per central
processing unit

Source: Montgomery Phister, Jr., *Data Processing Technology and Economics,* 2d ed. (Bedford, Mass.: Digital Press, and Santa Monica Publishing Co.), pp. 257, 266, 602, 607.

a. In figures 2-2 through 2-5 real price indexes are calculated by dividing component price in current dollars by the GNP implicit price deflator from *Economic Report of the President, February 1985,* p. 236.

computer characteristics, can then be estimated statistically, and shifts in price over time interpreted as the effects of technological progress.[7]

The approach adopted here is to focus on the components of a computer system and not on any specific implementation of the technology of the day. Appendix A explains in detail how such an index of the cost of information processing (IP) capacity might be constructed. Basically, this capacity is viewed as an output of the components installed within. Measures of the average cost of installed components were

7. For an extensive discussion of the application of hedonic methods to estimating a quality-adjusted price for computers, see Jack E. Triplett, "Price and Technological Change in a Capital Good: A Survey of Research on Computers" (U.S. Department of Commerce, Bureau of Economic Analysis, 1986).

Figure 2-3. *Real Price Indexes for Major System Components, 1957–78*

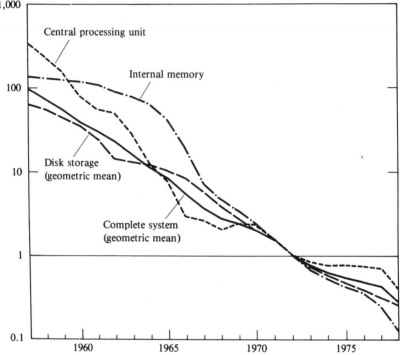

Logarithmic scale, 1972 = 1

Sources: See appendix tables A-3, A-5.

corrected with a rough index reflecting how information processing *bandwidth* (bits of information processed per unit time) has changed for each component over the years. Improvements in computer architecture, as well as in the speed of electronic circuitry, are presumed to be captured in the price index for central processor information processing capacity. Improvements in memory and input-output systems are reflected in the indexes of price and performance derived for these items.

To measure how the price of computing capacity has changed in real terms relative to all other prices in the economy, these indexes can be deflated by a price index showing the general level of prices for all goods and services in the economy. The implicit price deflator for the gross national product has been used to do so, and the results are graphed in figure 2-3. Note the logarithmic scale.

Declining Costs

The overall price index for computing capacity has dropped at a remarkable rate. In nominal (current dollar) terms, costs have declined at well over 20 percent a year for a sustained twenty-year period! That is to say, the dollar cost of these services has declined by a full order of magnitude (a factor of ten) every eight years. In real (constant dollar) terms, the decline has been even sharper—about 28 percent per year—dropping an order of magnitude every seven years. Without a doubt, this has been one of the steepest sustained declines in an important price in the history of industrial society.

The torrid pace of technological progress has not been uniform, however. The rate of advance slowed below the average during the late 1960s and early 1970s and picked up in the mid-1970s. This observation is confirmed by fitting a straight line to the overall performance measure displayed in figure 2-3 and plotting residuals.

Figure 2-3 also reveals the trend in prices for key components in computing systems. The steepest declines from 1955 to 1965 were in the cost of central processing units. From the mid-1960s on, this decline slows considerably and lags behind the overall continued progress. Most of the key improvements on the basic Von Neumann serial architecture had been introduced by the mid-1960s, and improvements in the performance of central processing units took on a more incremental character, driven by continued improvements in the price performance of electronic circuitry.

The price of internal memory capacity was roughly constant during the late 1950s, then declined sharply in the early 1960s. The memory technology of the day was ferrite cores, and this is largely consistent with other data on IBM's manufacturing costs for core memories during the same period.[8] Since the mid-1960s, semiconductor memories have replaced ferrite cores, and the cost of semiconductors has fallen even faster than the overall cost of computers.

The most important technology for peripheral, secondary memory has been the hard disk, moving-head file. Since its introduction on a large scale in the late 1950s, its effective cost has declined at roughly the

---

8. See Emerson W. Pugh, *Memories That Shaped an Industry: Decisions Leading to IBM System/360* (Cambridge: MIT Press, 1984), p. 245.

Figure 2-4. *Real Price Indexes for Other System Components, 1957–78*

Logarithmic scale, 1972 = 1

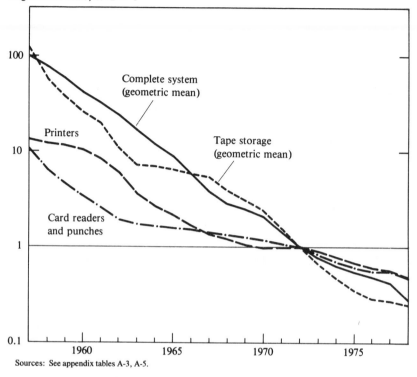

Sources: See appendix tables A-3, A-5.

same rate as the overall index of information processing cost. The cost improved at a considerably faster rate in the 1970s.

Input-output technologies have seen much smaller price performance improvements over the years. Punched card equipment and line printers, after significant gains from 1955 to 1965, slowed to a very gradual, marginal rate of improvement in cost per unit of work capacity (see figure 2-4).

Table 2-1 summarizes the overall improvement in systems and component price performance. The average declines over the entire 1957–78 period in the real cost of data processing capacity have been computed by fitting a straight line to the data in figures 2-3 and 2-4. Annual trends in real prices have been declines of 37 percent for internal memory capacity, 32 percent for central processor computing capacity, 28 percent for moving-head files, 28 percent for magnetic tape storage, 16 percent for line printers, and 12 percent for punched card equipment.

Table 2-1. *The Declining Cost of Computer Hardware, 1957–78*[a]

System component	Percent decline in real, quality-corrected cost per year
Central processing unit	32
Internal memory	37
Disk storage[b]	28
Tape storage[c]	28
Printers	16
Card readers and punches	12
Complete computer system[d]	28

a. Regressions of the form $\ln P = a - b \cdot year$ were run using the price indexes constructed in appendix A. For disk storage, tape storage, and complete computer system, a geometric mean of high and low bounds is presented. Price index P was deflated to real terms using the implicit GNP price deflator. Coefficient b can be interpreted as a trend rate and is reported in this table.

b. High series, 35; low series, 20.

c. High series, 31; low series, 24.

d. High series, 30; low series, 27.

These indexes of the declining cost of computing power present a fairly reasonable picture of cyclical changes in price performance over time (see figure 2-5). The first cycle occurred around 1962, when a series of moderately rapid declines in cost slowed down. This marks the end of the Second Generation of computers. (These machines incorporating transistor technology perhaps should be called the 2.5 Generation.) The next cycle of rapid technological advance peaked around 1966 and dissipated through 1969; this clearly was the Third Generation and coincided with the diffusion of the very successful IBM System 360 into the national computer stock. The next, more modest round of technological advance peaked around 1972, about the time IBM System 370 was sold in large numbers. The 370 incorporated more advanced integrated circuits into the 360 architecture. The Japanese called this the 3.5 Generation. Finally, in the late 1970s a fourth cycle of rapid technological progress began.

Using very different methodologies, others have obtained similar price-performance estimates. Gregory Chow studied only newly introduced computer models and used regression methods to relate "box" price (that is, the price for central processing units and main memory) to multiplication time, memory size, and memory access time (a subset of the system characteristics shown in table 2-2). Chow found that the real cost of computers between 1955 and 1965 declined on average 20 percent per year.[9] IBM researchers, using sophisticated extensions of Chow's methods, show computer box prices between 1972 and 1984

9. Gregory C. Chow, "Technological Change and the Demand for Computers," *American Economic Review*, vol. 57 (December 1967), p. 1130.

Figure 2-5. *Rates of Change in Computer System Cost, 1958–78*

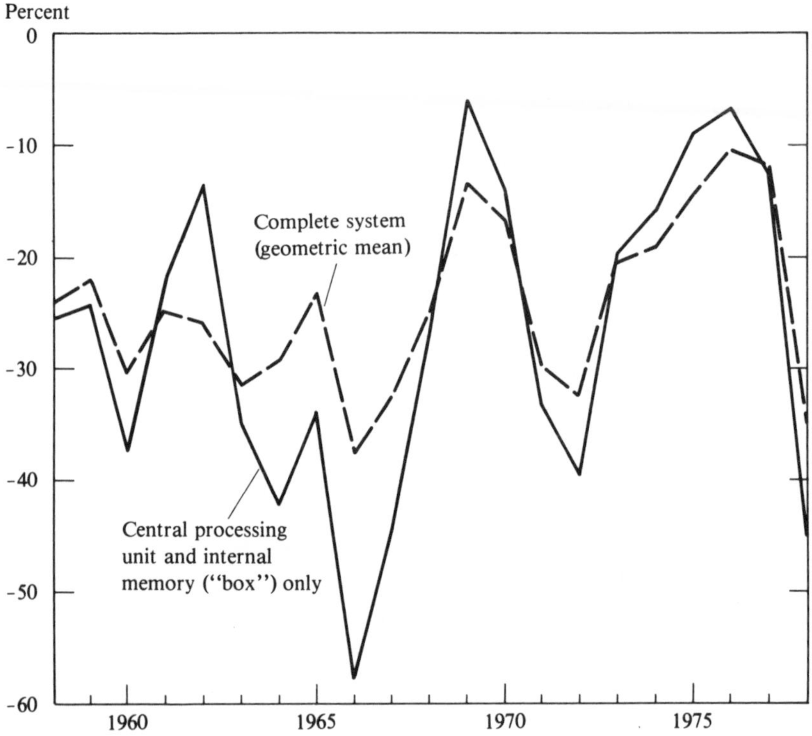

Percent

Sources: See appendix tables A-3, A-5.

declining an average of 18 percent per year—23 percent in real terms.[10] A fixed weight index of computer characteristics for new models was used by K. E. Knight. Price for given performance dropped at a remarkably steady average rate of 25 percent per year from the mid-1950s to mid-1960s, at slower rates in the early 1970s, and at quicker rates again in later years.[11] W. J. Baumol and his collaborators, on the

10. Rosanne Cole and others, "Quality-Adjusted Price Indexes for Computer Processors and Selected Peripheral Equipment," *Survey of Current Business,* vol. 66 (January 1986), pp. 41–50. These indexes have been divided by the GNP implicit price deflator to calculate a real rate of change. Annual rates of change were then averaged over the years in question.

11. See William F. Sharpe, *The Economics of Computers* (Columbia University Press, 1969), pp. 342–43; and Kenneth E. Knight, "A Functional and Structural Measurement of Technology," *Technological Forecasting and Social Change,* vol. 27 (May 1985), p. 125. Sharpe notes that a variety of other studies seem to show substantially greater improvement in box performance through the early 1960s, some as high as 100 percent per year (pp. 322–33).

Table 2-2. *Computer Production in Relation to Gross National Product, 1958–85*

Year	U.S. computer shipments as percent of GNP[a]	Year	U.S. computer shipments as percent of GNP[a]
1958	0.30	1972	0.59
1959	0.33	1973	0.61
1960	0.38	1974	0.68
1961	0.40	1975	0.59
1962	0.40	1976	0.64
1963	0.41	1977	0.69
1964	0.45	1978	0.78
1965	0.45	1979	0.91
1966	0.59	1980	1.03
1967	0.51	1981	1.09
1967	0.55	1982	1.21
1968	0.55	1983	1.25
1969	0.62	1984	1.40
1970	0.57	1985	1.27
1971	0.56		

Sources: For 1958–67, unpublished data from the Bureau of Labor Statistics for input output industries; for 1967–82, U.S. Bureau of the Census, *1982 Census of Manufactures, Industry Series: Office, Computing, and Accounting Machines* (GPO, 1985), p. 35F-S; for 1983–85, partial (but almost complete) shipments data in U.S. Bureau of the Census, *Current Industrial Reports: Computers and Office and Accounting Machines, 1985* (GPO, 1986), p. 1, expanded under assumption that the ratio between partial shipments and industry totals was the same in 1983–85 as in 1982. GNP is from *Economic Report of the President, February 1986*, p. 252.

a. Shipments are by standard industrial classification (SIC) industries 3573 and 3574.

basis of an assortment of fragmentary studies, argue for a long-term 25 percent annual decline in nominal information processing cost.[12] Only Paul Stoneman's study of British computers finds a considerably slower rate of advance, but his population may be considerably different, and his methods are somewhat suspect.[13]

Elasticity of Demand

To estimate an economic return from advances in computer technology, it is first necessary to describe how a drop in price (or improvement

12. See William J. Baumol, Sue Anne Batey Blackman, and Edward N. Wolff, "Unbalanced Growth Revisited: Asymptotic Stagnancy and New Evidence," *American Economic Review*, vol. 75 (September 1985), pp. 813–14.

13. Stoneman's data refer to commercial British computers, and technological advance in these machines may have lagged. His regression equation linking price to computer characteristics includes a highly significant term relating price to physical system size, which is highly suspect given the shift to semiconductor technology. Paul Stoneman, *Technological Diffusion and the Computer Revolution: The UK Experience* (Cambridge: Cambridge University Press, 1976), chap. 3.

Figure 2-6. *Quantity of U.S. Computer Systems Capacity*
Installed per Unit Output, 1957–78[a]
1972 dollars

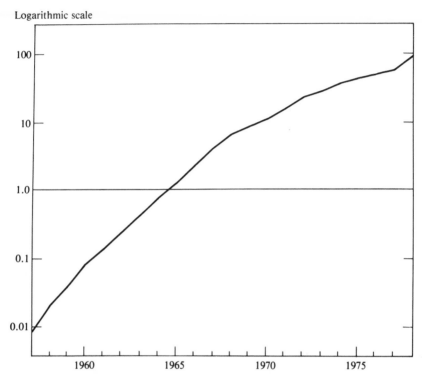

a. Computer systems and GNP are deflated to 1972 dollars using the price index for computer systems reported in table A-5, col. 7, and the implicit price deflator for GNP from *Economic Report of the President, February 1985*, p. 236.

in performance) affects demand. One can then infer what the value to society of this price decline might be.

By dividing estimates of the value of the stock of computer systems by an index of quality-corrected computer price, an implicit quantity index for the total information processing capacity in use in the U.S. economy can be constructed. This series can be divided by real output of American goods and services, and an estimate calculated of information processing capacity used per dollar of U.S. GNP (see figure 2-6). Note the slower pace at which information processing capacity was installed during the first half of the 1970s. This coincided with the slowdown in the decline in real price for computing capacity noted earlier. American computing capacity per unit of goods and services produced rose at a 41 percent per year trend rate between 1957 and 1978.[14]

Recall that during this period the real cost of computing capacity fell by about 28 percent annually. The price elasticity of demand for information processing capacity can be estimated by dividing the rate of change in the computing capacity per unit American output by the rate of decline in its relative cost. The price elasticity of demand was around 1.46. In other words, a 1 percent decline in cost was associated with about a 1.5 percent increase in demand for computer capacity. If other factors caused any of the increasing use of IP per unit of output, one would expect the true price elasticity to be somewhat lower.

The changes in price for information processing capacity are so large, however, that they probably swamp the effects of year-to-year changes in other factors that might influence demand. Suppose that demand for information processing capacity is derived from use as an input to production of other goods and services. The demand for information processing services (assumed to be proportional to information processing capacity) will depend on the volume of production of goods and services (that is, GNP) and the prices of other inputs relative to the IP services price. If there are constant returns to scale in the production of goods and services (that is, at any moment in time, a doubling of all inputs, including IP services, results in a doubling of output), demand for IP services (IP) can be expressed as:

$$(2\text{-}1) \qquad\qquad IP = i(P_I, P')\, Q.$$

Function i represents demand for IP per unit of output of final goods, as a function of the price of IP services, P_I, and a vector of the prices of all other inputs, P'. The total output of goods and services is Q (and $i = IP/Q$).

For convenience, let all prices be measured in real terms, that is, relative to the price of output.[15] Given the assumption of constant returns to scale, the price elasticity of IP, total demand for information processing capacity, is exactly the same as the price elasticity of i, demand per unit

14. A regression equation of the form ln $(IP/GNP) = a + b \cdot time$ ($time$ being a variable with value 1957 in 1957, 1958 in 1958, and so on) was fit to this data. The results were log $(IP/GNP) = -804$ (36) + 0.41 (0.018) $\cdot time$, $R^2 = 0.96$, Durbin-Watson = 0.12. Numbers in parentheses are reported standard errors.

15. Since i must be homogeneous of degree zero in prices, all the prices in 12.1 can be divided by the price of output without affecting i.

of output produced. If changes in P_I are very much larger than changes in any elements of P', then changes in i are well approximated when only the effects of P_I are considered. A similar argument suggests that changes in the price of IP services, P_I, are well approximated by the effects of changes in the cost of IP capacity.[16]

Another simple approximation of the price elasticity of demand might be calculated by looking at how IP demand per unit of output has varied with IP price. A simple regression of the natural logarithm of IP demand on IP price produces an elasticity estimate of 1.45, almost exactly the same as the cruder approximation of price elasticity first calculated.[17]

Chow estimates that the price elasticity of U.S. computer demand from 1955 to 1965 was 1.44.[18] His somewhat more sophisticated analysis takes into account lags over time between price declines and their effects on investment.

A price elasticity in the 1.4 to 1.5 range seems appropriate when considering demand for computing power. A rather conservative estimate that ascribes increases in computing demand to factors other than cost declines might reduce this elasticity estimate by a third; a fairly conservative lower bound would be 1.0.

Social Benefits

Thus far the advance in computer technology has been carefully documented. As noted, the resources invested in computer-related R&D have led to a trend decline of about 28 percent per year in the real cost of computing power (that is, the cost relative to that of other goods and services). A conservative lower bound for this decline might be 20 percent.

16. The notation $\cdot$ indicates first derivatives with respect to time (that is, $d(\ )/dt$). Suppose, for notational convenience only, that there is only one other input with price P'; then $\dot{i} = \dot{P}_I \cdot [di/dP_I + di/dP' \cdot (\dot{P}'/\dot{P}_I)]$. If $\dot{P}'/\dot{P}_I$ is approximately zero (or is very small), effects other than those of P_I can be ignored. The cost of IP services equals the price of a unit of IP capacity times a function containing as its arguments the depreciation rate, the cost of raising funds, the expected inflation rate, and parameters reflecting the tax treatment of new investments. Changes in all these other variables are again very small relative to the decline in the cost of IP capacity.

17. The regression results were $\ln IP/GNP = 3.05\ (0.093) + -1.45\ (0.039) \cdot \ln P_I$, $R^2 = 0.99$, Durbin-Watson $= 0.18$. P_I is measured in real terms (that is, it is deflated by the GNP deflator).

18. See Chow, "Technological Change and the Demand for Computers," pp. 1117–30.

Figure 2-7. *Social Benefits from the Decline in Computer Cost*

Dollars

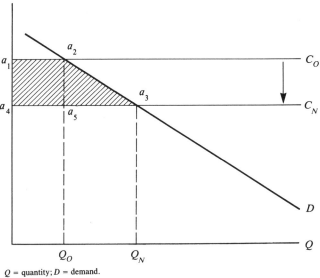

Q = quantity; D = demand.

But what social benefits can be reaped from this technological progress? If product markets were perfectly competitive so that prices were equal to the marginal costs of production, then the social gains would be passed on in their entirety to consumers (see figure 2-7). One year's technological progress would lower unit costs for information processing services from their old level, C_O, to their new level, C_N. The rectangle $a_1 a_2 a_5 a_4$ represents the benefit to consumers from the savings on the information processing used to produce their goods and services. Because information processing services would be produced more cheaply, they might then be substituted for other, more expensive inputs (and cheaper goods using information processing services might replace other final goods that are consumed). The benefit from widened use of cheaper information processing is represented by triangle $a_2 a_3 a_5$.[19] The

19. Technically, the demand curve in figure 2-7 should be a compensated demand. It should represent the demand for information processing services when lump-sum taxes are imposed on consumers to keep their total satisfaction constant. Surplus calculations using market demand are a very good approximation of the theoretically correct calculations using compensated demands, unless income effects are very large. Robert D. Willig, "Consumer's Surplus Without Apology," *American Economic Review*, vol. 66 (September 1976), pp. 589–97.

total benefit received by consumers ("consumer's surplus") is trapezoid $a_1\, a_2\, a_3\, a_4$.[20]

This consumer's surplus, CS, can be measured using a second-order approximation[21] as

$$(2\text{-}2) \quad F(C_O, C_N) = \frac{CS}{C_O \cdot IP} = \frac{(C_O - C_N)}{C_O} \cdot \left[1 + \left(\frac{(C_O - C_N)}{C_O} \cdot \frac{E}{2} \right) \right].$$

with $F(C_O, C_N)$ the function giving CS as a fraction of the value of consumption of information processing services at the original cost, C_O, and E as the price elasticity of computing demand.

If parameters are judged to be optimistic (E is 1.5 and cost decline is 30 percent), then the annual benefit from technological advance would amount to about 37 percent of base value (old technology) consumption of computing services per dollar of GNP. If the parameters are considered to be conservative (E is 1.0 and cost decline is 20 percent), then the annual benefit would be 22 percent. The result hinges on the magnitude of cost declines and is little affected by price elasticity.

During the early 1980s, shipments by U.S. computer producers rose to well over 1 percent of GNP (see table 2-2). The rental value of the stock of computers used in the United States probably ranged from 1.5 percent to 2 percent of GNP.[22] The benefit from one year's technological change—equivalent to 20 percent to 40 percent of expenditure on computer use—would amount to 0.3 percent to 0.8 percent of GNP, a

20. See Richard Schmalensee, "Another Look at the Social Valuation of Input Price Changes," *American Economic Review*, vol. 66 (March 1976), pp. 239–43; Stephen E. Jacobsen, "On the Equivalence of Input and Output Market Marshallian Surplus Measures," ibid., vol. 69 (June 1979), pp. 423–28; and Dennis W. Carlton, "Valuing Market Benefits and Costs in Related Output and Input Markets," ibid., vol. 69 (September 1979), pp. 688–96. The results are extended to a regulated industry in Timothy F. Bresnahan, "Measuring the Spillovers from Technical Advance: Mainframe Computers in Financial Services," *American Economic Review*, vol. 76 (September 1986), pp. 742–55.

21. This can be derived from the second-order terms of a Taylor series expansion of consumer's surplus as a function of prices. It was used in Zvi Griliches, "Research Costs and Social Returns: Hybrid Corn and Related Innovations," *Journal of Political Economy*, vol. 66 (October 1958), pp. 419–31.

22. In 1978 annual rent on IBM equipment was about one-third of purchase costs and the value of installations was about 5.7 times the value of computer shipments in the United States, about the same as in 1975 and 1977 but down from 6.1 in 1976. These same values suggest that shipments of 1 percent of GNP are equivalent to rental value of 1.9 percent of GNP. See Montgomery Phister, Jr., *Data Processing Technology and Economics*, 2d ed. (Bedford, Mass.: Digital Press, 1979), pp. 601, 637.

rather large amount when compared with measured GNP growth rates in recent years (although advances in computer technology have largely gone unmeasured when GNP growth is computed). This rate of technological advance has been maintained during the past few decades, which suggests that improved computer technology has contributed to substantial welfare gains in relation to all other forms of economic growth.[23]

The Rate of Return on Investments

Private firms have constantly invested their own resources in computer innovation, believing the profits so created more than outweigh their cost. Society—acting through government—has also invested considerable public resources in this never ending stream of progress. The requirement to turn a profit is not built into the process by which these funds have been committed. Indeed, it would be counterproductive in addressing the economic rationale for society making these investments (for example, if social return exceeds private return because of the public good aspects of technology).

It is reasonable then to ask whether the return to society, from a purely economic standpoint, has justified the full cost to society of investing in the continuing development of the computer. If the purely economic benefits do not justify the cost, that does not close the issue, however. After all, the benefits to national security may be the most important. But if economic benefits alone make the investments a rational choice, then the defense applications need not be invoked to justify the expenditure.

Implicit in the following discussion is this assumption: public investment in computer technology has been productive. If America had relied solely on private investments in computer R&D, the pace of technological progress would not have been as strong.

But it is not assumed that R&D activity is efficient in the sense of achieving the maximum return from a given expenditure. Instead, consider all R&D as one giant, economy-wide research project, and consider whatever duplication, fragmentation, and waste that exist as

23. In the financial services sector alone, the benefits to consumers from technological progress in computers over a fourteen-year period (1958–72) may have amounted to between 500 and 2,000 times the value of computer expenditure in that sector. See Bresnahan, "Measuring the Spillovers from Technical Advance."

an institutional given, a structural feature of the market and nonmarket mechanisms that generate research and development in the United States. The more or less continuous progress in computing technology has resulted from a continuous history of investments in computer R&D.

A Simple Framework

Appendix B explains in detail why the resources committed to computer R&D can be justified on purely economic grounds. Plausible parameter values are inserted into a simple analytical framework. The results shed considerable light on the differing roles of domestic and foreign markets in contributing to the private and social returns to investment in the technology.

The starting point is the simplified view of benefits to consumers shown in figure 2-7. A rate of return calculation must be further modified to reflect additional complications. To calculate the rate of return more accurately, the following factors must be considered:

—The benefit recurs year after year into the indefinite future. A rate of return should include the discounted sum of these future benefits.

—The overall economy is growing. Figure 2-7 will measure the benefit per unit of national product. As output of goods and services grows, so too will the benefit.

—There is usually a time lag (or *gestation lag*) between when R&D expenditures are undertaken and when the results first hit the market in the form of an improved product or process and begin earning a return. The longer the time lag, the lower the return, since the resources invested in R&D could have been put to alternative uses.

—To recoup its investment in R&D, a computer company must have exclusive control over the improved technology created by that expenditure for some period of time. During that time it must charge a price in excess of its manufacturing costs to earn at least enough to cover its R&D expenses. This technological rent adds to the social welfare calculations an additional element, a so-called "producer's surplus" (the difference between total revenues and the total costs of production). This private return must be counted as an element of the social return to R&D over and above the benefits perceived by computer users. Part of this private return is realized through domestic sales, the remainder in foreign markets.

—Sales in foreign markets account for a substantial portion of worldwide sales of American computer firms—about 40 percent to 50 percent in recent years (see table 1-4). For the purpose of estimating rate of return, 80 cents in foreign sales is assumed for every dollar of domestic sales (that is, 44 percent of worldwide sales in foreign markets).

—Ultimately, new technology does get beyond the boundaries of the firm. Because of the ease with which competitors have been able to imitate successful computer innovations, there is only a short window of time during which the innovator can claim a technological rent from exclusive use of new technology. After this period (henceforth called the *diffusion lag*), imitators can copy the innovation at low or no cost.

—Models of imperfect competition in a research-intensive good tend to be quite complex. There is no agreed upon standard analysis. Results are very dependent on the precise nature of assumptions about the characteristics of firms, their reactions to the decisions of other firms, and the extent to which research investments can be transferred and sold.

The approach adopted in appendix B will be to model market structure in two ways. The first is to vary the portion of the decline in cost that is captured as profit by an innovating firm. If the innovation immediately were to become available at no cost to a large number of firms (the industry is perfectly competitive), this parameter (henceforth referred to as the *capture rate*) will equal 0. Naturally, private investment in innovation could not be sustained in the long run in this case. If the innovating firm has exclusive control over the innovation, the capture rate will equal 1.[24] Alternative models of market structure will result in intermediate values for the capture rate within these two extremes, and by estimating rates of return with a spectrum of alternative values, some idea of plausible magnitudes for rates of return may be obtained.

The second approach will be to hypothesize that the market for computers is contestable. In other words, if the fixed costs of entry into the industry can be fully recovered when a firm exits and liquidates its assets, another firm can enter the industry without obstruction if greater than normal returns are being earned by existing firms. Although economies of scale in the use of R&D may give the largest firm a cost advantage, competitors can enter the industry if above normal profits are being earned, undercut the old prices, displace the dominant firm,

---

24. This presumes that the innovation does not lower the cost of production below the marginal revenue that would have been received by a monopolist selling at the old level of output. See appendix B.

Table 2-3. *Estimated Rates of Return on Investments in Computer R&D*[a]

Percent unless otherwise specified

Sales	Demand elasticity	Savings as percent of preinnovation cost	Fixed capture rate model[b]		Contestable markets model[c]	
			Social return	Private return	Social return	Capture rate
Normal foreign	1.5	30	69	37	67	10
	1.0	20	52	18	51	18
No foreign	1.5	30	65	18	65	18
	1.0	20	49	2.1	49	13

a. In both models the growth rate of the economy is 4 percent, the gestation lag is two years, and the diffusion lag is three years. See appendix tables B-3, B-4.

b. Capture rate is 20 percent.

c. Private rate of return is 15 percent.

and still earn above average profits. Even if no entry occurs, the threat of entry will put downward pressure on prices charged by the dominant firm, until technological rents are just sufficient to provide the normal rate of return on investments with the risk and return characteristics appropriate to that industry.

The requirement that the private rate of return equal a "normal," competitive return makes the capture rate an endogenous parameter, jointly determined by the assumed normal rate of return and assumptions about the other parameters mentioned earlier. A conservative, high bound on normal rate of return for the computer industry was estimated by taking the actual rate of return on equity in a good business year. Given a capture rate determined by the assumed contestability of computer markets, a social rate of return could then be calculated.

Table 2-3 summarizes the results of estimating social and private rates of return on investments in computer technology. A range of plausible values—generally spanning the range from very conservative to somewhat optimistic—was used to obtain the gestation and diffusion lags, economic growth rates, elasticities of demand, and the magnitude of technological advance. Excessively large estimates of private and public resources invested in computer R&D were used to give the rate of return simulations a downward bias. When taking the capture rate as a parameter, the private rate of return was determined by the model; alternatively, when the contestability assumption was used (and the private rate of return therefore taken as a parameter), the capture rate was determined endogenously by the model. Social rates of return were generally found to be quite high—in the 50 percent to 70 percent range under fairly conservative assumptions. A complete discussion of the results may be found in appendix B.

Estimates of social rates of return are most sensitive to assumptions about the magnitude of technological advance and the gestation lags delaying the fruits of research expenditure. They are relatively insensitive to assumptions about demand elasticities, economic growth, the private capture of technological rents, and the extent of foreign markets. Private rates of return, on the other hand, are extremely sensitive to all these factors. Calculations of private return will vary greatly with assumptions about market structure and the economic environment.

Table 2-3 also estimates the rates of return as if there were no foreign sales. Three major points emerge from this experiment. First, the social benefit perceived in domestic markets by U.S. consumers over the long haul far outweighs the private rents received from foreign (as well as domestic) sales. Foreign sales contribute only marginally to social return. Second, foreign operations play a major role in private return. Third, foreign markets can be crucial to the case for policies to increase private capture of the benefits of innovation. Appendix B shows that in the fixed capture rate model, raising the capture rate increases social return with a large foreign market; quite the opposite occurs with no foreign sales.

Some Comparisons

Perhaps the most credible direct calculations of returns to industrial innovation are those produced by Edwin Mansfield and his collaborators for a broad variety of low- and high-tech products.[25] The analytical framework presented in this chapter is an extension of their work. While they found social rates of return in the hundreds of percent on particular products, the median social return was considerably lower, about 56 percent. The median private rate of return was about 25 percent.

Mansfield's direct estimates of rates of return are based upon individual firm data on particular applied research projects. This data must exclude the costs of more basic research not attributable to a single project, carried out both within the firm and outside, which may have important effects on innovation. Since econometric studies frequently

---

25. See Edwin Mansfield and others, "Social and Private Rates of Return from Industrial Innovations," *Quarterly Journal of Economics,* vol. 91 (May 1977), pp. 221–40. This approach, in turn, builds on Griliches, "Research Costs and Social Returns."

have suggested much higher rates of return on the most basic research,[26] it is natural to believe that the returns calculated on particular applied research and development expenditures may be somewhat overestimated. The benefits of basic research were counted, but the costs (though only a small fraction of all R&D) were not.

Studies that have attempted to count both the social benefits and the costs of innovation in an entire sector are more rare. These studies, largely confined to agriculture, have counted the costs of basic research investments, as well as public investments in R&D. Zvi Griliches's pioneering study of R&D on hybrid corn in America concluded that a social rate of return in the 35 percent to 40 percent range was appropriate.[27] More aggregate studies of postwar investments in American agricultural R&D have found social rates of return between 40 percent and 50 percent.[28] Recent empirical results for American manufacturing suggest private rates of return on R&D between 11 percent and 16 percent, and social returns between 26 percent and 38 percent.[29] Private returns on such investments in Japan fall in about the same range.[30] Thus by the standard of either firm or sectoral studies, investments in computer R&D have yielded social returns at the high end of measured rates.

Summary

Domestic and foreign markets play vastly different roles in justifying R&D investments, depending on whether the private or social interest is considered. From the social viewpoint, the benefits of an innovation

26. See, for example, Edwin Mansfield, "Basic Research and Productivity Increase in Manufacturing," *American Economic Review*, vol. 70 (December 1980), pp. 863–73; and Zvi Griliches, "Productivity, R&D, and Basic Research at the Firm Level in the 1970s," ibid., vol. 76 (March 1986), pp. 141–54.

27. See Griliches, "Research Costs and Social Returns," p. 425.

28. Alain de Janvry and Jean-Jacques Dethier summarize these studies in *Technological Innovation in Agriculture: The Political Economy of Its Rate and Bias* (Washington, D.C.: The World Bank, 1985), chap. 4.

29. See E. Wolff and M. I. Nadiri, "Interindustry Effects and the Return to R and D in Manufacturing," mimeo, 1984, and "Linkage Structure and Research and Development," mimeo, 1984, as cited in M. Ishaq Nadiri, "Economics of R and D Investment," *NBER Reporter*, Summer 1985.

30. See Kazuyuki Suzuki, "Knowledge Capital and the Private Rate of Return to R&D in Japanese Manufacturing Industries," *International Journal of Industrial Organization*, vol. 3 (1985), pp. 293–305.

yielding a permanent cost decline will accumulate forever, and their cumulative sum is little affected by the relatively short lags between when investments in innovation are made and when their full benefit is passed on to consumers. Since the temporal window (the "diffusion lag") during which technological rents are reaped by producers is so short, profits on foreign and domestic sales (which become a component of social return during this period) are largely irrelevant to the social argument for making these investments. Most of the social benefit is derived from the savings on the cost of U.S. information processing services being passed on to U.S. consumers.

Quite a different logic rules when private return is considered. The key factors determining an innovation's private profitability are the length of time over which technological rents can be captured and the size of the market in which those rents can be collected. The benefits that continue to be passed on to American consumers long after this private rent has been eroded and dissipated are a social windfall quite irrelevant to a firm making a business decision to invest in an R&D project. Foreign sales then become a substantial factor in the private return on an R&D investment. When R&D investments result in smaller cost gains, or yield profits over shorter and more distant time periods, substantial foreign sales will be a critical factor. Without foreign sales, it would appear, such marginal investments in technology would not be made.

Thus foreign markets are of small significance to the social argument for undertaking research but of major importance to private investment decisions. The social rate of return on investment in computer technology appears to be quite high—on the order of 50 to 70 percent, when conservative assumptions about key parameters are used.

In purely economic terms, the research effort has been well worth the costs. The marked interest that governments have shown in computer technology, even where no obvious strategic motive is evident, should therefore come as no surprise.

CHAPTER THREE

Federal Support for Computer Technology

THE ROLE of the federal government in the forty-year history of the U.S. computer industry has been complex and not without irony. Some military programs ultimately were not justifiable in terms of narrow defense objectives, yet their returns were enormous in terms of the technologies created and spun off into the civilian economy. These military projects led otherwise fierce competitors to cooperate on the development of complex, computer-based defense systems. This largely unplanned diffusion and sharing of technology has, decades later, become a conscious objective of national technology policy.

A Brief History

Between 1945 and 1955 the U.S. government dominated computer development. All major computer technology projects in the United States were supported by government and military users. Between 1955 and 1965, however, a commercial, business-oriented market for computers grew rapidly, drastically reducing the government's share of the action. Government users still dominated in high-performance, large-scale scientific computers, and advanced technology projects paid for by the federal authorities accounted for much of the technical advance in computers.

From 1965 to 1975, as the commercial computer market matured, competition in this technology-intensive industry stepped up. Only a few firms firmly entrenched in specific market niches survived. Entry into the hardware competition was largely confined to firms specializing in new, low-end applications (often based on *minicomputers*) and high-end, very large-scale computers (*supercomputers*). The government played little direct role in the entry of the cheaper, low-end hardware producers, but a very direct and significant role in the high-end, supercomputer marketplace. The government's role in supporting computer technology declined, consistent with a general pattern of reduced support for technology as a result of the costly Vietnam War. Federal support for computer R&D shifted to advanced, precommercial, leading-edge concepts, more exotic technologies, and support for basic research.

Since 1975 hardware costs have continued to decline. Today the computer is a low-cost, mass-produced good. The economic fundamentals of competition in the commercial marketplace have restructured the industry at home and abroad. A new generation of advanced computer products focused on so-called "artificial intelligence" concepts based on government-funded research and development of the 1970s and early 1980s has just come to market. And a new round of heavy investment by the military in advanced computer technology promises future returns.

In the United States five federal agencies have historically provided the bulk of the resources channeled into computer research and development. In rough order of importance, they are the Department of Defense (DOD); the Atomic Energy Commission (AEC) and its institutional successors, the Energy Research and Development Agency (ERDA) and the Department of Energy (DOE); the National Science Foundation (NSF); the National Aeronautics and Space Administration (NASA); and the National Institutes of Health (NIH). This chapter examines the R&D programs of these agencies and their continuing impact on the development of computer technology. The next chapter analyzes other types of government programs that have affected the development of computer technology, such as government procurement, indirect fiscal and financial incentives favoring the computer industry, and policies directly regulating the nature of competition in the marketplace.

The Legacy of the Fifties

As noted earlier, the first American computers, installed in the 1950s, were built for military users. The huge research effort mobilized in wartime, at first whittled down to more modest proportions, was expanded after the Soviet H-bomb test in 1949 and the outbreak of the Korean War in 1950. But it was by no means inevitable that the Defense

Department assume all responsibility for computer development. For a brief period after the war the Commerce Department and its technical arm, the National Bureau of Standards (NBS), pushed for a research and development program oriented to the needs of U.S. industry. It was proposed that all the research undertaken in wartime be catalogued and made available to private businesses that had not directly participated in the defense research program. The first full-fledged, working computer in the United States was built inside the NBS, although the proposed "encyclopedia" of wartime R&D was never published.

These attempts to sponsor the development of new technologies with an explicitly commercial orientation were abruptly terminated in the early 1950s. A huge political tempest, the so-called "AD-X2 scandal," was the reason.[1] In retrospect it is clear that the fundamental issue was whether the government had any business meddling in industry, interfering, as it were, with the normal operation of free market forces. The now widely accepted economic rationale for government support for research and development had not even been articulated at that point.

For many years government support for research and development was politically acceptable only if phrased in terms of some strategic or defense objective. The major exceptions to this rule were the National Science Foundation, created in 1950 to fund basic research in universities, and the national institutes established for health research. Since computer science did not even become a "legitimate" academic discipline until the mid-1960s, virtually all government-sponsored R&D in the field was sponsored, in one way or another, by the military. Support for investment in advanced computer technology has largely continued to be phrased in terms of defense and strategic objectives. This is a historical legacy with a strong and powerful hold on the present.

Funding Research and Development

Table 3-1 details funding for mathematics and computer science research since 1967 by government agency sponsoring the research.[2]

1. The makers of the battery additive AD-X2 objected when the results of tests of its efficacy were made public by the National Bureau of Standards. See Rexmond C. Cochrane, *Measures for Progress: A History of the National Bureau of Standards* (Washington, D.C.: NBS, 1966), p. 487, on the proposed "encyclopedia."
2. Funding for mathematics and computer science have been combined for several

Unfortunately, these statistics and those presented in table 3-2 do not include information on support for development efforts by product field. Two significant trends are apparent in table 3-1. First, federal research funding began a steep slide in 1967, when statistics first became available. The nadir was 1974–75. Government research support did not recover to its 1967 level until 1982.

Second, the Defense Department has continued to lead the federal research effort. In recent years the National Science Foundation, the second largest federal patron of computer research, has expanded its support to roughly 40 percent of the Defense Department's math and computer science budget. The brunt of the budget cutbacks of the late 1960s and early 1970s was borne by Defense. Its share of research obligations dipped from 70 percent of government funding in 1967 to 47 percent in 1978. Nonmilitary users spearheaded the resurgence in support in the 1970s. In the mid-1980s, with new military computer research initiatives, that share rose again sharply.

The most uneven profile in research funding is that of NASA, which has jockeyed for third place in the funding competition with the Department of Energy and its predecessors. The decline of NASA's share in the late 1960s coincided with the completion of the lunar exploration program, and the resurgence of the mid-1970s coincided with NASA's commitment to the experimental and very expensive ILLIAC IV supercomputer. This machine was dismantled at the end of the 1970s and so too was NASA's computer research budget. Construction in the early 1980s of NASA's massively parallel processor (MPP) and its numerical

---

reasons. First, separate figures were not available until 1975, and even since then a considerable portion of the research has not been separately classified. Second, the boundaries between computer science and applied mathematics are exceedingly vague. Research in certain areas of mathematics (particularly numerical analysis, complexity theory, logic, statistics, and coding theory) is closely associated with computer research. Classification decisions vary considerably among institutions. Moreover, large classification errors are known to have occurred in the published statistics for university-administered FFRDCs (federally funded research and development centers) for 1980. Personal communication with Ms. Judith Coakley, NSF, 1984. See also National Science Foundation, *National Patterns of Science and Technology Resources, 1982,* NSF 82-319 (Government Printing Office, 1982), table 58.

Only half of funding for basic mathematics research as reported by NSF has gone to "fundamental mathematics" in recent years, according to Edward E. David, Jr., in "The Federal Support of Mathematics," *Scientific American,* vol. 252 (May 1985), p. 46. All research by the NIH in math and computer science is classified as math in the published statistics, although development of artificial intelligence applications, including expert medical systems, is known to have been funded.

Table 3-1. *Federal Funding of Mathematics and Computer Science Research, Fiscal Years 1967–86*
Federal obligations in millions of 1982 dollars

Year	Total federal obligations	Percent funded by					
		DOD	DOE[a]	NASA	NSF	NIH	All five
1967	357	70	5	5	15	2	97
1968	313	67	5	3	16	3	94
1969	271	69	6	2	16	3	96
1970	226	64	6	1	18	3	93
1971	241	60	5	1	24	3	93
1972	260	59	4	0	22	4	89
1973	232	61	4	1	19	4	89
1974	211	61	4	1	21	5	92
1975	211	57	5	2	23	5	92
1976	250	58	4	3	22	5	91
1977	291	48	4	13	21	4	90
1978	299	47	4	8	21	4	84
1979	267	54	4	1	21	3	84
1980	281	57	5	2	22	3	89
1981	297	53	5	1	22	3	85
1982	350	54	4	7	19	3	87
1983	403	53	5	12	17	3	90
1984	408	49	5	14	18	3	90
1985	519	53	8	11	17	3	91
1986	555	58	5	9	17	2	92

Sources: National Science Foundation, Division of Science Resources Studies, *Federal Funds for Research and Development; Federal Obligations for Research by Agency and Detailed Field of Science: Fiscal Years 1967–1986* (GPO, 1985), pp. 5, 11, 13, 19, 25, 27, 31, 37, 39, 45, 51, 53. The GNP deflator is from *Economic Report of the President, January 1987*, p. 248. The data for 1985–86 are NSF estimates based on the president's budget.

a. Figures before 1977, when the Department of Energy was created, refer to the Atomic Energy Commission (1967–73) and the Energy Research and Development Administration (1974–76).

aerodynamic simulator (NAS) boosted the agency's computer research once again.

Much of the military research money in the 1970s went to development projects, but this pattern shifted somewhat in the 1980s. Table 3-2 charts the structure of federal funding for university and college research, traditionally the repository for most of the nation's basic research. Since at least the early 1970s, federal funds have accounted for about three-quarters of math and computer research and development performed in universities and colleges.[3] Roughly 40 percent of the total government math and computer research budget has gone to support academic research. In the early 1970s Defense and the NSF accounted for roughly

3. See National Science Foundation, *Academic Science/Engineering, 1972–83*, NSF 84-322 (GPO, 1984), tables B-3, B-4.

Table 3-2. *Federal Funding of Mathematics and Computer Science Research in Universities and Colleges, Fiscal Years 1973–86*[a]

Year	As percent of all such federal funding[b]	Percent funded by					
		DOD	DOE[a]	NASA	NSF	NIH	All five
1973	43	47	4	1	45	3	100
1974	46	51	2	1	40	4	98
1975	46	43	3	3	45	4	98
1976	37	38	1	2	53	4	98
1977	37	40	4	1	48	4	97
1978	37	42	4	1	48	4	99
1979	42	47	5	1	43	3	99
1980	39	41	4	3	47	4	100
1981	43	46	4	2	43	3	99
1982	40	49	4	3	41	3	99
1983	41	52	3	3	38	2	99
1984	41	53	3	3	37	3	99
1985	43	55	6	3	33	2	99
1986	45	59	3	3	32	2	100

Sources: NSF, *Federal Obligations for Research by Agency*, pp. 5, 31; and National Science Foundation, Division of Science Resources Studies, *Federal Funds for Research and Development; Federal Obligations for Research to Universities and Colleges by Agency and Detailed Field of Science: Fiscal Years 1973–1986* (GPO, 1985), pp. 5, 9, 11, 17, 19, 21, 23, 27, 29, 35, 37, 39. The data for 1985–86 are NSF estimates based on the president's 1986 budget.
    a. Percent of federal obligations.
    b. Excludes funding for development.

equal shares of support to academe. With the sharp resurgence of military-sponsored computer research in the early 1980s, however, defense agencies again dominate the funding of academic projects.

To understand the nature of the computer research reflected in these figures, it is necessary to trace the evolution of support in the major federal agencies. First the primary programs sponsored by the Department of Defense will be discussed and then those of the minor agencies, where contributions have been significant despite a relatively low share of the overall federal budget.

The Defense Department

Defense Department funding made the United States a world leader in computer technology in the 1950s. This early work was largely funded or supervised by the Office of Naval Research (ONR).[4] By the end of

4. See Mina Rees, "The Computing Program of the Office of Naval Research, 1946–1953," *Annals of the History of Computing*, vol. 4 (April 1982), pp. 103–13.

the decade, however, this office had passed most of the responsibility for basic research to the military services. Before commercial computers came on the market in large numbers, all three services built their own general purpose computers for in-house research use.

The original research projects were primarily one-of-a-kind demonstration projects. Their names read like alphabet soup: the ENIAC, EDVAC, ILLIAC, the Institute for Advanced Studies (IAS) computer, Whirlwind, and the OARAC. Other projects were developed for volume production—for example, the Engineering Research Associates' 1103, the UNIVAC I, the many computers built for the Air Force's SAGE air defense system, and the Philco Corporation's TRANSAC computers.[5] The end of this first phase in defense support, skewed toward developing very expensive experimental computers, is 1961. That year the Army's Ballistic Research Laboratories Electronic Scientific Computer (BRLESC), the last of these big projects, was delivered at a cost of $3 million.[6] After 1961 costly defense computers were relatively rare, and they were usually oriented toward a special application rather than general purpose computation.[7]

The Air Force, along with the Office of Naval Research, played an especially important role among the military services in the late 1940s. In 1947 Project SCOOP, intended to model and solve large-scale systems problems for military and industrial applications, was launched. SCOOP supported the development of the first computers within the National Bureau of Standards. Computer methods for solving equation systems and optimization problems can be traced back to SCOOP's seminal work.[8]

The development of numerically controlled machine tools also began

5. See Kenneth Flamm, *Creating the Computer: Government, Industry, and High Technology* (Brookings, forthcoming).

6. See Martin H. Weik, "A Fourth Survey of Domestic Electronic Digital Computing Systems," Report 1227 (Aberdeen Proving Ground, Md.: Ballistic Research Laboratories, 1964), pp. 36–39.

7. Post-1961 examples include a limited experimental version of the parallel SOLOMON computer built in the early 1960s for the Air Force; ILLIAC IV, a larger-scale descendant of SOLOMON, delivered in 1972 and operational in 1975; the specialized PEPE parallel processor designed to process radar data for antiballistic missile defense; the massively parallel processor built by Goodyear Aerospace in 1983 for NASA, successor of the STARAN image processing computer built by Goodyear for the Air Force; and the S-1 parallel multiprocessor computer being developed at the Lawrence Livermore National Laboratory under Navy sponsorship.

8. Bruce W. Arden, ed., *What Can Be Automated?* (Cambridge: MIT Press, 1980), pp. 86–87.

in the early 1950s. Heavy promotion of this technology by the Air Force eventually resulted in the creation of the robotics and computer-controlled machine tool industries. The Air Force has continued to be the primary government funding source for efforts to automate manufacturing technologies.[9]

The most expensive computer of the period was MIT's Whirlwind. It set the contemporary standard for performance and reliability. From Whirlwind emerged the largest project of the 1950s, the Air Force's SAGE air defense system. Teamed on this huge system were MIT, IBM, the Bell Telephone Laboratories, and Burroughs. The project made important advances in both fundamental concepts and manufacturing practice. Computer graphics, timesharing, digital communications, and the ferrite core memory all have roots in the SAGE project.

National Security Agency

Deep within the Defense Department, the National Security Agency (NSA) played a critical role in the development of high-performance computers during the 1950s. It supported early computer work at ERA, Raytheon, and Technitrol; solid state and transistorized computers built by Sperry Rand and Philco; IBM's Stretch supercomputer; customized coprocessors and peripherals going into NSA's massive Harvest computer installation; and one of the first remote job-entry systems designed by Sperry Rand.

In the mid-1950s NSA also sponsored the largest basic electronics research program of the time. The agency had a direct stake in this research. Early computers had mainly employed electronics technology developed for radar applications. It was already becoming evident that advance in electronic components was the key to rapid technological advance in computers. As the cryptological workload expanded, the capacities of even the most advanced computers were being stretched to their limits. In late 1956 NSA launched Project Lightning with the

9. Much of this early history is traced in David F. Noble, *Forces of Production: A Social History of Industrial Automation* (Knopf, 1984). See also Karl L. Wildes and Nilo A. Lindgren, *A Century of Electrical Engineering and Computer Science at MIT, 1882–1982* (MIT Press, 1985), pp. 218–25. The Air Force began its integrated computer-aided manufacturing (ICAM) program in 1978 and its computer-integrated manufacturing (CIM) program in 1984. See Office of Technology Assessment, *Computerized Manufacturing Automation: Employment, Education, and the Workplace* (Washington, D.C.: OTA, 1984), chap. 8.

objective of developing components for computers a thousand times faster than the installations (including Stretch) already under development. Budgeted at $25 million over five years, Project Lightning accounted for a large part of the electronic component work under way in the United States at the time, and it included research on exotic components, basic materials, and computer architecture.[10]

Ultimately, Lightning research had little impact on the evolution of commercial computers. Rapid advances in semiconductor technology, largely fueled by the demands of other government users, made the use of silicon transistors and integrated circuits far more cost effective than the more exotic technologies. With certain exceptions, NSA's role in U.S. computer development was greatly reduced, although the agency remained a good customer for technological innovation produced elsewhere.[11]

After a long hiatus until the early 1980s, NSA regained a highly visible position on the frontiers of computer research. In late 1984 the agency announced the construction of its $12 million Supercomputing Research Center (SRC) in Greenbelt, Maryland, to be administered by the Institute for Defense Analysis. The classified research at this huge facility includes parallel architectures for high-speed computation and optical processing devices. A goal of a ten-thousandfold increase in computational speed has been suggested by NSA officials. If published reports on staffing

10. Many of the technologies were not being investigated in depth in academic and industrial labs. The results were reported in scientific publications to encourage the growth of a sophisticated technical community. The main projects included magnetic thin-film devices and tunnel diodes at Sperry Rand, tunnel diodes at RCA, supercooled (cryogenic) logic devices at IBM, high-speed rotary switches at Philco, tunnel diode-transistor logic at General Electric, basic materials and computer architecture research at MIT, and high-frequency pulse techniques at the University of Kansas and Ohio State University. More than 160 technical articles, 320 patent applications, and 71 university theses came out of the Lightning research. See Samuel S. Snyder, "Computer Advances Pioneered by Cryptologic Organizations," *Annals of the History of Computing*, vol. 2 (January 1980), pp. 67–69. The cost of Lightning, $25 million, was a considerable investment in basic research at the time. At IBM roughly $26 million was spent from 1954 to 1963 on the development of commercial memory products. See Emerson W. Pugh, *Memories That Shaped an Industry: Decisions Leading to IBM System/360* (MIT Press, 1984), p. 212.

11. NSA did fund research on advanced logic and packaging technology for the high end of the IBM System 360 in the early 1960s. See Franklin M. Fisher, John J. McGowan, and Joen E. Greenwood, *Folded, Spindled, and Mutilated: Economic Analysis and U.S. v. IBM* (MIT Press, 1983), pp. 297–98; and Franklin M. Fisher, James W. McKie, and Richard B. Mancke, *IBM and the U.S. Data Processing Industry: An Economic History* (Praeger, 1983), pp 157–58.

levels are correct, the expenditures at this institute will probably range between $10 and $15 million per year.[12]

Defense Advanced Research Projects Agency

In 1958, roughly the time when NSA was reducing its sponsorship of leading-edge computer research, a new organization was formed within the Defense Department to develop advanced technologies for defense applications. In response to the Soviet Union's Sputnik launch of 1957, the Advanced Research Projects Agency (Defense was added to its name in 1972) was established to oversee the military space program.[13] After President John F. Kennedy's election in 1960, DARPA was given a charter to pursue basic and applied research in a broad variety of fields of military interest.

From space-related research the agency branched into materials science, and in 1961 the predecessor to its Information Processing Techniques Office (IPTO) was organized. The first director of this office was J. C. R. Licklider, a psychologist and computer systems expert who had worked with Leo Beranek on speech problems at Harvard University's psychoacoustics laboratory during World War II. Later Licklider and Beranek joined Richard Bolt and Robert Newman at MIT. The four men's association continued at the Cambridge, Massachusetts, consulting firm Bolt, Beranek, and Newman (BBN), where Licklider began to work full time in the late 1950s. At BBN Licklider oversaw the development of one of the first timesharing computer systems, based on a

12. Michael Schrage, "Md. Supercomputer to Help NSA Encrypt, Crack Codes," *Washington Post,* Washington Business section, December 3, 1984; Rudolph A. Pyatt, Jr., "R&D Center Set for P.G.," *Washington Post,* November 28, 1984; and Rudolph A. Pyatt, Jr., "Supercomputer a Coup for the Region," ibid., November 30, 1984. See also "Senior Member Paul B. Schneck: NASA's Illiac to Supercomputers of NSA, in Pursuit of Parallelism," *The Institute,* vol. 9 (April 1985), p. 12; *Communications of the ACM,* vol. 28 (April 1985), p. A-40; and *Datamation,* vol. 31 (January 15, 1985), p. 66.

Datamation reported that the SRC staff will include about one hundred scientists and engineers and seventy technicians. According to National Science Foundation, *Research and Development in Industry, 1982,* NSF 84-325 (GPO, 1984), table B-35, the average research cost per scientist and engineer in the machinery industries (which include computers, historically close to the sectoral average) was about $103,000. With inflation and other cost increases, this suggests $10 million to $15 million as a reasonable ballpark estimate today.

13. All references in this chapter to the agency—pre- and post-1972—will be to DARPA. See Eric J. Lerner, "Technology and the Military: DOD's Darpa at 25," *IEEE* [Institute of Electrical and Electronics Engineers] *Spectrum,* August 1983, pp. 72–73.

Digital Equipment Corporation (DEC) PDP-1. His mission at IPTO was to build a number of "centers of excellence" for basic research in computer science that would improve the command, control, communications, and intelligence systems required by an increasingly technological military.[14]

In fiscal 1965 the research budget of the Information Processing Techniques Office was a hefty $14 million a year. Research topics included computer graphics and display systems, interactive computing and timesharing systems, and the new field of artificial intelligence. By fiscal 1970 IPTO's budget had increased to $26 million and by fiscal 1973 to $39 million. During the next decade IPTO's funding for computer research nearly quadrupled (see table 3-3).[15]

In the early days of the Kennedy administration, the secretary of defense established primacy over the individual military services as the chief funding authority for military science. In fiscal 1961 the Office of the Secretary of Defense and the centralized defense agencies, dominated by DARPA, controlled 24 percent of the R&D budget for military sciences; by 1965 that share had risen to 50 percent.[16]

Military research funding declined in the early 1970s. But DARPA's dominance became even more complete in computer science, in contrast to other disciplines. Table 3-4 shows that since the mid-1970s, when data became available, IPTO's budget has accounted for most DOD-supported basic research and roughly 40 to 50 percent of applied research

14. Interviews with R. Fano, F. Corbató, and J. C. R. Licklider, MIT, February 15, 16, 1984; and with Robert Kahn, DARPA, July 6, 1984. See J. C. R. Licklider, "Man-Computer Symbiosis," *IRE Transactions on Human Factors in Electronics,* vol. HFE-1 (March 1960); John McCarthy, "Reminiscences on the History of Time Sharing," March 1983; and Wildes and Lindgren, *A Century of Electrical Engineering,* pp. 257, 303–08, 347–48. One of the first centers of excellence jointly funded by the Army, Navy, and Air Force was MIT's Research Laboratory of Electronics, the first interdepartmental lab at MIT. Its early postwar research included microwave technology and machine translation of languages.

15. See Richard J. Barber Associates, *The Advanced Research Projects Agency, 1958–1974* (Alexandria, Va.: Defense Technical Information Center, 1975), fig. ix-1. The Defense Department appears to classify budget category 6.1 (research) as basic research, budget category 6.2 (exploratory development) as applied research, and budget categories 6.3 to 6.5 (advanced development, engineering development, management and support, and operational systems development) as development. See Department of Defense, *Basic Research Program* (GPO, n.d.), pp. 1–3. In practice, these categories are rather fluid, and appropriated funds are often transferred from one category to the next.

16. *Report of the Committee on the Economic Impact of Defense and Disarmament* (GPO, 1965), table A-7.

Table 3-3. *IPTO Funding for Computer Research, Fiscal Years 1974–84*[a]

Millions of current dollars

Year	Excluding strategic computing		All, including strategic computing
	Basic research	Applied research	
1974	13	25	38
1975	12	22	35
1976	14	20	35
1977	15	20	35
1978	18	22	40
1979	22	26	48
1980	21	31	51
1981	27	33	60
1982	38	41	79
1983	45	46	94
1984	46	41	135

Source: Graph supplied by DARPA.

a. IPTO is the Information Processing Techniques Office of the Defense Advanced Research Projects Agency.

in math and computers. Because of definitional difficulties, these statistics should be regarded as estimates. Nonetheless, they make clear that DARPA plays the key role within the military in setting computer research priorities.[17]

DARPA's large-scale involvement in developing new computer tech-

17. DARPA's share of the military services' basic research funding between fiscal 1979 and fiscal 1984 averaged 13 to 16 percent. The basic research budget of the individual services is spread across many fields, including physics and astrophysics, mechanics and aeronautics, oceanography, biology and medicine, and chemistry. By contrast, DARPA's budget is limited to five out of fourteen research areas: materials, electronics, computer science, terrestrial sciences, and behavioral sciences. In computer and behavioral sciences DARPA is the largest single funder of basic research in the military.

For basic research in math and computer sciences, the DARPA share was 60 percent in fiscal 1980, 63 percent in fiscal 1981, and between 40 and 43 percent during fiscal years 1982 to 1984. The services have considerable mathematics funding included in their research programs; the DARPA program is classified as computer science in its entirety. Thus DARPA's share of computer research is considerably higher, although certainly somewhat lower than the figures in table 3-4. Department of Defense, *Basic Research Program* (GPO, c. 1983); ibid. (GPO, 1980); and unpublished tables furnished by the Office of the Secretary of Defense.

Table 3-4 is constructed by taking DARPA IPTO budget categories 6.1 and 6.2 and calculating their size relative to support for computer science research from all defense sources. To measure defense computer science support, unassigned funds in the math and computer science areas have been distributed to math and computer science in the

Table 3-4. *IPTO Funding as Percent of Defense Department Support for Computer Science Research, Fiscal Years 1976–84*[a]

Year	Type of research		
	Basic	Applied	All
1976	108	48	65
1977	140	37	53
1978	112	39	56
1979	106	42	48
1980	97	38	49
1981	100	42	57
1982	112	40	58
1983	84	42	57
1984	83	42	89

Sources: NSF, *Federal Obligations for Research by Agency*, pp. 67, 93, 123, 149; and graph supplied by DARPA.

a. Figures may exceed 100 percent because not all IPTO research is classified as "computer science," although most clearly is.

nology in the mid-1960s was *not* focused on particular military applications. At the time the agency was heavily committed to supporting basic research with long-term importance, even if there was no immediate military application.[18] Internal reports argued that because the Defense Department was a major user of computers, acceleration of technological developments within the commercial computer industry in the United States would have important, second-order consequences. Namely, it would benefit military procurement of commercial products.[19]

same proportion as the funds actually assigned in these two areas. This is not a precise measure of DARPA's relative importance since not all of IPTO's budget was spent on items that are clearly computer science; IPTO supported programs in microelectronics, for example. Other offices within DARPA, particularly the Strategic Technology Office and Tactical Technology Office, also sponsored research on systems with a significant computer component. In 1986 IPTO was restructured as the Information Science and Technology Office (ISTO).

18. The most prominent example was DARPA's support of the radiotelescope observatory in Arecibo, Puerto Rico. Dr. Jack Ruina, a former director of DARPA, acknowledged that the project "has no immediate applications that the Services are immediately interested in, but some terribly important applied science. . . . If we weren't going to do it, nobody was—and that's all there was to it." Barber Associates, *Advanced Research Projects Agency*, p. VI-24.

19. To quote the agency's official history: "ARPA's description of the FY 1966 IPT program . . . justified the program on grounds that the DOD was a very large user of computer technology rather than stressing any unique military applications. In fact, it was boldly asserted that DOD was a beneficiary of the research largely in a secondary sense, that is, IPT's work would improve the quality of products of commercial manufacturers and DOD would ultimately benefit as a buyer of such products." Ibid., pp. VII-32–VII-33.

The funding style of DARPA has been to concentrate resources on key areas and in a few major research organizations with proven capabilities. Criticism in recent years of the highly concentrated, non-competitive, and informal nature of computer research funding by DARPA has prompted the agency to make some changes. Major areas of the Strategic Computing Initiative (SCI), DARPA's latest computer research effort, were opened to competitive bidding in large part because of this persistent criticism.

Centers of excellence for computer research across the country greatly benefited from healthy injections of DARPA funds. They included MIT, Stanford University, Carnegie-Mellon University, the University of California at Berkeley, the University of Michigan, the University of Utah, SRI International, and the Systems Development Corporation (SDC). The actual impact on university research budgets was often significantly greater than the nominal funding levels might suggest because DARPA often provided advance funding for contract work carried out later.[20] The best way to gauge DARPA's contribution is to assess some of the computer technology innovations derived from these research efforts.

TIMESHARING. Early on IPTO initiated a large-scale program on computer timesharing. Timesharing refers to a computer operating system that slices up a computer's processing time and offers it to numerous users rather than dedicating use of the machine to a single user for a long period of time. By reducing idle resources, it makes computing less expensive. It also gives all users the illusion of simultaneous access to a large computer, making real-time interaction economically feasible.

At Bolt, Beranek, and Newman, Licklider had been involved in developing one of the earliest timeshared computer operating systems, and he was convinced of the potential value of increasing the real-time interaction between human beings and computers. Early prototype timesharing systems were developed with the SDC, where $6 million was expended to create a rudimentary system for the IBM Q-32 military computer.[21] The first demonstration of this system was made in 1963.

20. In some cases in the mid-1960s DARPA provided up to four years of advance funding to universities. Ibid., p. VII-3.

21. Ibid., pp. V-49–V-50. The IBM Q-32 "super-SAGE" computer was a solid state replacement for the Q-8 SAGE computer. Although four were built, they were never installed, since the proposed upgrade of the system to a transistorized computer was never approved. The Q-32 was a white elephant at the time, and SDC was in the middle

By 1962 timesharing on the small DEC PDP-1, mentioned earlier, had become operational at BBN. With backing from IBM and the National Science Foundation, MIT simultaneously developed the much larger CTSS (compatible timesharing system) to run on a modified IBM 7090 computer.[22]

In late 1962 all these exciting developments came together: senior MIT faculty and DARPA officials negotiated a large-scale contract for an MIT-based computer research project with a timesharing focus. The research effort was named Project MAC for machine-aided cognition and multiple-access computer (or, as some joked, more assets to Cambridge).

Project MAC was a large and well-funded effort. Its initial grant from DARPA for a little over $2 million per year was quickly raised. Funding peaked at $4.3 million in 1969, slumped to under $3 million in 1973, and rose again in the late 1970s.[23] This pattern of declining research expenditure in the early 1970s and recovery in the late 1970s characterized defense-funded research in general and was a direct outcome of the budgetary claims and costs of the Vietnam War.[24] To this day DARPA continues to supply the bulk of the funding for computer science research at MIT.[25]

---

of funding problems as the SAGE project wound up. DARPA accepted the transfer of these resources from the Air Force as an entry into computer systems development. Claude Baum, *The System Builders: The Story of SDC* (Santa Monica, Calif.: Systems Development Corporation, 1981), pp. 90–92.

22. McCarthy, "Reminiscences"; Corbató interview; and Alan Oppenheimer, "The Development of Time-Sharing—An M.I.T. Perspective," MIT, 1981. CTSS was originally developed for the IBM 709. Later it moved to a 7090 and then to a specially modified IBM 7094. IBM had supported this effort by giving MIT hardware; NSF funded much of the research through grants to the MIT computation center.

23. See MIT, *Report of Sponsored Research, Fiscal Year 1981* (MIT, 1981). Project MAC's research staff peaked in 1967 at 400. Robert M. Fano, "Project MAC," in Jack Belzer, Albert G. Holzman, and Allen Kent, eds., *Encyclopedia of Computer Science and Technology*, vol. 12 (New York: Marcel Dekker, 1979), p. 347.

24. See June 8, 1967, letter from the acting director of DARPA, Peter Franken, to Howard Johnson, the president of MIT, in Collection AC 12 of the MIT archives. Johnson wrote: "As you know, the Department of Defense commitment in Southeast Asia has required significant changes in the DoD budget. For Fiscal Year 1968, the impact on ARPA has been substantial." Advance funding for future fiscal years, as a standard contracting practice, had been eliminated as an economy measure, and MIT was so notified. Further cuts in funding followed in later years.

25. Project MAC gave rise to two computer research laboratories at MIT: in 1971 the Artificial Intelligence Laboratory and in 1976 the Laboratory for Computer Science (LCS). In 1981, $3.8 million of LCS's $6.1 million budget came from the Defense

Project MAC initially copied CTSS but later refined, adapted, and expanded the original system. MIT contracted in 1964 with General Electric to construct a modified GE 635 computer for which a more advanced and ambitious timesharing system was to be built. This system was dubbed Multics for multiplexed information and computing service. In 1965 the Bell Telephone Laboratories joined the project. Bell and MIT performed most of the design and software work, while GE was responsible for the hardware.[26]

Building the Multics system—almost ten times the size of the standard IBM operating systems for large mainframes—took much longer than had been imagined. The complete system, including utility programs, ran more than ten million instructions. Not until 1969 did an initial version become operational, and not until the early 1970s was a version reliable enough for commercial use available. Bell quit the project in 1969, when it became clear that a commercial production system was several years away. Some of the Multics researchers at Bell then reacted by developing a much simpler timesharing system for small DEC computers. This brainstorm evolved into the UNIX operating system, today an emerging force in the computer world.[27]

While Multics was never adopted on a large scale commercially, research on this computer system strongly influenced the design of operating and, especially, timesharing systems. Researchers in Europe and Japan as well as the United States followed the Multics developments closely. Project MAC research papers had a wide circulation. Innovations demonstrated on the system included a complex virtual memory

---

Department, roughly $0.8 million from private sources, and the remainder from other government agencies. For the Artificial Intelligence Laboratory $2.5 million of its $2.7 million 1981 budget came from DOD, $0.07 million from private sources, and the balance from NSF. See MIT, *Report of Sponsored Research, Fiscal Year 1981.*

26. IBM, although approached by MIT, was not sufficiently interested in the MAC proposal to make required changes in its System 360 hardware. Once it realized this serious error, IBM started its own large internal timesharing project and made the necessary hardware changes in its next line of computers, the System 370. See Bob O. Evans, "IBM System/360," *Computer Museum Report*, no. 9 (Summer 1984), p. 16; Fisher, McKie, and Mancke, *IBM and the U.S. Data Processing Industry*, pp. 159–67; and Fano interview. See also Fano, "Project MAC," p. 349.

27. See Peter J. Denning and Robert L. Brown, "Operating Systems," *Scientific American*, vol. 251 (September 1984), p. 96. General Electric sold its mainframe computer business to Honeywell in 1970, but collaboration between MIT and Honeywell on Multics continued until 1977. Honeywell adopted the GE architecture for its mainframe computer products and in 1973 came out with its first commercial version of the Multics system. Fano, "Project MAC," p. 349.

arrangement, an advanced multiuser file system, a large library of utility programs, and considerable work on enhancing and verifying the security of the operating system.[28] Perhaps more important, numerous user application programs were developed as part of Project MAC—programs to manipulate algebraic equations symbolically, to prove theorems, to design, to perform structural and stress analysis on various types of physical structures, to assist in electronic circuit analysis and simulation, and to do simple word processing. Descendants of many of these programs are widely used today in a variety of scientific and engineering tasks.

Although DARPA's largest projects were at MIT and SDC, the agency also helped fund Project Genie at the University of California, Berkeley (a program that developed timesharing systems for small Scientific Data Systems [SDS] minicomputers),[29] and, at BBN, the advanced TENEX operating system for the large DEC-10 computer. This system subsequently had an important effect on the design of DEC's commercial TOPS-20 timesharing system.[30] In short, DARPA's influence was pervasive. Of twelve general purpose timesharing systems catalogued in a 1967 survey article, six (including the most sophisticated and advanced systems) were sponsored by DARPA.[31]

NETWORKS. Computer networks are communications systems that tie together the resources associated with many different computer systems; all resources are available to a user located at any single node of the network. In a sense networks are a logical extension of the timesharing

28. The virtual memory system allowed application programs to function as if available memory were much larger than the memory actually attached to the processor. It featured an automatically managed three-level memory system, controlled sharing and protection of data and programs accessed by multiple users, and the ability of the system to reallocate its resources dynamically without interruption. Fano, "Project MAC," p. 349.

29. Interview with Dr. Robert Spinrad, February 13, 1984; and B. W. Lampson, W.W. Lichtenberger, and M. W. Pirtle, "A User Machine in a Timesharing System," *Proceedings of the IEEE*, vol. 54 (December 1966), pp. 1766–74. After finishing its timesharing system for the IBM Q-32 computer, SDC went on to develop a high-security timesharing system known as ADEPT for the IBM and GE computers for DARPA and the Air Force. See Baum, *System Builders*, pp. 118–19.

30. C. Gordon Bell, J. Craig Mudge, and John E. McNamara, *Computer Engineering: A DEC View of Hardware Systems Design* (Bedford, Mass.: Digital Press, 1978), p. 511.

31. See T. James Glauthier, "Computer Time Sharing: Its Origins and Development," *Computers and Automation*, October 1967, p. 25.

concept. Many users can simultaneously access the specialized resources of numerous computers rather than those of a single machine.[32]

The involvement of DARPA in computer networks evolved directly from its timesharing program in the mid-1960s. A preliminary study in 1965 at MIT's Lincoln Laboratory, under a DARPA contract, laid out some of the basic concepts for a *packet-switched communications network*, proposed as an experimental link between the existing prototype timesharing systems.[33]

In 1966 DARPA funded the development of an experimental network that linked the Q-32 computer at SDC to the MIT TX-2 computer. The experiment was a success, and development proceeded at a rapid pace.

32. The more traditional method of setting up communications between two points is a so-called *circuit-switched network*. When information is to be transmitted, a control system sets up a physical circuit between two points, which is then dedicated to the transmission until it is completed. The circuit is then taken down. With this technology a fixed portion of the bandwidth (information handling capacity) of the communications channel is dedicated to the transmission, whether or not it is actually in use, until completed.

33. A packet-switched communications network is essentially a way of timesharing another scarce and expensive hardware resource, a telephone line, or other communications link. Information to be transmitted is broken up into small, discrete packets, each tagged with the address of its source and destination, its order within the entire message, and error-correcting codes that provide a check on the integrity of the transmitted packet and permit some moderate levels of noise to corrupt the transmission and still be decipherable by the receiver. The individual packets can then be sent out in any order, over many different routes, to their destination, where they are reassembled into the original message. The information handling capacity of communications links is more fully used with packet switching.

Packet switching was first proposed in the early 1960s by Paul Baran and his associates at the Rand Corporation as a way of ensuring reliable communications over a system in which many links were likely to fail, as in the event of nuclear war. Reliability and survivability were the primary objectives in these studies, commissioned by the Air Force. The packet-switching concept was rediscovered simultaneously in the United States and England in the mid-1960s. Donald Davies of the National Physical Laboratory (NPL) independently devised a scheme similar to that developed under DARPA auspices. Both proposals were presented at the same conference in 1967, and the DARPA proposal was altered to incorporate some of the features of the NPL design.

The British researchers were given much less in the way of resources to implement their design than was available to DARPA. By the end of 1969 a first version of the wide area (that is, linking geographically remote nodes) ARPANET was up and running, while a local (that is, within the laboratory) implementation of the British ideas at NPL was not in operation until 1973. See Lawrence G. Roberts, "The Evolution of Packet Switching," *Proceedings of the IEEE*, vol. 66 (November 1978), pp. 1307–13; Bolt, Beranek, and Newman, Inc., *A History of the ARPANET: The First Decade*, report 4799 (DARPA, April 1981).

Larry Roberts, the principal architect of the full network (christened ARPANET), became manager of IPTO's computer research in 1969, and the primary contract for the system was awarded to BBN. Specialized communications hardware was developed by Honeywell under subcontract.[34] By 1973 the basic ARPANET system was operational. Two years later the management of the network was transferred to the Defense Communications Agency.[35]

By 1969 the cost of the computer hardware required for dynamic management of communications circuits had fallen to the point where it was cheaper to use the ARPANET technology than a direct line or dedicated telephone circuit to link two computers.[36] In 1972 BBN formed a subsidiary, known as Telenet, to provide commercial packet-switched data communications; service was first introduced in late 1975. Public telephone companies in the United States and other countries later introduced similar services modeled on the ARPANET.[37]

In the early 1970s DARPA also supported the development of packet-switched communications over radio frequencies as well as telephone lines. The initial focus of this research was the ALOHA Net run by the University of Hawaii. It connected remote computer terminals to a central computer on the island of Oahu. Although packet-switched radio communications have yet to become a significant commercial technology (important as they are in military applications),[38] the method devised to control the network—known as *collision* or *contention control*—has become important in the design of local area networks (LANs). ETHERNET, perhaps the most widely supported commercial LAN system, uses a variation on the collision control system first devised for

34. Specialization in merging computers with communications applications became a major feature of Honeywell's business strategy (and that of the Japanese firm to which it was linked, NEC).

35. Bolt, Beranek, and Newman, *History of the ARPANET*, pp. III-66–III-67.

36. See Lawrence G. Roberts, "Data by the Packet," *IEEE Spectrum*, February 1974, p. 50.

37. Larry Roberts left his position as head of IPTO to become president of Telenet. BBN later sold Telenet to GTE. The ARPANET software was in the public domain. U.S. firms offering packet-switched network services based more or less directly on ARPANET concepts include Tymnet, Graphnet, IT&T, and AT&T. Other commercial packet-switched networks include TRANSPAC in France, EPSS in the United Kingdom, CTNE in Spain, DATAPAC in Canada, and JIPNET (a very faithful copy of ARPANET) in Japan. See Bolt, Beranek, and Newman, *History of the ARPANET*, pp. III-99–III-102; and Roberts, "Evolution of Packet Switching."

38. See Robert E. Kahn and others, "Advances in Packet Radio Technology," *Proceedings of the IEEE*, vol. 66 (November 1978), pp. 1468–96.

the ALOHA Net.[39] The most widely used protocol for transporting data between computers over commercial computer networks is taken directly from the ARPANET system.[40]

DARPA-funded computer research also had an important impact on the design of other commercial local area networks. The use of DECsystem-10 in DARPA computer projects formed the research base for its proprietary DECnet functions.[41]

Electronic mail and message systems, increasingly ubiquitous in the modern office, were a largely unexpected outcome of the ARPANET experiment. Moreover, DARPA-sponsored researchers were given relatively free access to the ARPANET. Because of the preeminence of DARPA in funding basic computer science research in the United States, most computer research institutions were ultimately linked on ARPANET. Working papers and brief communications could be distributed widely and rapidly in electronic form within the U.S. computer research community, a standard to which workers in other information-intensive areas aspired.

ARTIFICIAL INTELLIGENCE. Machine or artificial intelligence (AI) can be simply defined as techniques to make machines act smarter. Technologies in this area include the programming and architecture of "smart" systems, design and analysis systems ("expert" systems), studies of language, learning and vision, and manipulation and reasoning about objects.[42]

Studies of artificial intelligence began as early as the 1950s, but the cost of computing at that time discouraged widespread use of computers on problems with little immediate practical application. The main excep-

39. ETHERNET was actually invented at Xerox's Palo Alto Research Center (PARC). Its principal designer, R. Metcalfe, came to PARC from Project MAC and drew on work he had done for his doctoral dissertation. See David D. Clark, Kenneth T. Pogran, and David P. Reed, "An Introduction to Local Area Networks," *Proceedings of the IEEE,* vol. 66 (November 1978), pp. 1501–02; and interview with A. Fraser, Bell Laboratories, April 30, 1984.

40. It is known as TCP/IP. See William E. Seifert, "Choosing a Transport Protocol," *Systems and Software,* June 1985, pp. 87–90. Another commonly used protocol, devised for Xerox's ETHERNET, also has many elements drawn from work on the ARPANET.

41. C. G. Bell and others, "The Evolution of the DECsystem-10," *Communications of the ACM,* vol. 21 (January 1978), pp. 45, 57.

42. See Patrick H. Winston, "Perspective," in Patrick H. Winston and Karen A. Prendergast, eds., *The AI Business: The Commercial Uses of Artificial Intelligence* (MIT Press, 1984), pp. 1–13; and "Artificial Intelligence," in Arden, ed., *What Can Be Automated?*

Table 3-5. *Federal Expenditures in Advanced Computer Research by Subject Area, Fiscal Years 1983–85*[a]
Millions of dollars

Subject area	1983	1984	1985 (estimated)	Estimated 1985 expenditures by federal agency						
				Defense			Energy	NSF	NASA	Commerce
				All	DARPA	NSA[b]				
Computational mathematics	15.8	16.8	17.9	5.3	0.0	0.0	9.0	1.0	1.4	1.2
Machine architecture[c]	20.0	28.8	55.2	38.9	20.4	12.0	8.0	3.7	4.6	0.0
Machine intelligence and robotics	28.8	42.0	61.6	46.9	34.1	0.0	1.0	5.1	7.0	1.6
Distributed computing and software systems	24.7	38.9	49.0	41.4	17.8	0.0	2.2	4.5	0.9	0.0
VLSI design and special purpose computing	24.2	27.0	28.3	23.9	19.6	0.0	0.0	2.4	2.0	0.0
Data management	10.0	8.6	10.2	4.5	2.4	0.0	0.9	3.1	1.7	0.0
Theoretical computer science	9.2	11.9	16.0	4.4	3.1	0.0	0.3	11.3	0.0	0.0
Network and research facilities	34.1	46.9	53.7	29.5	26.7	0.0	1.0	16.0	2.2	5.0
Performance evaluations and models	6.6	6.0	6.4	0.3	0.0	0.0	0.0	4.0	1.1	1.0
Total	173.4	226.9	298.3	195.1	124.1	12.0	22.4	51.1	20.9	8.8

Source: *Report of the Federal Coordinating Council on Science, Engineering, and Technology Panel on Advanced Computer Research in the Federal Government*, June 1985, pp. A-1, A-3, B-3.
a. Advanced computer research includes basic research and exploratory development in a small subset of the fields encompassed by information processing technology. Much computer network research, the Defense Department's Ada and STARS programs, Strategic Defense Initiative research, and mission-specific computer research activities are specifically excluded.
b. Only NSA's Supercomputing Research Center.
c. Most research in computer architecture is in parallel multiprocessor computer designs. In fiscal 1984, $23.4 million was in such parallel designs, out of $28.8 million in this category. See *Report*, pp. 14, B-2.

tion was in the area of machine translation of foreign languages; the Air Force sponsored a significant research program on this subject.

The essence of much intelligent behavior is real-time interaction with the environment or other human beings. Hence the development of timesharing, which permitted low-cost interaction with very expensive large computers, was a precondition for progress in artificial intelligence research.

DARPA has always been the major supporter of AI research. As table 3-5 shows, the agency currently supplies about 55 percent of government funding for research on artificial intelligence and robotics; other military sources furnish another 20 percent. Much of this funding has been concentrated in three universities that are centers of excellence in computer science: MIT, Stanford, and Carnegie-Mellon.[43] Other beneficiaries of DARPA funds included SRI International, BBN, and Xerox's PARC.[44] One remarkable feature of DARPA's record is that the research payoff has been very long term. It was not until the early 1980s that commercial products using artificial intelligence began to emerge from

43. See Marvin Denicoff, "Sophisticated Software: The Road to Science and Utopia," in Michael L. Dertouzos and Joel Moses, eds., *The Computer Age: A Twenty-Year View* (MIT Press, 1979), p. 376; and Clifford Barney, "A 'New' Technology Goes Back 27 Years," *Electronics,* November 3, 1983, p. 131.

44. Much of the highly influential work at PARC—including powerful, user-friendly work stations, the ETHERNET local area network, and the Smalltalk programming language—built on work financed by DARPA elsewhere. DARPA contracts directly financed much of PARC's work on refinements of the Lisp language, the fundamental tool of artificial intelligence research in the United States, and the establishment on its premises of a "silicon foundry" to turn out integrated circuits. Robert Taylor, a former head of IPTO, first organized computer research at PARC and set its agenda. Interviews with Spinrad and Licklider. See also Tekla Perry and Paul Wallich, "Inside the PARC: The 'Information Architects,' " *IEEE Spectrum,* October 1985, pp. 62–75.

Private firms with long-standing research programs that have built on this DARPA-funded research base in artificial intelligence include DEC and the Bell Telephone Laboratories. DEC developed its well-known XCON expert system for configuring computers in collaboration with the Carnegie-Mellon computer science department. Although IBM supported early research on artificial intelligence in the 1950s and early 1960s, it largely phased it out during the late 1960s and early 1970s. One of IBM's very first commercial offerings in the area, Intellect, a natural language front-end to its data base management software, was actually secured from an outside vendor. See Tom Manuel and Michael B. Rand, "Has AI's Time Come at Last?" *Electronics Week,* February 4, 1985, pp. 52–53. IBM did launch a major effort in the area of speech recognition. See M. Mitchell Waldrop, "Natural Language Understanding," *Science,* vol. 224 (April 27, 1984), p. 373; and Raj Reddy and Victor Zue, "Recognizing Continuous Speech Remains an Elusive Goal," *IEEE Spectrum,* November 1983, p. 87. At the end of the 1970s, interest in data bases and logic programming led IBM to renew its AI effort. Interview with Dr. Glen Bacon, IBM, June 8, 1984.

the laboratory—twenty years after DARPA's investments in the field began.

In 1971 the agency started the SUR (speech understanding and recognition) projects. Budgeted at $3.5 to $4 million per year over a five-year period, this was the first major, concerted effort to develop a practical speech understanding system.[45] Originally planned as a sequence of two five-year projects, SUR involved parallel design efforts at BBN, the Lincoln labs, SRI International, SDC, and Carnegie-Mellon University. The original goal of the project was to accept and understand connected speech from many different speakers. The system was to use a selected vocabulary of one thousand words and an artificial syntax on a highly limited task, with a less than 10 percent error rate at speeds well under real time on a fast computer. At that time a fast computer operated at a computational rate of one hundred mips (million instructions per second).

The original group of five contractors was weeded down to three, and two of the systems produced by the survivors performed at levels close to the original goal.[46] Nonetheless, the computational requirements for the prototypes far exceeded the feasible cost for operational systems, and the second phase of the project was canceled in 1976. Speech recognition research in subsequent years continued to build on concepts pioneered in the SUR projects. Until very recently, only IBM had continued large-scale research in the area.[47] On the SUR projects DARPA set specific performance goals at the outset of research. This was rare. Other examples include the ILLIAC IV supercomputer and most recently the Strategic Computing Initiative.

Commercial computer products have recently begun to emerge from

45. Interview with Licklider. See also "Understanding Spoken Language," in Avron Barr and Edward A. Feigenbaum, eds., *The Handbook of Artificial Intelligence,* vol. 1 (Stanford, Calif.: HeirisTech Press, 1981), pp. 323–61; Reddy and Zue, "Recognizing Continuous Speech"; Lee D. Erman and others, "The Hearsay-II Speech-Understanding System: Integrating Knowledge to Resolve Uncertainty," in Bonnie Lynn Webber and Nils J. Nilsson, eds., *Readings in Artificial Intelligence* (Palo Alto, Calif.: Tioga Publishing, 1981), pp. 349–89.

46. The survivors from the first round of competition were Carnegie-Mellon, BBN, and a joint SRI-SDC team. The most sophisticated system, designed by BBN and running on a PDP-10, operated at 1/700 real time. The Carnegie-Mellon system, running on a PDP-11, almost ran in real time, but had a limited vocabulary and very limited transition possibilities between words.

47. See Robert Rosenberg, "Speech Technology Takes Slow but Steady Commercial Course," *Electronics Week,* April 22, 1985, pp. 34–35; and Reddy and Zue, "Recognizing Continuous Speech," pp. 84–87.

government-sponsored research on artificial intelligence. Computers with special instruction sets optimized for running programs written in artificial intelligence languages are now available. As of the mid-1980s, four American firms were selling computers with special architectures designed for programming in the artificial intelligence language Lisp.[48]

Today useful software written in Lisp exists in the marketplace. The largest commercial market for artificial intelligence concepts is in "expert" systems. Commercial products in vision and speech recognition and natural language understanding are a focus of current development efforts. The firms commercializing these advances are largely made up of computer science professors and graduate students with artificial intelligence research experience, largely financed by DARPA contracts, in the major AI labs of the 1970s—Stanford, MIT, Carnegie-Mellon, Xerox's PARC, SRI International.[49]

ADVANCED COMPUTER ARCHITECTURE. By the mid-1960s the basic serial computer architecture had been developed and refined, and computer designers began to explore the possibility of hooking together numerous processors to speed up computation on large problems. The first multiprocessor computers produced commercially ran independent programs concurrently, sharing data and expensive hardware resources (examples include the Burroughs B5000 and D825 computers, the English Electric KDF-9, and the Machines Bull Gamma 60).

In a pioneering paper in 1962, Daniel Slotnick explored a new concept:

48. In early 1981 specialized Lisp computers were announced by three American firms: Xerox Corporation; Symbolics, Inc., of Cambridge, Massachusetts; and LISP Machine, Inc., a California company. Xerox's dialect of Lisp, Interlisp, was developed with DARPA support. The designers of a DARPA-funded prototype Lisp machine built at MIT were the founders of Symbolics. The company LISP Machine also purchased the rights to manufacture MIT's Lisp machine. (Racal Ltd., in England, has made a similar arrangement to use the MIT technology.) These three companies have since introduced second-generation Lisp hardware products. In late 1984 a well-established firm, Texas Instruments, joined the ranks of Lisp machine vendors with its TI Explorer System, again using technology and an architecture licensed from MIT. "Artificial Intelligence Machines Burst Out of the Lab," *Business Week,* October 1, 1984, p. 109; Tom Manuel and Stephen Evanczuk, "Commercial Products Begin to Emerge from Decades of Research," *Electronics,* November 3, 1983, pp. 127–29; Edith Meyers, "Moving Beyond LISP," *Datamation,* vol. 30 (June 15, 1984), p. 64; and "High-Performance Four-User System That Runs Under Lisp Brings Down the Cost per User," *Electronics Week,* August 6, 1984, p. 84.

49. See M. Mitchell Waldrop, "Artificial Intelligence (1): Into the World," *Science,* vol. 223 (February 24, 1984), pp. 802–05; and Karen A. Frenkel, "Toward Automating the Software-Development Cycle," *Communications of the ACM,* vol. 28 (June 1985), pp. 578–89.

linking multiple processors together to simultaneously execute small parts of a single large program. A ten-processor experimental prototype of Slotnick's design, the SOLOMON computer, was built under Air Force sponsorship in the early 1960s.[50] In 1966 DARPA awarded a contract to Slotnick, then at the University of Illinois, to design a 256-processor, parallel computer known as the ILLIAC IV. This machine never achieved its goal: a speed of one billion floating-point operations per second (one *gigaflop*). A scaled-down version, with only sixty-four processors, was installed in 1972 at a cost of $31 million. This machine, one of the most expensive computers ever made, achieved only fifteen megaflops, about one-tenth of the original performance objective.[51] It was delivered to NASA, where it was used to solve aerodynamic flow problems and predict weather.[52]

Although a failure in terms of its design goal, ILLIAC IV was not without accomplishments. It pioneered the use of high-performance ECL (emitter-coupled logic) chips and all-semiconductor memory,[53] spurred the development of computer-assisted design techniques for its circuitry, and pushed the technology of printed circuit boards with a complex, fifteen-layer design. Much of this component technology was in wide commercial use within five years. In spite of its costly experience with the ILLIAC IV, DARPA continued to fund innovative research on multiprocessor computer architecture.[54]

50. R. W. Hockney and C. R. Jesshope, *Parallel Computers: Architecture, Programming and Algorithms* (Bristol, U.K.: Adam Hilger, 1981), pp. 16–19; and interview with Sidney Fernbach, May 9, 1984.

51. See Howard Falk, "Reaching for a Gigaflop," *IEEE Spectrum,* October 1976, p. 69. These costs include only expenses as of ILLIAC's initial installation in 1972. Further modifications and other work were necessary, and the system was not in regular and stable operation until 1975. It was dismantled in 1979.

52. Computers breaking the gigaflop barrier were first announced in 1984. See Tom Manuel and Charles L. Cohen, "Information Technologies Race to Merge," *Electronics Week,* September 24, 1984, p. 58. These machines were the Cray X-MP/48, an enhanced four-processor version of the Cray-1, and the NEC SX-2, delivered in 1985.

53. The first 256-bit RAM chip was produced by Fairchild for the ILLIAC IV. See Stan Augarten, *State of the Art: A Photographic History of the Integrated Circuit* (Ticknor and Fields, 1983), p. 24.

54. Texas Instruments later built a supercomputer, the Advanced Scientific Computer (ASC), using improved versions of integrated circuits intended for ILLIAC IV. The semiconductor memory chips developed for ILLIAC IV were also the basis for commercial semiconductor memories later marketed by Fairchild. See R. Michael Hord, *The Illiac IV, the First Supercomputer* (Rockville, Md.: Computer Science Press, 1982), app. D. At Carnegie-Mellon, the classical and perhaps most important experimental

This work led to the development in the late 1970s of "clustered" computer systems, independent computers joined together in a high-speed network, sharing expensive system resources, but accessed by the user as if they were a single ultrapowerful computer. In reality, however, work is distributed among the component computers. The VAXcluster system introduced by DEC in 1983 is a good example of a commercial incarnation of this type of system.[55]

General parallel computation on a large scale—that is, many processors working on different parts of a single problem in a flexible way that permits general application to a large class of problems—did not appear on the commercial market until the mid-1980s. The first product marketed of this general type, Denelcor's HEP-1 computer introduced in the early 1980s, was the commercialization of a machine built for the Army's Ballistic Research Laboratories.[56]

In 1985 BBN announced a DARPA-sponsored commercial multi-processor system, the Butterfly. A commercial parallel computer based on DARPA- and DOE-funded research at the California Institute of Technology (Caltech) was announced by Intel at roughly the same time. Still other commercial, massively parallel machines funded by DARPA monies were shipped in 1986 by Floating Point Systems and Thinking Machines.[57] As has often been the case, advances in component tech-

---

multiple processor system, known as C.mmp, was built in the early 1970s and followed by later experiments with a ten-processor and fifty-processor "Cm*" system of clustered computers. All was done with DARPA support. At BBN, as part of the work on ARPANET, a modular system based on multiple Lockheed military SUE computers, lashed together into a single system, was built and dubbed the Pluribus. At MIT, an advanced network to link together numerous computers in a distributed processing system, as well as designs for specialized computers to run the symbolic Lisp programming language, were sponsored by DARPA. See Bell, Mudge, and McNamara, *Computer Engineering,* pp. 393–403, 469–77; and Daniel P. Siewiorek, C. Gordon Bell, and Allen Newell, *Computer Structures: Principles and Examples* (McGraw-Hill, 1982), pp. 346–49, 918. The CHAOSNET and the work on Lisp machines are described in MIT, *Report of the President,* various years from 1976 on.

55. See Geoffrey L. Cohler, "A Star Is Born," *Digital Review,* April 1985, pp. 35–38.

56. The fate of pioneers is not always a happy one. Denelcor teetered toward bankruptcy in 1985. See J. Robert Lineback, "Parallel Processing: Why a Shakeout Nears," *Electronics,* October 28, 1985, p. 34.

57. See Linda Monroe, "Cornell Refusal Fires Up $50 Billion Debate," *The Oregonian,* February 6, 1986; *Defense Department Authorization and Oversight, Authorization of Appropriations for Fiscal Year 1987: Research, Development, Test, and Evaluation—Title II,* Hearings before the House Armed Services Committee, 99

nology were what made these commercial products feasible. The cost of small microprocessors had dropped to the point where experimental systems made up of hundreds of microprocessors joined together by high-speed communications links were affordable.[58]

Research on the organization and programming of massively parallel computers is a central focus of government-supported computer research today. DARPA is vigorously promoting other parallel computer designs at MIT, Stanford, Caltech, Berkeley, Carnegie-Mellon, and Rochester.[59] As table 3-5 shows, more than 70 percent of federal research and development on computer architecture was paid for by the Department of Defense in fiscal 1985, mainly by DARPA.

After years of federally sponsored research, these new ideas on parallel architecture have finally interested private firms. IBM announced a major project involving these futuristic architectural concepts in 1985. This project was largely based on the Ultracomputer research project at New York University, which was supported initially by the National Science Foundation.[60]

GRAPHICS, DESIGN, AND PRODUCTIVITY TECHNOLOGY. The field of computer graphics traces its origins to the advanced displays developed for MIT's Whirlwind and the SAGE computers in the 1950s. The first computer graphics system was "Sketchpad," developed by I. Sutherland on the TX-2 computer at the Lincoln lab and funded by an NSF

Cong. 2 sess. (GPO, 1986), p. 296; and DARPA, *Strategic Computing: Second Annual Report* (Arlington, Va.: DARPA, 1986), pp. 22-23.

58. Craig D. Rose, "Butterfly Gets 60 MIPS from 128 Processors," *Electronics Week,* May 13, 1985, p. 20. In May 1985, 16 systems with 227 processors had been installed by BBN, with another 48 systems with 423 processors on order.

The Intel iPSC, based on the experimental Caltech Cosmic Cube architecture, was brought to market in early 1985. See Robert Rosenberg, "Super Cube," *Electronics Week,* February 11, 1985, pp. 15–17; Michael A. Dornheim, "Caltech, JPL Advancing Supercomputer As Low-Cost Tool in Aerospace Work," *Aviation Week and Space Technology,* April 22, 1985, pp. 93–101; and Benjamin M. Elson, "Intel Offers New Family of High-Speed Computers for Scientific Applications," *Aviation Week and Space Technology,* March 4, 1985, pp. 81–83.

59. DARPA was supporting computer architecture research at these institutions in 1983. See Mark A. Fischetti, "U.S. Research: Fostering the Next Generation of Computing," *IEEE Spectrum,* vol. 20 (November 1983), pp. 59–63. For an extensive review of federally supported research on parallel computation, see Paul B. Schneck and others, "Parallel Processor Programs in the Federal Government," *Computer,* vol. 18 (June 1985), pp. 43–56.

60. See Tobias Naegele, "Parallel Design Gets IBM Seal of Approval," *Electronics,* August 26, 1985, p. 16. The architectural concepts were so costly to test that even IBM sought support from DARPA.

grant to the MIT mechanical engineering department. Its success sparked great interest, and CAD (computer-aided design) became a major focus of activities related to Project MAC at MIT. The first commercial computer graphics system and language, Automated Engineering Design or AED, was developed at MIT as part of this effort; the developers of AED founded a commercial software house, Softech, which has since become an influential player in the software marketplace.[61]

Sutherland went on to replace J. C. R. Licklider as head of IPTO in 1964, and advanced computer graphics remained an important item on DARPA's agenda. In the 1960s the University of Utah, the Lincoln lab, Rand, and SRI pursued significant work on graphics.[62] Sutherland later cofounded the firm Evans and Sutherland specializing in graphics and simulation technology. DARPA has continued to fund research in the area of flight simulation and training technology, and Evans and Sutherland and MIT have remained a fruitful source of innovation in advanced computer graphics systems.

Numerous computer-based engineering design aids are the descendants of systems developed at Project MAC. Examples include the structural design language STRUDL, part of the ICES civil engineering design system; the electronic circuit design system CIRCAL; the algebraic computation system MACSYMA; and the silicon compiler SCHEME. Other integrated-circuit design tools primarily funded by DARPA include the MacPitts silicon compiler developed at the Lincoln lab; Bristle Blocks developed at Caltech; the SLED layout editor engineered at Evans and Sutherland and the University of Utah; and SPICE, a widely used program to simulate integrated circuits developed at Berkeley.[63]

61. See M. David Prince, "Man-Computer Graphics for Computer-Aided Design," *Proceedings of the IEEE,* vol. 54 (December 1966), pp. 1698–1708; "Computer Graphics Comes of Age: An Interview with Andries Van Dam," *Communications of the ACM,* vol. 27 (July 1984), pp. 638–48; Robert R. Everett, "WHIRLWIND," in N. Metropolis, J. Howlett, and Gian-Carlo Rota, eds., *A History of Computing in the Twentieth Century* (Academic Press, 1980), pp. 365–84; Wildes and Lindgren, *Century of Electrical Engineering,* p. 225; and interview with Licklider.

62. Licklider interview; Prince, "Man-Computer Graphics"; and "Computer Graphics Comes of Age." While most of the funding for these projects came from DOD, not all of it came from DARPA. Results of the DARPA work included the Rand "tablet" and the SRI "mouse," graphics input devices that are now commonly used with personal computers. Leon E. Wynter, "Defense Agency's Research Role Stirs Debate," *Wall Street Journal,* October 24, 1985.

63. A commercial version of MacPitts, MetaSyn, is marketed by Metalogic of Cambridge, Massachusetts. See Paul Wallich, "On the Horizon: Fast Chips Quickly,"

DARPA also has been a major funder of research in robotics, automated assembly, machine vision, and other intelligent sensor systems. Early work at SRI and Stanford University's Artificial Intelligence Laboratory (SAIL) was very important in the evolution of commercial robotics and vision systems. Since the early 1970s MIT's Artificial Intelligence Laboratory has supported a large program in machine vision and programmable automation. The first prototype optical disk drives for reading and writing digital data were also developed under DARPA sponsorship in the mid-1970s.[64]

ADVANCED MICROELECTRONICS. Since the late 1970s another important DARPA priority has been the so-called "silicon foundry." DARPA researchers since 1980 have been able to use a silicon compiler to design a chip and assemble a data file containing the technical specifications required to fabricate an integrated circuit.[65] This file is transmitted over the ARPANET to the agency's MOSIS (metal-oxide semiconductor implementation system), which uses it to prepare the photolithographic masks needed to manufacture the chip. Batched in economic lots with designs conceived by other researchers, this chip is then sent to a commercial fabrication facility where small numbers of experimental chips are produced. The objective is to permit cost-effective fabrication of new types of integrated electronic devices by designers lacking easy access to the very costly production facilities required for full-scale

---

IEEE Spectrum, March 1984, pp. 28–34. Silicon Compilers, Inc., of Los Gatos, California, markets a commercial version of this Bristle Blocks. See also Paul Wallich, "The One-Month Chip: Design," *IEEE Spectrum,* vol. 21 (September 1984), pp. 30–34; and Denise Caruso, "Startup ECAD Thinks Big in CAD/CAE Marketplace," *Electronics Week,* May 13, 1985, pp. 44–45. For a description of SPICE, see Laurence W. Nagel, "SPICE: A Computer Program to Simulate Semiconductor Circuits," Electronics Research Laboratory Memorandum ERL-M520 (University of California at Berkeley, n.d.). SPICE development was funded by the Sprague Electric Company, the NSF, and DARPA.

64. For robotics at MIT, see *Report of the President,* various years. See also Robert U. Ayres, Leonard Lynn, and Steve Miller, "Technology Transfer in Robotics Between the U.S. and Japan," in Cecil H. Uyehara, ed., *Technological Exchange: The U.S.-Japanese Experience* (Washington, D.C.: University Press of America, 1982), pp. 89–91; and U.S. Department of Commerce, *A Competitive Assessment of the U.S. Disk Storage Industry* (GPO, 1985), pp. 10–11.

65. See John Markoff, Phillip Robinson, and Donna Osgood, "Homebrew Chips," *Byte,* May 1985; and Wallich, "The One-Month Chip," pp. 364–66. The original MOSIS facility was located at Xerox's PARC in 1980; it has since been moved to the University of Southern California's Information Sciences Institute. Commercial brokers offering services similar to MOSIS have entered the market recently.

semiconductor production. Access to these facilities was expanded to NSF-supported researchers, then to any government user, and most recently to virtually any researcher in the United States. If successful, the MOSIS service will pioneer the economic production of custom electronics in small batches.

At a more fundamental level, the Department of Defense in general and the Defense Advanced Research Projects Agency in particular have been the primary supporters of U.S. research on semiconductors constructed of exotic (that is, nonsilicon) materials. In the late 1970s the military funded roughly two-thirds of all research on semiconductors made from the compound gallium arsenide (GaAs), the most important of these technologies.[66] Because such structures are more resistant to certain types of radiation than are silicon devices, military interest in GaAs is often associated with radiation hardness, a subject of little commercial interest right now except in space-based and nuclear applications. Because the electrons in gallium arsenide devices display an extremely high mobility—five to ten times that in silicon—they may be much faster than similar structures fabricated in conventional silicon.[67] DARPA has also funded research on even more speculative technologies, such as chips using organic-based polymeric films.[68]

Manufacturers of supercomputers are currently developing designs based on gallium arsenide technology. The first commercial gallium

66. In late 1982 it was estimated that since 1977, when federal support for gallium arsenide began to rise sharply, DOD and NASA expenditure amounted to perhaps $35 million out of a total of $60 million spent in the area. Among commercially oriented labs, IBM and Bell labs have been leaders in basic gallium arsenide research. See Arthur L. Robinson, "GaAs Readied for High-Speed Microcircuits," *Science*, January 21, 1983, pp. 275–77.

67. See Hockney and Jesshope, *Parallel Computers*, pp. 367–68. Whether other factors are likely to limit the actual gains from using gallium arsenide with very fine device geometries is disputable. See National Research Council, National Materials Advisory Board, *An Assessment of the Impact of the Department of Defense Very-High-Speed Integrated Circuit Program*, Report NMAB-382 (Washington, D.C.: National Academy Press, 1982), app. G, p. 123; and Robert W. Keyes, "What Makes a Good Computer Device?" *Science*, October 11, 1985, p. 141. Because silicon technology is so advanced and developing rapidly, leading-edge silicon geometry may continue to be substantially smaller than that of gallium arsenide, in which case the shorter interconnections between circuit elements implemented in silicon will compensate, to some extent, for slower speeds.

68. DARPA funded a major research facility to investigate the use of polymeric films at Case Western Reserve University in early 1984. See David Olmos, "DOD Finances Case Western Biochip Research Center," *Computerworld*, September 3, 1984, p. 26.

arsenide chips are just starting to be produced in the United States and not surprisingly in firms whose technological roots are firmly planted in the defense sector. Further development of advanced microelectronics technology is a major priority of DARPA: one-quarter of the $49 million dollar budget for the first year of its new Strategic Computing Initiative went into pilot gallium arsenide fabrication lines and another 5 percent into other microelectronics research. To ensure that the technology begins to find its way into the marketplace, DARPA required that only 60 percent of the chips produced be allocated to the Defense Department, with the other 40 percent to be marketed freely to other customers.[69]

THE STRATEGIC COMPUTING INITIATIVE. The current centerpiece of DARPA's support for computer technology is the Strategic Computing Initiative, first presented to Congress in early 1983. Many believe support for the initiative was largely a reaction to Japan's announcement in 1981 of its "Fifth Generation" program. Congress, in approving the program, was deadset on ensuring the United States' industrial competitiveness.[70] According to DARPA, the Strategic Computing Initiative's objective, "first, and foremost, is to advance machine intelligence technology across a broad front to maintain with assurance the U.S. technical lead

69. In the United States the Cray-3 computer is being designed with gallium arsenide chips, and Cray is developing its own, in-house gallium arsenide capability. Jan Johnson, "ETA Leaves Home," *Datamation,* vol. 30 (October 1983), pp. 80–81; Larry Waller, "GaAs ICs Bid for Commercial Success," *Electronics,* June 14, 1984; and "GigaBit Unveils GaAs Product Line," *Defense Electronics,* July 1984, p. 33. GigaBit Logic, the first commercial semiconductor firm to specialize in GaAs products, was formed by a team of researchers who left Rockwell. See also DARPA, *Strategic Computing: First Annual Report* (Arlington, Va.: DARPA, 1985), p. 7. The gallium arsenide program was switched to the strategic defense initiative in fiscal 1985. See Michael Schrage, "Computer Effort Falling Behind," *Washington Post,* September 5, 1984; and Alton K. Marsh, "Honeywell Will Produce Gallium-Arsenide Chips," *Aviation Week and Space Technology,* May 6, 1985, p. 125.

70. See DARPA, *Strategic Computing—New-Generation Computing Technology: A Strategic Plan for its Development and Application to Critical Problems in Defense* (Arlington, Va.: DARPA, October 1983); M. Mitchell Waldrop, "The Fifth Generation: Taking Stock," *Science,* November 30, 1984, p. 1063; and Jonathan Jackey, "Washington: The 'Star Wars' Defense Won't Compute," *Atlantic,* vol. 255 (June 1985), p. 24. Former Congressman Ed Zschau, who was chairman of the Republican task force on high technology, thus expressed these reservations about the program: "My concern is that specific technological breakthroughs—other than what's in people's heads—may be classified because they're considered to have military significance and therefore may be difficult to get out into the private sector. I would feel more comfortable if there were two military applications and one commercial one." See Willie Schatz and John W. Verity, "DARPA's Big Push in AI," *Datamation,* vol. 30 (February 1984), p. 50.

in advanced computer technology through the next decade."[71] In widely quoted public statements, former DARPA director Robert Cooper described the initiative as "buying an insurance policy against IBM management's decision not to pursue machine intelligence through the 1990s."[72] The head of the Strategic Computing Initiative, Clint Kelley, has stated that the capture of international market share based on advanced computer technologies "is the absolute salient issue confronting this program and, in fact, confronting all research of this nature in the country."[73]

The project, originally budgeted at $145 million in fiscal 1986, but cut back to $104 million, is expected to cost about $600 million in its first five years and over $1 billion if extended for a decade.[74] The program is heavily weighted toward increased support for the research areas that traditionally have been the preserve of DARPA: artificial intelligence, innovative parallel architecture for symbolic computing applications, advanced microelectronics, and new hardware. Out of the ordinary are the dramatic increases in public resources to be invested in these fields and the specific military applications, complete with ambitious performance objectives, in which these technologies are to be used. Computing technology accounted for 31 percent of the 1987 DARPA budget request, or $263 million, replacing directed energy weapons (largely transferred to the Strategic Defense Initiative organization in 1984) as DARPA's major effort.[75]

In fact, many computer scientists believe that the military "test bed" applications of the program may be decades away.[76] One application is

71. DARPA, *Strategic Computing: First Annual Report*, p. 1.

72. See "Darpa Chief Calls U.S. Supercomputer Effort 'Insurance Policy' after IBM Drops Research," *The Institute*, vol. 8 (April 1984), p. 1; and Jake Kirchner, "Japan No Big Threat to U.S. Vendors, Darpa Chief Says," *Computerworld*, March 5, 1984, p. 23.

73. Elizabeth Corcoran, "Strategic Computing: Far from the Finish Line," *The Institute*, vol. 10 (December 1986), p. 8.

74. See Schatz and Verity, "DARPA's Big Push in AI," pp. 48–50; Corcoran, "Strategic Computing"; and DARPA, *Strategic Computing: First Annual Report*, p. 7.

75. Philip J. Klass, "DARPA Envisions New Generation of Machine Intelligence Technology," *Aviation Week and Space Technology*, April 22, 1985, p. 46; and *Defense Department Authorization and Oversight*, Hearings, p. 281.

76. At a conference in Santa Cruz in March 1984, attended by computer scientists in government, academia, and industry, the consensus was that the military applications objectives were unachievable within the stated time horizon. See "Researchers Differ on Strategic Computing," *The Institute*, vol. 9 (May 1985), p. 1. See also Willie Schatz and John W. Verity, "Weighing DARPA's AI Plans," *Datamation*, vol. 30 (August 1,

a "pilot's associate" that would be able to help a combat pilot manage his craft under battle conditions in real time by understanding and responding to continuous natural speech commands in a noisy, stressed, and hostile environment. This application lies far, far beyond the current capabilities of any actual system. Another unlikely target for 1990 is an autonomous, driverless vehicle able to travel with other moving vehicles up to sixty kilometers per hour and navigate as far as fifty kilometers away using visual sensors.[77] The third application is a series of expert systems in naval battle management that can communicate with naval officers through speech and graphic interfaces. This is perhaps the most readily achievable objective, given the relative maturity of expert systems technology compared with complex speech and image understanding systems. About 80 percent of the expenditure in the program from 1984 to 1988 was slated to be invested in "technology base" and "infrastructure," and only 20 percent in military applications.[78] Economic and industrial spinoffs were a conscious objective of the program's planners.[79]

1984), pp. 34–43; and Mark Stefik, "Strategic Computing at DARPA: Overview and Assessment," *Communications of the ACM,* vol. 28 (July 1985), pp. 690–704. DARPA officials have apparently revised their view of the feasibility of these applications. See Schrage, "Computer Effort Falling Behind." Air Force scientists also seem to be backing away from any commitment to producing a prototype system in the near term: "The Pilot's Associate is not developmental hardware, but is targeted for next-generation aircraft, beyond the Advanced Technology Fighter. . . . Therefore, we will do the initial Pilot's Associate work in non-real time. When we get capable machines, we will bring them into the program. We will begin with symbolic machines knowing we will have to go to real-time machines later." Dr. Donald L. Moon, Air Force Avionics Laboratory, quoted in Kenneth J. Stein, "DARPA Stressing Development of Pilot's Associate System," *Aviation Week and Space Technology,* April 22, 1985, pp. 71, 74.

77. One computer scientist is quoted as follows: "I think you can expect to see one of these vehicles moving independently in a constrained environment at a reasonable speed in the near future, but moving independently in the real world which is occupied by other moving objects and differing terrain, well that's quite a way off." See "Car with Six Wheels and No Driver Leading to New Generation of Robots," *New York Times,* May 6, 1985. Within DARPA the autonomous land vehicle appears to be viewed as the application most likely to be implemented according to plan. According to Schrage, "Computer Effort Falling Behind," DARPA is "very pleased" with the vehicle's progress. Lynn Conway, former chief scientist for the program, said, "We have a fair degree of confidence that we can plan and produce the autonomous vehicle hardware on schedule." See Waldrop, "Fifth Generation," p. 1063.

78. See Stefik, "Strategic Computing at DARPA," p. 696.

79. As Waldrop states, "The theme of industrial involvement is echoed again and again at DARPA headquarters. 'It's our most important objective,' says [DARPA head] Cooper. The research means nothing to the rest of the Pentagon until there is an

In some respects the Strategic Computing Initiative represents a change in the way DARPA operates. Traditionally, much of the agency's support has gone to the academic research community. But the lion's share of strategic computing funds (48 percent of the 1984 and 1985 budgets) went to industry.[80] The emphasis on "milestones" and concrete "deliverables" marks a clear shift toward more applied, developmental work. Previous DARPA programs (ILLIAC IV and the SUR projects) held too firmly to rigidly set goals in areas where technological limits were poorly defined. They were less than fully productive because the freedom to change direction was renounced at the start.

Office of the Secretary of Defense

Although DARPA has clearly played the leading role in military support for computer technology since the early 1960s, it has not been the only actor in the Defense Department.

During the late 1970s the Office of the Secretary of Defense (OSD), independently of DARPA, began considerable efforts to upgrade computer-related technology within DOD. The first of these programs was the development of the Ada language, intended to be the single future standard for all military systems applications (at the time there were about 400 incompatible languages in use). The mounting costs of software production and maintenance convinced OSD that significant economies could be achieved through software standardization. After an extensive specification process begun in 1975, a large, multipurpose language developed at CII-Honeywell-Bull was chosen in 1979.[81] After further testing and evaluation, the specifications were frozen into a standard in 1983. Although there is considerable debate over the utility and size of the Ada instruction set, there is little doubt that military support for the language will encourage its widespread use in the future.[82]

---

industrial base to provide the hardware, he says. Moreover, getting industry involved is the key to spin-offs in the private sector." Waldrop, "Fifth Generation," p. 1063.

80. See DARPA, *Strategic Computing: First Annual Report*, p. 7; and *Strategic Computing: Second Annual Report*, p. 26. Forty-three percent of the budget went to universities in 1984 and 41 percent in 1985.

81. See "ADA: Past, Present, Future: An Interview with Jean Ichbiah, the Principal Designer of Ada," *Communications of the ACM*, vol. 27 (October 1984), pp. 992–93. Though the Ada initiative was hatched in the Office of the Secretary of Defense, its development and refinement were managed by DARPA.

82. Debate over Ada focuses primarily on the size and complexity of the language— it is designed to do all things for all people—and the difficulty of producing an efficient

This is not the first time Defense Department designs have influenced the development of programming languages. In the late 1950s a DOD task force designed the specifications for the common business-oriented language (Cobol).[83] By requiring general purpose computers purchased for the military services to have facilities for programming in Cobol, and insisting that logistics and other business-like applications be written in Cobol, the services gave the language an important boost. Cobol became and remains the de facto standard for business applications. Similarly, the Jovial language, developed for the Air Force by the Systems Development Corporation for command-control applications in 1959, was adopted by the Navy and Air Force as their standard command-control systems language.[84] Although used extensively by the services, NASA, and industry, it was by nature a very specialized instrument and had far less impact on industrial users than had Cobol.

In 1982 the Ada program was joined by other new programs as part of a more generalized software initiative run by OSD. The intention was to improve productivity, reliability, and adaptability in DOD software development, and the program was dubbed STARS (software technology for adaptable, reliable systems). In fiscal 1984 the effort was budgeted at $60 million. Funding was expected to soar to a sustained level of $100 million (constant 1984 dollars) per year by fiscal 1987, but it held steady at roughly the fiscal 1984 level.[85] A major focus of the program is the development of software production technology and productivity-enhancing software development tools to be transferred to the private sector. As part of this effort, a five-year, $103 million contract establishing a Software Engineering Institute at Carnegie-Mellon University was announced in 1985. With a staff of 250, the primary mission of the institute is to develop new software tools and methods.[86]

---

compiler. As of mid-1985, a practical production-quality compiler had not been released. See "More on Is Ada Too Big?" *Communications of the ACM*, vol. 28 (July 1985), pp. 752–53; and Brad Bass, "Ada Is Falling Short, Report Says," *Government Computer News*, vol. 6 (February 13, 1987), pp. 1, 12–13.

The artificial intelligence applications written for the strategic computing program will almost certainly be written in the AI language Lisp or Prolog. In spite of the intended universality of use, Ada is not appropriate for development of AI applications.

83. See Jean E. Sammet, *Programming Languages: History and Fundamentals* (Englewood Cliffs: Prentice-Hall, 1969), pp. 330–34.

84. See Baum, *System Builders*, pp. 55–57.

85. Edith W. Martin, "Strategy for a DoD Software Initiative," *Computer*, March 1983, p. 58; and *National Defense Authorization Act for Fiscal Year 1987*, House Conference Report, 99 Cong. 2 sess. (GPO, 1986), pp. 419–33. Much of the funding was transferred from the army into the strategic defense initiative in fiscal 1987.

86. George Leopold, "CMU Starts DOD Software Center," *Electronics Week*,

The centerpiece of defense research in the mid-1980s is the Strategic Defense Initiative (SDI), a multibillion-dollar program to devise a space-based (hence the nickname "Star Wars") ballistic missile defense. Some of the work on parallel computer architecture at Caltech's Jet Propulsion Laboratory became a focus for efforts to develop command and control systems for SDI. In 1985 researchers at a number of academic institutions, including Stanford, Caltech, Carnegie-Mellon, and MIT, were jointly granted an initial $9 million contract to pursue research on parallel architecture and optical computers to be used for a space-based ballistic missile defense.[87] Another group, formed in 1985 to research "novel materials," will focus on compact electronic packaging for use in computing systems and new semiconductor materials. Yet another SDI-related effort, run by DARPA's Strategic Technology Office, is aimed at constructing a fast gallium arsenide thirty-two-bit microprocessor for use in a satellite-based defense computer.[88]

In recent years OSD has also supported a major initiative in conventional, silicon semiconductor technology, the VHSIC (very high speed integrated circuit) program. It was launched in 1978 in response to intelligence estimates that the United States' lead in semiconductor technology had slipped from five to ten years to three to five years. Industry sources were convinced that the program was as much a response to Japan's VLSI (very large scale integration) program begun in 1977 as to any challenge from the Soviet Union, and it was sold to Congress as a response to industry's eroding technological leadership. By fiscal 1989 close to one million dollars will have been invested in the program. The VHSIC program has speeded up the pace of development of design tools, high-performance production equipment, and semi-

February 4, 1985, p. 27. One of the first projects of the institute is to investigate the concept of a "software factory," one of the very few areas in which the Japanese software industry may be ahead of U.S. practice. See D. Brandin and others, *JTECH Panel Report on Computer Science in Japan* (La Jolla, Calif.: Science Applications International Corporation, 1984), pp. 3-3–3-5.

87. Other participants include the Batelle Columbus Laboratories, Georgia Tech, the Lincoln lab, the Naval Ocean Systems Laboratory, and the universities of Dayton and Alabama. See David E. Sanger, "Universities Given 'Star Wars' Computer Research," *New York Times*, April 24, 1985; and R. Jeffrey Smith, "Academic Consortia Receive First Star Wars Grants," *Science*, May 10, 1985, pp. 696–97.

88. "SDI Pursues Hypercube Technology Effort," *Aviation Week and Space Technology*, March 4, 1985, p. 81; and Richard Halloran, "Research Planned on Missile Defense," *New York Times*, May 18, 1985. Members include GE, SUNY Buffalo, and the Naval Research Laboratory. On the satellite-based defense computer, see Clifford Barney, "DARPA Eyes 100-MIPS GaAs Chip for Star Wars," *Electronics Week,* May 20, 1985, p. 22.

conductor device designs, but some critics question whether the types of products and technologies developed are the most commercially promising.[89]

This discussion has stressed the major programs in computer-related technologies run by the Office of the Secretary of Defense. It is important to note, however, that significant development efforts in all these fields have also been made by the individual military services. The Air Force, in particular, recently announced the creation of two consortia in the field of artificial intelligence, funded out of $22 million budgeted for AI research in fiscal 1985. In one arrangement a group of eight northeastern universities was awarded an $8.2 million contract to undertake artificial intelligence research on specific technologies over the next five years.[90]

And in 1985 the establishment of an institute to apply artificial intelligence to manufacturing problems was announced. This is a cooperative venture by industry, university, and government researchers. An Air Force contribution of $1.5 to $2 million per year is to be matched with industry funding for a total of $6 to $8 million per year.[91]

The Atomic Energy Commission

From the outset the newly developed digital computers were used in nuclear weapons design. The first problem run on ENIAC in 1945 was as part of the nuclear bomb research in Los Alamos. The computational requirements for such problems prompted the AEC to support computer development, especially since that very first problem proved to be far

89. See Ray Connolly, "Pentagon to Fund Major IC Program," *Electronics*, September 14, 1978, p. 81; "VHSI Proposal Finds Willing Audience," *Electronics*, September 28, 1978, pp. 89–90; Glen R. Fong, "The Potential for Industrial Policy: Lessons from the Very High Speed Integrated Circuit Program," *Journal of Policy Analysis and Management*, vol. 5 (1986), p. 277; General Accounting Office, *GAO Assessment of DOD's Very High Speed Integrated Circuits (VHSIC) Technology Program*, Report to the Secretary of Defense (Gaithersburg, Md.: GAO, 1985), pp. 4–5; National Research Council, *Assessment of the Impact;* "VHSIC Hits New Levels of Acceptance," *Electronics Week*, February 25, 1985, p. 13; Phillip R. Brannon, "VHSIC Commercial Potential Gets Brighter," *High Technology*, vol. 5 (May 1985), p. 56; and Leslie Brueckner with Michael Borrus, "Assessing the Commercial Impact of the VHSIC (Very High Speed Integrated Circuit) Program," Roundtable on the International Economy (Berkeley: University of California, 1984), pp. 44–50.

90. John Wengler, "Northeast AI Research Gets Air Force Boost," *Electronics Week*, February 4, 1985, p. 29.

91. "Wright Laboratories Broadens Advanced Technology Initiatives," *Aviation Week and Space Technology*, April 22, 1985, p. 79.

beyond the abilities of ENIAC.[92] The AEC and its institutional successors, the Energy Research and Development Agency and the Department of Energy, have been and continue to be a major force behind the development of high-performance scientific supercomputers.

To meet the atomic program's computational needs, a series of computers copied from the pioneering Institute for Advanced Studies computer were constructed and installed at laboratories pursuing nuclear research. Machines built as part of this program included the MANIAC I, built at the Los Alamos National Laboratory, the Oak Ridge National Laboratory's ORACLE, the Argonne National Laboratory's AVIDAC, and the ILLIAC I at the University of Illinois. Another copy of the Institute of Advanced Studies computer was built at the Air Force's Project RAND. Although based on the IAS design, considerable new work went into systems built for all of these computers.[93] Because the development process for these machines turned out to be so protracted, completed machines built elsewhere were often commandeered for nuclear weapons work as well. Weapons design jobs were run on SEAC soon after it was completed at the National Bureau of Standards, and the calculations needed for the United States' first thermonuclear weapons were actually cranked out on the floor of the UNIVAC factory in Philadelphia.[94]

In the mid-1950s the AEC began a second round of state-of-the-art computer projects involving design and construction of new model computers at selected universities and research labs.[95] As a commercial

92. See the interview with Stanley Frankel, October 5, 1972, conducted by Robina Mapstone, available in the Smithsonian Institution archives.

93. See J. C. Chu, "Computer Development at Argonne National Laboratory," James E. Robertson, "The ORDVAC and the ILLIAC," and N. Metropolis, "The MANIAC," all in Metropolis, Howlett, and Rota, *History of Computing,* pp. 345–46, 347–64, 457–64.

94. See Ralph J. Slutz, "Memories of the Bureau of Standards' SEAC," in Metropolis, Howlett, and Rota, *History of Computing,* pp. 471–77; and *Computers and Their Role in Energy Research: Current Status and Future Years,* Hearings before the House Committee on Science and Technology, 98 Cong. 1 sess. (GPO, 1983), p. 163. The IAS and Argonne computers were completed in 1951, the Los Alamos and Illinois machines in 1952, and the Oak Ridge machine in 1953.

95. At Los Alamos design and construction of MANIAC II was begun in 1955, completed in 1957, and at Argonne, GEORGE was built. See Metropolis, "MANIAC," pp. 457–64; "History of Computing at Los Alamos," in Los Alamos National Laboratory, *Annual Report 1982,* pp. 90–95; and Herman H. Goldstine, *The Computer: From Pascal to von Neumann* (Princeton University Press, 1972), p. 307. ILLIAC II was built at the University of Illinois from 1957 to 1962; MERLIN (used for on-line control of physics

computer industry emerged, AEC support for computer development largely shifted to contracts with industry.

With the importance of advanced computers to its mission becoming increasingly clear, the AEC set up a formal computer research program in 1956. Shortly thereafter the agency contracted with private firms to develop and produce supercomputers—the Sperry Rand LARC for the Livermore lab, IBM's Stretch for Los Alamos. The AEC's computer research budget in the late 1950s was not extraordinarily large—perhaps $5 to $6 million per year.[96] Nonetheless, both these projects greatly influenced computer design.

The purchase of high-performance supercomputers by the AEC was the backbone for the development of this particular market in the 1960s. Development of Control Data Corporation's 6600—the machine that dominated supercomputing throughout the decade—was financed by AEC advance payments and purchased by the Livermore lab in 1964. Two of the first four built, in fact, were delivered to the AEC.[97] From the early 1960s to the mid-1970s, the commission was the central player in a series of expensive, lengthy, and often delayed development projects with Control Data that drove forward the state of the art in advanced supercomputers.[98]

---

experiments) at the Brookhaven National Laboratory from 1956 to 1959; and a later copy, the RICE computer, at Rice University in the early 1960s, along with MANIAC III at the University of Chicago. Interview with Spinrad; Robertson, "The ORDVAC and the ILLIAC"; Weik, "A Fourth Survey"; K. Curtis and others, "John R. Pasta, 1918–1981: An Unusual Path Toward Computer Science," *Annals of the History of Computing,* vol. 5 (July 1983), pp. 224–38. The ILLIAC III, a specialized computer for image processing applications, was designed and built with AEC support in the early 1960s but destroyed by fire before it was completed. See B. H. McCormick, "The Illinois Pattern Recognition Computer—ILLIAC III," *IEEE Transactions on Computers,* vol. EC-12 (December 1963), pp. 791–813.

96. Curtis and others, "John R. Pasta"; and interview with Fernbach.

97. Sidney Fernbach, "A Brief History of Supercomputers," draft, n.d., p. 3.

98. Livermore in 1963 bought the first Control Data 3600, a smaller machine with a compatible architecture, to develop software for the 6600. In anticipation of the 3600, Livermore had bought Control Data's first product, the 1604.

The successor to the 6600, the 7600, also was purchased first by Livermore in 1969, and software development was initiated on a 6600 prior to its delivery. Fernbach interview; Fisher, McKie, and Mancke, *IBM and the U.S. Data Processing Industry,* p. 93.

In the mid-1960s, when Westinghouse was considering the development of the ILLIAC IV supercomputer design, Livermore had set aside $5 million to invest in that project. When Westinghouse declined, the entire effort was absorbed by DARPA instead. Thus when Control Data sought support for the development of a vector processing

Seymour Cray, a principal designer of the Control Data supercomputers (the 1604, 3600, 6600, and 7600) left the corporation in the early 1970s to start his own firm, Cray Research. By 1976 he had developed, without any financial support from the government, the Cray-1. To make a sale he was forced to put the first Cray-1 into place at Los Alamos, free of charge, to be tested. The machine performed outstandingly, and Los Alamos bought it.[99]

The contribution of the national laboratories to scientific computing has not been confined to underwriting development of, or serving as first purchaser for, high-performance hardware. In 1964 the Livermore lab developed OCTOPUS, one of the first local area networks to link remote users to central computer facilities. This network was probably the first sophisticated general purpose computer network built.[100]

Even more important, the AEC and DOE national laboratories developed much of the software used in high-performance scientific computing. Top-of-the-line supercomputers had generally been deliv-

---

computer to be known as the STAR 100, Livermore had both an interest and available funds. Control Data was awarded a contract for the STAR by the AEC. It was not to be a happy experience. Development was delayed, the AEC had become uncharacteristically tight-fisted about releasing funding for the project, and the prototypes at first did not work properly. Fernbach interview; interview with James Thornton, February 7, 1984; and Fernbach, "Brief History of Supercomputers."

Finally, in 1974, the machine was delivered. Four were built, of which two were delivered to the Livermore lab, one to NASA, and the fourth was used by Control Data. The machine performed well on problems easily formulated in terms of vector operations and poorly on conventional scalar processing. A high-performance scalar unit was added to the design in the late 1970s, and the machine was renamed the Control Data Cyber 203. This design was further upgraded in 1982 to the Cyber 205, then marketed as the only other commercial competition for the Cray-1 supercomputer. Hockney and Jesshope, *Parallel Computers*, pp. 12–13; and Fernbach, "Brief History of Supercomputers," p. 6.

In 1983, Control Data spun off its supercomputer product line into a subsidiary, ETA, which is currently developing the successors to the Cyber 205. See Office of Technology Assessment, *Information Technology R&D: Critical Trends and Issues* (OTA, 1985), p. 60. It is certainly no coincidence that Engineering Technology Associates can trace its lineage back to Engineering Research Associates, formed by the Navy to build high-performance computing equipment after the war.

99. The Cray-1 is descended from the CDC 7600 architecture, which Control Data had dropped for the STAR 100. See Los Alamos, *Annual Report*; and Fernbach, "Brief History of Supercomputers," p. 7.

100. C. Gordon Bell and Allen Newell, *Computer Structures: Readings and Examples* (McGraw-Hill, 1971), pp. 504, 507; and Siewiorek and others, *Computer Structures*, p. 393. A possible rival might be the network built by NSA in the late 1950s and early 1960s to pull together the machines of its Harvest computer complex, about which almost no details have been published.

ered to their first users with little software. Livermore developed an operating system, a timesharing system, and applications software for the Control Data machines it pioneered. The first Cray-1 was delivered to Los Alamos without software; researchers there developed both an operating system and applications software. The Cray Time Sharing System (CTSS), the main timesharing system for the Cray-1, was developed at Livermore, and it is a direct descendant of a system developed for the 6600 twenty years earlier.[101]

The DOE labs have been an important source of numerical analysis software for mathematical computations. High-quality matrix manipulation subroutines, developed and distributed gratis by the Argonne National Laboratories (with funding from DOE and NSF), are widely used in industrial, government, and academic computing installations across the United States.[102]

The Atomic Energy Commission's share of federal spending on math and computer research has held fairly constant at between 4 and 6 percent (see table 3-1). In the early-to-mid-1970s the AEC retreated from its traditional, center-stage role in supercomputer funding. Its reluctance to take a financial risk on Control Data's STAR 100 and the Cray-1 was in marked contrast to direct research support to Sperry Rand, ERA, and IBM in the 1950s and advance payments to Control Data in the 1960s. One knowledgeable observer thus explains the change:

In the 40s and early 50s the direct federal government funding of supercomputer development leaned heavily on the vast reservoir of electronic technology developed under government auspices during World War II. In the late 50s and 60s the pattern changed to government supported base technology development and the placing of government orders in advance of development by small companies which risked their future on technical success with supercomputers. During the most recent decade the federal government's approach has been to buy its supercomputers at arm's length from established suppliers who take the full risk for their development, and it's no

101. See Fred W. Dorn, "The Cray-1 at Los Alamos," *Datamation*, vol. 24 (October 1978), p. 115. Dieter Fuss and Carol G. Tull, "Centralized Supercomputer Support for Magnetic Fusion Energy Research," *Proceedings of the IEEE*, vol. 72 (January 1984), p. 37.

102. These are the LINPACK and EISPACK routines. See W. J. Cody, "Observations on the Mathematical Software Effort," in Wayne R. Cowell, ed., *Sources and Development of Mathematical Software* (Englewood Cliffs, N.J.: Prentice-Hall, 1984), pp. 1–14.

coincidence that the rate of progress has slowed. . . . This 'try before you buy' policy is now common in government procurements.[103]

By the late 1970s the government's research funding had again picked up, large purchases of new generation supercomputers for the nuclear laboratories were made, and new initiatives developed. For the first time since the 1950s, the national labs began to develop their own prototypes of new hardware for high-speed computation.

The largest of these was the S-1 computer, developed at the Livermore lab under Navy sponsorship with additional technical and research support from MIT and other outside contractors.[104] Although originally justified in terms of high-speed signal processing applications, the machines currently produced in the S-1 program are general purpose, parallel, multiprocessor computers with a broad variety of uses.[105] From 1975 to 1982 roughly $30 million (in 1982 dollars) was invested in the program; from 1980 through 1983 annual spending on the S-1 amounted to roughly $5 to $6 million (current dollars); from 1984 to 1988 planned funding was about $7 million per year.[106] The S-1 project will probably be at least as costly as the ill-starred ILLIAC IV, with considerably less visible results. Other experimental work on computer hardware is also supported at Los Alamos and Livermore.[107] Unfortunately, the commercial industry has been little influenced by any of these projects.[108]

103. William C. Norris, "A Conducive Environment for Supercomputers," paper presented at the Frontiers of Supercomputing Conference, Los Alamos National Laboratory, August 18, 1983, p. 4.

104. See the descriptions of activities at the Laboratory for Computer Science in MIT, *Report of the President,* 1976 and 1977.

105. The S-1 was being evaluated for use in symbolic computing, as well as for artificial intelligence applications, by DARPA in 1984. It fell well short of the Cray-XMP (a dual processor version of the Cray-1) in performance on these applications. See DARPA, *Strategic Computing: First Annual Report,* p. 6. It was also being justified as a component of the Strategic Defense Initiative.

106. *Computers and Their Role in Energy Research,* Hearings, p. 271. 1975 dollars have been converted to 1982 dollars using the GNP deflator. See also OTA, *Information Technology R&D,* p. 58; *Supercomputers,* Hearings before the House Committee on Science and Technology, 98 Cong. 1 sess. (GPO, 1983), p. 282. DOE began to cosponsor the S-1 project in the early 1980s, and funding is currently split evenly between DOE and the Navy.

107. At Los Alamos researchers were developing their own experimental parallel processing system, known as PUPS (parallel microprocessor system), and leasing a HEP-1 (a parallel machine produced by Denelcor, Inc.). See "Supercomputers: Who'll Be the Fastest with the Fastest?" *Physics Today,* vol. 37 (May 1984), pp. 62–63.

108. One exception has been the development of software used for computer logic design. By late 1983, 160 copies of this automated design system, known as SCALD

The National Aeronautics and Space Administration

NASA's level of support for computer research has varied considerably over the years. In the early and mid-1960s the space program was one of the principal markets for advanced computer systems. At IBM, NASA replaced the Defense Department as the primary customer for the IBM Federal Systems Division; at Scientific Data Systems in the 1960s NASA represented 40 percent of the division's market.

Much of NASA's work could be applied by its large contractors, especially IBM, to software development and programming. In hardware, NASA's research focus was on redundant and fault-tolerant computers. Research supported in these areas later provided concepts used in commercial systems designed for nonstop transaction processing and processors used in systems that needed to be highly reliable. The experimental STAR (self-test and repair) computer, delivered by the Caltech Jet Propulsion Laboratory in 1969 on a NASA contract, established the leading-edge for fault-tolerant techniques in the 1960s.[109]

By the late 1960s the space program had peaked, and NASA-funded computer research began to decline rapidly. By 1972 it had virtually halted. With the exception of its work on the ILLIAC IV in the mid- and late 1970s, NASA did not revive its computer research until the early 1980s, with development of multiple processor systems for image processing and a large-scale supercomputer facility to develop advanced techniques for numerical modeling of aerodynamic structures.[110] By 1987 NASA's numerical aerodynamic simulator handled computations requiring the performance of one gigaflop per second. The simulator is expected to be a dependable market for future advanced supercomputers as they are developed.[111] The design of aerodynamic structures—aircraft,

(structured computer-aided logic design), had been released to industry. See *Supercomputers,* Hearings, p. 196. The SCALD system is being supported commercially by Daisy Systems, Valid Logic Systems, and Mentor Graphics, the industry leaders, as well as other firms. Interview with Lowell Wood, Lawrence Livermore National Laboratory, February 13, 1984.

109. Siewiorek, Bell, and Newell, *Computer Structures,* p. 442.

110. In 1979 NASA awarded a contract to Goodyear Aerospace to build a special purpose multiprocessor system, the massively parallel processor. Completed in 1983, the MPP uses 16,000 specialized processors, operating in parallel, to process imaging data received from NASA sensors orbiting in space. See the testimony of Jack L. Kerrebrock, in *Computers and Their Role in Energy Research,* Hearings, pp. 83–84.

111. Ibid., p. 84; and Victor L. Peterson, "Impact of Computers on Aerodynamics Research and Development," *Proceedings of the IEEE,* vol. 72 (January 1984), pp. 78–79.

vehicles, and ships—is being revolutionized as mathematical models replace the time-consuming and costly evaluation of physical models in wind tunnels.

In software development NASA's expert system LUNAR, constructed to help geologists analyze moon rocks, provided a foundation for natural language understanding techniques later financed by DARPA.[112] NASA also underwrote the development of the finite-element method of modeling physical structures—now the most widely accepted approach to such problems—and the computer program NASTRAN.[113]

The agency is contemplating developing new computer systems, using artificial intelligence techniques. Congress in 1984 required NASA to set aside 10 percent of the cost of its proposed space station for developing advanced automation and robotics, and a recent advisory committee report recommended raising the funding level for expert systems, robotics, and other artificial intelligence applications from $800 million to $1.3 billion, or 13 percent of projected space station costs.[114]

The National Science Foundation

Organized in the early 1950s, the National Science Foundation did not begin to play any role in computer development until the end of the decade. Given the traditional orientation of the NSF toward established

112. See George Johnson, "Solving the Problem of Meaning," *APF Reporter,* vol. 8 (Spring 1985), pp. 22–26. NASA and DARPA had also supported at Stanford University the early development of the DENDRAL expert system for inferring the structure of chemical compounds from mass spectrograms. Funding was later picked up by NIH. See Bruce G. Buchanan and Edward A. Feigenbaum, "Dendral and Meta-Dendral: Their Applications Dimension," in Webber and Nilsson, eds., *Readings in Artificial Intelligence,* p. 320. Barr and Feigenbaum, *Handbook of Artificial Intelligence,* pp. 292–94.

113. NASA's lofty ambitions were clear: "It is the intent that this procurement will provide NASA with the most modern and efficient program that can be developed within the state of the art." See Richard H. MacNeal, "Some Organizational Aspects of NASTRAN," *Nuclear Engineering and Design,* vol. 29 (1974), p. 255.

A NASA-commissioned study put the total development costs through 1974 (including maintenance) at about $6.6 million and users' cost savings at about $150 million per year in expenses in the early 1970s. See Mathematica, Inc., *Quantifying the Benefits to the National Economy from Secondary Applications of NASA Technology,* NASA Contractor Report CR-2673 (Washington, D.C.: NASA, 1976), pp. 110–26.

114. Alton K. Marsh, "NASA Space Station Effort Drives Expert Systems Research at Johnson," *Aviation Week and Space Technology,* April 22, 1985, pp. 59–63; and "NASA Report Urges Developing Robotics, Software for Station," *Aviation Week and Space Technology,* April 22, 1985, p. 63.

Table 3-6. *National Science Foundation Grants for Computer Facilities, Fiscal Years 1956–70*
Millions of current dollars

Year	Grants	Year	Grants
1956	0.136	1964	4.657
1957	0.030	1965	4.935
1958	0.211	1966	8.899
1959	2.201	1967	11.825
1960	2.296	1968	10.605
1961	2.200	1969	6.500
1962	4.180	1970	6.533
1963	5.974		

Source: Joseph Fennell, "Computer Facilities Grants FY'56–FY'70," memo to file, NSF, June 24, 1970.

academic disciplines and peer review by well-respected figures in a particular discipline, this is not very surprising. It was not until the mid-1960s, after all, that the first computer science departments were established as separate entities at American universities.[115] Computer science as an independent research area did not gain recognition within NSF until the 1970s.[116]

Between 1956 and 1970 NSF pumped about $71 million into computer facilities at U.S. colleges and universities (see table 3-6). This would be about $200 million in 1982 dollars. Most of the foundation's early support for computer research focused on applications to particular science and engineering problems.[117] A small amount of funding, minor when com-

115. For a discussion of what constitutes *computer science,* see Allen Newell, Alan J. Perlis, and Herbert A. Simon, "Computer Science" (letter to the editor), *Science,* September 22, 1967, pp. 1373–74. Often computer science programs were cross-disciplinary. At MIT and Berkeley, for example, computer science was established as a subfield within the Electrical Engineering Department. At Stanford computer science became a division within the Mathematics Department in the early 1960s and a separate department (perhaps the first) in 1965. See the interview with Albert Bowker of May 21, 1979, available in the Charles Babbage Institute at the University of Minnesota.

116. An Office of Computing Activities, primarily focused on computer applications, was first established at NSF in 1967. Personal communication from Joseph Fennell, September 1985. Nevertheless, the NSF did play an important role in certain key areas of computer development at a much earlier date. The Office of Naval Research had taken over much of the computer-related research sponsored by the National Bureau of Standards (including the Institute for Numerical Analysis at UCLA) after its fall from political grace in the early 1950s. ONR itself had been given caretaker responsibilities for basic academic research in anticipation of the establishment of the NSF, and over the course of the 1950s it gradually transferred much of this activity to the NSF and other federal agencies.

117. See *Supercomputers,* Hearings, p. 275. Not all NSF funds went into the

pared with the institutional computing program, went to unsolicited proposals in the field of computer science. The National Science Foundation became and remains the principal funder of work in theoretical computer science. It also funded computer-related research topics in applied mathematics that were not funded by the Defense Department and the AEC (including the theory of automata, complexity theory, the theory of algorithms, and automatic theorem-proving).[118]

The first visible push into computers came in late 1967 when President Lyndon Baines Johnson parceled out about $22 million in annual funding.[119] Roughly half went into institutional computing facilities, one-quarter into computer science, and the remainder into special projects.

The late 1960s and early 1970s marked a dramatic shift in NSF research policies. The rationale for its institutional computing program had been to expand the use of computers in academic research. This did not necessarily include sustaining the use of the equipment once in place. Amid rampant budget-cutting pressures, the program was ended in 1970, and academic institutions were asked to budget computer support into their regular research funding. The strict accounting standards of the Office of Management and Budget had to be followed, and restrictions on the types of costs that could be covered by the rates charged were imposed by federal overseers. The net impact (hastened by the development of cheap and increasingly powerful minicomputers) was a shift toward smaller, decentralized computing facilities and a decline in the use of larger computers on federal grants. In 1966–67 roughly one-third

---

purchase of hardware; much of the $783,825 that went to MIT as part of this program was put into research. Several grants in the early 1960s supported the development of CTSS. At Dartmouth these institutional computer grants, along with private funding from General Electric, paid for the development of the interactive Basic timesharing system. See Joseph Fennell, "Computer Facilities Grants FY '56–FY '70," memo to file, June 24, 1970; interview with Kent Curtis, March 23, 1984. One of the earliest applications was weather modeling (still a major user of supercomputer resources), and the National Center for Atmospheric Research was set up in the early 1960s to facilitate the application of large computers to these problems. Curtis interview; David L. Williamson and Paul N. Swarztrauber, "A Numerical Weather Prediction Model—Computational Aspects of the Cray-1," *Proceedings of the IEEE,* vol. 72 (January 1984), pp. 56–67. An NSF grant to the MIT Mechanical Engineering Department provided the initial stimulus for the pioneering Sketchpad CAD system.

118. See "Theory of Computation," in Arden, ed., *What Can Be Automated,* p. 291; and Curtis interview. Funding of theoretical computer science was small relative to the institutional computing program—perhaps $100,000 to $200,000 per year and certainly under a million dollars as late as 1967. Curtis interview.

119. Personal communication from Joseph Fennell, September 1985.

of computing expenditures at major universities had been paid for by federal funding compared with 10 percent in 1976–77.[120]

Passage by Congress of the Mansfield Amendment to the military procurement authorization for fiscal 1970 had an immediate and powerful impact on government support for basic research. It effectively limited Defense Department support for research to "studies and projects that directly and apparently relate to defense needs."[121] Although dropped from procurement authorizations in following years, the measure continued to influence funding priorities for many years to come.

The Mansfield Amendment transferred support for basic research from the Defense Department to the civilian federal agencies.[122] To make up for "drop-outs" from the defense budget, Congress did appropriate additional funding for the NSF, but it fell far short of the funding the Defense Department had provided: perhaps 25 to 50 cents of additional funding were appropriated for every "drop-out" dollar.[123] Computer research, because of its traditionally heavy reliance on DOD funding, was particularly hard hit by these developments.

The National Science Foundation reorganized its research funding in the mid-1970s, and computer science emerged as definite winner. Applications of computers to the sciences, which had accounted for 30 to 40 percent of the NSF computer research budget, were shifted to other programs, and the overall computer program budget was left essentially unchanged. In effect, this amounted to a large increase in computer research funding. Since then, NSF support for computer research has continued to grow at phenomenal rates. From a budget of

120. Curtis interview; National Science Foundation, *A National Computing Environment for Academic Research* (Washington, D.C.: NSF, 1983), pp. 4–5, citing studies by John Hamblen and Carolyn Landis.

121. See David, "Federal Support of Mathematics," for an analysis of the impact of this measure on basic research in mathematics.

122. The Mansfield Amendment is often mentioned as a key factor affecting research support in the early 1970s. It is, however, easy to attribute too much influence to this measure. The Mansfield Amendment applied only to basic research, yet funding of all types of Defense Department research and development went into steep decline in the late 1960s and early 1970s.

Only 4 percent of DOD projects failed the Mansfield test (none was in DARPA). The Department of Defense clearly funded procurement at the expense of R&D during the Vietnam War, and the Mansfield Amendment may have been used as justification of sorts for some policies dictated by the economics of the war. See Barber Associates, *Advanced Research Projects Agency,* pp. VIII-20–VIII-21.

123. David, "Federal Support of Mathematics," p. 45; and Curtis interview.

around $15 million in fiscal 1975 and fiscal 1976, computer science funding grew to almost $40 million in fiscal 1985.[124]

During the military buildup of the early 1980s, defense research support grew even faster than NSF funding, and the foundation's share of the total slipped rapidly. In spite of the enormous gains in NSF funding for computer science, its share of total federal support by 1983 had declined to the level of 1970 (see table 3-1). The National Science Foundation remains the only federal funding source with a primary focus on academic institutions. In fiscal 1983, 92 percent of its math and computer science research support went to universities and colleges, compared with 41 percent at DOD, 27 percent at DOE, 10 percent at NASA, and 36 percent at NIH.[125]

New computer initiatives at NSF promise to increase funding for computer-related research activities considerably. In 1984 NSF announced a five-year, half-million-dollar grant to help establish a joint industry-university Optical Circuitry Cooperative at the University of Arizona. This was only one of twenty such joint research programs to be established by NSF. A five-year, $16 million program to establish long-term support for four new centers for experimental computer science was also announced, a further expansion in a program that had established fourteen new research facilities since 1980. In 1985 NSF launched an initiative to increase the availability of supercomputers to U.S. researchers—a five-year, $200 million program to establish National Advanced Scientific Computing Centers at four institutions, to be matched by roughly equal funding from industrial and other sources. This program supplements other funding for supercomputer time given to six supercomputer facilities in 1984 and 1985. All of these new initiatives emphasize university-industry cooperation.[126]

124. Among the noteworthy software packages developed with NSF support were SAS, SPSS, and TROLL, which are now in wide use by social scientists engaged in statistical analysis.

125. National Science Foundation, *Federal Funds for Research and Development: Fiscal Years 1983, 1984, and 1985,* vol. 33, Report NSF 84-336 (GPO, 1985), table C-84.

126. See the following NSF publications: "NSF Funds Establishment of Center for Optical Circuitry Research," press release NSF PR84-69, November 7, 1984; "NSF Grants $15.9 Million to Four Universities for Experimental Computer Science Research," press release NSF PR84-35, June 8, 1984; "NSF Selects Four Institutions to Be National Advanced Scientific Computing Centers," press release PR85-12, February 26, 1985; and "NSF Funds Will Give Researchers Easier Access to Supercomputers," press release PR85-28, May 2, 1985.

The National Institutes of Health

The National Institutes of Health have developed a narrow but important set of computer applications and software. In the 1960s NIH supported the Health Sciences Computing Facility at UCLA, a major center for computational research and services in the 1960s and early 1970s.[127] The widely used Biomedical Data (BMD) statistical software package was written at this center.

In 1965 NIH funded a facility at Stanford University known as ACME (advanced computer for medical research), originally dedicated to real-time analysis of biomedical research data.[128] Nobel Prize winner Joshua Lederberg, along with computer scientists at Stanford, had begun work (originally under NASA sponsorship) on the DENDRAL system, an attempt to use artificial intelligence techniques to construct an expert system to interpret mass spectrograms used in determining chemical structure.[129] Sponsorship of this work was picked up by NIH from NASA. By the early 1970s DENDRAL and a growing list of other experimental expert systems had loaded the ACME system to capacity. In 1973 NIH agreed to fund a new and expanded facility at Stanford University as a national resource for applications of artificial intelligence to medicine and biology.[130] The Stanford University Medical Experimental Computer (SUMEX) allocated 40 percent of its capacity to Stanford researchers, 40 percent to other users nationwide, and 20 percent to systems developers.

During the 1970s, research carried out at the SUMEX facility played a leading role in the development of expert systems technology. Significant work at Stanford that built on DENDRAL included the MYCIN expert system, for selecting suitable antibiotics for patients with serious infections, and PUFF, for diagnosing lung diseases. The DENDRAL system was one of the earliest successful applications of artificial intelligence and probably the first to enter commercial use. The MYCIN system actually outperformed human specialists in a series of clinical tests.[131]

127. NSF, *A National Computing Environment for Academic Research*, p. 4.
128. Gregory Freiherr, *The Seeds of Artificial Intelligence*, NIH Publication 80-2071 (GPO, 1980), pp. 18–19.
129. Buchanan and Feigenbaum, "Dendral and Meta-Dendral," pp. 313–22.
130. Freiherr, *Seeds of Artificial Intelligence*, pp. 18–19.
131. See Randall Davis, "Amplifying Expertise with Expert Systems," in Winston

Other important expert systems developed on the SUMEX facility include the CASNET Glaucoma specialist, built by researchers at Rutgers, and INTERNIST, a diagnostic system for internal medicine built by scientists at the University of Pittsburgh.[132] The vital importance of the NIH program in the field of expert systems is clear. Of sixteen well-known expert systems catalogued as part of a 1983 conference on the commercial uses of artificial intelligence, five were SUMEX projects (compared with two developed at MIT, two at Carnegie-Mellon, two at BBN, and one other non-NIH Stanford system).[133]

Summary

From this detailed history of government support for computer research, a clear pattern of funding emerges. A broad selection of agencies felt the pinch of common fiscal constraints from the late 1960s through the middle of the 1970s. Support for the major programs declined from the relatively generous levels provided in the early 1960s. Defense Department funding seems to have been quite sensitive to other budgetary claims, and its share of federal expenditures has been the most volatile among major funders. During the late 1970s, as international competition in technology-intensive products picked up, funding for computer-related research began to flow considerably more freely. Then in the mid-1980s, when deficits and budget cutting again became the top priority, it was the long-term research projects without direct military applications that took the brunt of the cuts. Funding for SDI was maintained by slashing DARPA's budget, in some cases as much as 25 percent below original requests.[134] The Strategic Computing Initiative was one of the programs cut back. The historical lesson is clear and oft repeated: when funding gets short, applications and development with direct relevance to defense objectives are favored over longer term, basic projects with only indirect military benefits.

and Prendergast, *The AI Business,* pp. 17–40; and Freiherr, *Seeds of Artificial Intelligence,* pp. 38–40.

132. Freiherr, *Seeds of Artificial Intelligence,* pp. 33–37, 44–48.

133. See Davis, "Amplifying Expertise," p. 28. The SUMEX systems are PUFF, INTERNIST, META-DENDRAL, DENDRAL, and MYCIN. The two MIT systems are MACSYMA and Programmer's Apprentice. The Carnegie-Mellon systems are HEARSAY-III and R1. BBN built Sophie and Steamer. TEIRESIAS was developed at the Stanford AI Lab.

134. Corcoran, "Strategic Computing," p. 8.

Table 3-7. *Major Computing-Related Programs of Three Civilian Federal Agencies, Fiscal Years 1984–87*
Millions of current dollars

Agency	1984	1985	1986[a]	1987[a]
NASA				
Numerical aerodynamic simulator	17	27	28	30
Information systems	9	16	16	21
Department of Energy				
Applied mathematical sciences	15	34	38	33
University research support	5	10	10	11
National Science Foundation				
Advanced scientific computing	6	23	24	30
Computer research in mathematics and physical sciences	27	32	31	37
Information science and technology	6	9	9	12
Design, manufacturing, and computer engineering	11	18	18	22
Emerging and critical engineering systems	33	35	35	43

Sources: National Science Foundation, Division of Science Resources Studies, *Federal R&D Funding by Budget Function: Fiscal Years 1984–86*, NSF 85-319 (GPO, March 1985), pp. 26, 39, 48, 49, 52, 54; ibid., *Fiscal Years 1985–87*, NSF 86-306 (GPO, March 1986), pp. 25, 30–31, 34, 36, 52; Office of Technology Assessment, *Supercomputers: Government Plans & Policies*, background paper (GPO, 1986), p. 14; and conversations with NASA.
  a. Estimated.

Although the sizable new investments in military computer programs are likely to dominate over the remainder of the decade, the trend has been offset by significant budget increases in some civilian programs (see table 3-7). "Supercomputing" services will become more widely available as a result of funding increases for NASA's numerical aerodynamic simulator and for the advanced scientific computing program at NSF. Between 1984 and 1986 support for research roughly doubled in the Department of Energy's university support budget, the NSF's computer engineering program, applied mathematical sciences in DOE, and information systems in NASA. More theoretical research, as represented in the NSF's computer science and math budget, was slated for a considerably slower rise. The current emphasis is on applications and engineering over theory and basic research.

Increased funding for computer-related research far outstrips growth in other research funds budgeted by government. Funding for computer science in universities and colleges (where most fundamental research is carried out) increased 110 percent from 1980 to 1984, compared with a 32 percent rise overall, a 17 percent growth in physical sciences, and absolute declines in social and environmental sciences. Federal resources are clearly being shifted out of other areas and into computers.

CHAPTER FOUR

Government Policy and the American Computer Industry

WITHIN all industrialized countries development of new technology has been shaped by a broad and varied mix of policies, extending well beyond support for research and development. The variation over time within a country is often as striking as the contrasts between nations. Organized, systematic explorations of technological frontiers brought about profound but largely unforeseen changes in the postwar economy. At first, deliberate, large-scale investments in technological innovation were made with military objectives in mind. Increasingly, however, attention has shifted to economic benefits.

In grappling with tensions between private and social gain, competition and cooperation, commercial and strategic advantage, nations have followed very different paths reflecting their unique political and economic institutions.

America's experience in computers, the subject of this chapter, can be usefully contrasted with that of industrial competitors in Japan and Western Europe (see chapter 5). The least common denominator of technology policy is a small set of measures with relatively direct effects on investment in the creation of technology. These programs have generally included direct support for research and development, government procurement of technology-intensive products, indirect fiscal and financial incentives favoring a chosen industry, and policies that directly regulate the nature of competition in the marketplace.

Research and Development

The last chapter discussed in detail computer-related research and development programs inside and outside of the U.S. government. It is useful to distinguish between applied R&D programs (technology demonstration projects with one or two prototype systems) and projects that have developed a major military system or other type of system to be procured in production volumes. Both types of programs have been of considerable historical importance in the United States. The disposition of patent rights to advances arising from federally funded research and development has varied considerably across agencies.

Since procurement frequently follows research and development, the boundary between the two is often vague. When procurement is accompanied by advance payments to support research and development (the case with virtually all projects in the early 1950s as well as with the Atomic Energy Commission's later contracts for the construction of the first supercomputers), the ambiguity is especially obvious.

This lack of a well-defined boundary is further obscured by the Defense Department's practice of funding "independent" research and development out of monies not specifically labeled as research expenditure.[1] Although hard figures are lacking, it appears that funding for independent research and development (IR&D) is growing. In fiscal 1960 it amounted to 2.7 percent of Defense's research, development, test, and evaluation (RDT&E) budget.[2] By fiscal 1969 it totaled over 5 percent of direct research and development obligations. By fiscal 1979 Defense's independent research and development costs in major defense contractors amounted to roughly 9 percent of its direct R&D contracts; at the National Aeronautics and Space Administration (NASA) IR&D accounted for 3 percent of its direct R&D expenditure.[3]

1. Although reimbursed out of federal funds, such R&D is counted by the NSF in its statistics as coming out of company funds. See National Science Foundation, National Science Board, *Science Indicators, 1982* (Government Printing Office, 1983), p. 94.

2. *Patent Practices of the Department of Defense*, Preliminary Report of the Subcommittee on Patents, Trademarks, and Copyrights of the Senate Committee on the Judiciary, 87 Cong. 1 sess. (GPO, 1961), p. 34. RDT&E budget expenditures for fiscal 1960 are taken from *The Report of the Committee on the Economic Impact of Defense and Disarmament* (GPO, 1965), table A-5.

3. For fiscal 1969 the IR&D budget is cited in Comptroller General of the United States, *Partial Report: In-Depth Investigation into Independent Research and Development and Bid and Proposal Programs* (General Accounting Office, 1974), p. 1. DOD research and development obligations are cited in National Science Foundation, Division of Science Resources Studies, *Federal Funds for Research and Development, Detailed Historical Tables: Fiscal Years 1955–1986* (NSF, 1985), p. 104. For fiscal 1979 see NSF, *Science Indicators, 1982*, p. 94. See also NSF, NSB, *Science Indicators, 1980* (GPO, 1981), pp. 68–69; Howard Emery Bethel, "An Overview of DOD Policy for and Administration of Independent Research and Development," Study Report (U.S. Defense

Despite this built-in "fuzziness" in measuring defense support for research, the shifting role of the U.S. government in computer research funding can be traced. Around 1950 computer projects were funded in the $15 to $20 million range by the federal government, with Engineering Research Associates (ERA) and the Massachusetts Institute of Technology (MIT) absorbing the lion's share of the support. Privately funded industrial computer research and development probably amounted to less than $5 million in 1950, the very dawn of the computer industry in the United States. At that time perhaps 20 to 25 percent of computer research and development was privately funded (see appendix C).

Industry Support

By 1954 company-funded computer research had tripled, into the $15 million per year range. Nonetheless, throughout the remainder of the 1950s private industrial research continued to be overshadowed by federal spending (see table 4-1).

In the sample of companies presented in table 4-1, 59 percent of all the R&D performed was paid for by public funds. Even at IBM, the dominant power in the emerging commercial computer market, government funded considerably better than half of its research and development.

During the 1960s, despite the increasingly commercial orientation of the computer market, government support for computer research continued to be of very great importance to the industry. As table 4-2 indicates, government funds paid for a sizable 35 percent of research and development at IBM in 1963, a year when the company poured enormous amounts of its own resources into the development of the commercial System 360 line. The government directly funded 50 percent of R&D in the data processing labs developing computers at Burroughs, and at Control Data it funded 40 percent.

NASA became a major focus for industrial research support, especially at IBM, in the early 1960s. The distribution of federal research

Systems Management School, Ft. Belvoir, Virginia, 1975); and *Independent Research and Development,* Hearings before the House Committee on Armed Services, 91 Cong. 2 sess. (GPO, 1970). To receive IR&D funding, a contractor must first submit individual R&D programs for government approval, subject to an overall negotiated ceiling on the funding. A prorated share of such expenditure is then reimbursed by the government, based on the share of government sales in all sales related to the approved R&D.

Table 4-1. *Government and Private Funding of Research and Development at Selected Companies, Fiscal Years 1949–59*
Millions of dollars unless otherwise specified

Company	Government funding[a]	Private funding	Government's share of total funding (percent)
General Electric	1,500	1,370	52
Sperry Rand	854	133	87
Bell Telephone and Western Electric	760	832	48
IBM[b]	397	184	68
Raytheon	325	38	90
RCA	275	324	46
Computer Control Corp.	2.1	0.4	84
Total or average	4,113.1	2,881.4	59

Source: *Patent Practices of the Department of Defense*, Preliminary Report of the Subcommittee on Patents, Trademarks, and Copyrights of the Senate Committee on the Judiciary, 87 Cong. 1 sess. (GPO, 1961), pp. 96, 100, 108, 117–18, 121, 127.
a. The amount awarded for contracts.
b. If actual expenditure of government funds is considered, the figures would change as follows: $254 for government funding, 58 percent for the government's share, and 58 percent for all company average.

funding across companies was highly uneven, however (see table 4-2). Virtually none of RCA's or Honeywell's large federal research contracts involved their computer labs. Their computer development research in the early 1960s was essentially self-financed. Once the Advanced Research Projects Agency (ARPA, later called DARPA when Defense was added to the name) came on the scene as technical czar for military research support in the early 1960s, it frequently directed military resources into academic institutions and smaller, less established private enterprises. (A good example was Bolt, Baranek, and Newman [BBN]; 35 percent of its R&D budget was funded by the government in 1963. A steady diet of government contracts had transformed BBN into a major computer and communications systems house, with $178 million in revenues in 1986, three-quarters of which flowed in from government contracts.)[4]

The federally funded share of industrial computer R&D had declined

4. For a recent profile of BBN see *The Value Line Investment Survey*, December 19, 1986, p. 2115. IBM also received ARPA funds in the early 1960s. Some of its early work on list-processing languages (Lisp, IPL5, Snobol) was carried out on ARPA contracts. See R. W. O'Neill, "Experience Using a Time-Shared Multi-Programming System with Dynamic Address Relocation Hardware," in *Proceedings of the AFIPS Spring Joint Computer Conference*, vol. 30 (Washington, D.C.: Thompson Books, 1967), p. 611.

Table 4-2. *Government and Private Funding of Research and Development at Selected Companies, with DOD, NASA, and AEC Share, Fiscal Year 1963*
Millions of dollars unless otherwise specified

Company	Private funding (percent)	Government funding (percent)	Number of R&D scientists & engineers	Department of Defense	National Aeronautics and Space Administration	DOD, Atomic Energy Commission, and NASA
RCA	. . .	. . .	. . .	111.4	42.2	153.6
Princeton Laboratory	70	30	421	. . .	. . .	. . .
Communications products	95	5	200	. . .	. . .	. . .
Astro electronics	100	. . .	3,202	. . .	. . .	. . .
Electrical components	75	25	710	. . .	. . .	. . .
Data processing	100	. . .	217	. . .	. . .	. . .
Home products	100	. . .	184	. . .	. . .	. . .
Recording instruments	100	. . .	20	. . .	. . .	. . .
IBM	65	35	a	10.0	36.1	46.1
Honeywell	. . .	. . .	. . .	31.9	3.2	35.0
Corporate HQ	85	15	93	. . .	. . .	. . .
Military products	50	50	64	. . .	. . .	. . .
Data processing	100	0	350	. . .	. . .	. . .
Burroughs	. . .	. . .	. . .	11.2	0.1	11.3
Control Division	40	60	21	. . .	. . .	. . .
Defense and Space Division	20	80	280	. . .	. . .	. . .
Data Processing Division	50	50	260	. . .	. . .	. . .
Control Data	60	40	550	8.9	2.5	11.3
Cubic Corporation	20	75	147	4.4	2.8	4.5
Packard Bell Electronics	30	60	38	0.2	2.8	3.0
Scientific Data Systems	100	. . .	60	0.2	1.6	1.9
Technitrol	60	30	46	1.4	0.3	1.6
NCR	86	14	437	1.6	. . .	1.6
Bolt, Baranek, and Newman	. . .	65	106	1.1	0.4	1.5
California Computer Products	70	30	n.a.	. . .	1.2	1.2

Source: *Impact of Federal Research and Development Programs, Study Number VI*, H. Rept. 1938, 88 Cong. 2 sess. (GPO, 1964), pp. 63–68, 166, 171, 175–76, 211–12, 214, 229, 231, 234–35, 239, 246.
n.a. Not available.
a. 17,000 including programmers and support people.

to roughly one-third of total expenditure by 1965, and it continued to decline during the rest of the decade. Figure 4-1 illustrates the importance of military research funding at the major computer firms of the era, IBM and the so-called BUNCH.[5] In companies with highly diversified product lines, such as Sperry and Honeywell, it is difficult to relate the percent-

5. BUNCH stands for Burroughs, Univac (Sperry), NCR, Control Data, and

Figure 4-1. *Defense Share of Defense- and Company-Funded R&D,*
Selected Companies, 1956–85[a]

Percent

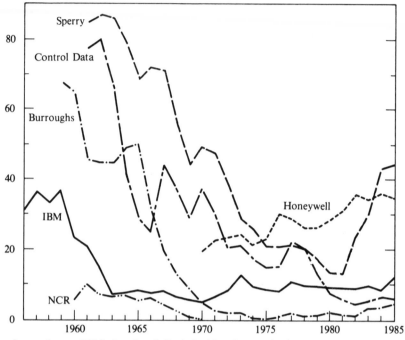

Sources: Company R&D funds are from the Standard and Poor Compustat data base and Montgomery Phister, Jr.,
Data Processing Technology and Economics, 2d ed. (Bedford, Mass.: Digital Press, and Santa Monica Publishing Co.,
1979), pp. 309, 311, 314. Defense RDT&E contract obligations to firms are from U.S. Department of Defense, Washington
Headquarters Services, Directorate for Information Operations and Reports, *500 Contractors Receiving the Largest
Dollar Volume of Prime Contract Awards for Research, Development, Test, and Evaluation* (GPO, various years); and
Patent Practices of the Department of Defense, Preliminary Report of the Subcommittee on Patents, Trademarks, and
Copyrights of the Senate Committee on the Judiciary, 87 Cong. 1 sess. (GPO, 1961), pp. 80–81.

a. Defense- and company-funded R&D is defined as expenditure on Department of Defense research, development, testing, and evaluation (RDT&E) contracts plus company-funded R&D expenditures. Defense RDT&E expenditures are calculated as 65 percent of Defense RDT&E contract obligations in a given year plus 35 percent of obligations
in the previous year. The expenditure rates that are applied to contract obligations are an approximation of the composite
Defense Department R&D expenditure rates reported in Department of Defense, Directorate for Program and Financial
Control, *Financial Summary Tables: Department of Defense Budget for Fiscal Year 1983* (DOD, 1982), section O, p. 2.
That report estimates that 59 percent of RDT&E appropriations are expended in the same fiscal year, 34 percent in the
following year, and the remainder in the following two years. Since obligations lag appropriations slightly (for RDT&E,
94 percent of appropriations are obligated in the same fiscal year, the remainder in the following year), the rates at which
obligations are expended are approximated by increasing the first-year share relatively more.

ages charted in the figure to support for computers other than in the most
general terms. Nonetheless, a dramatic falling off in military support for

Honeywell. In 1986 Sperry's computer line was absorbed into Burroughs (in turn
renamed Unisys), and Honeywell sold off its computer operations to its foreign associates,
Bull and Nippon Electric Corporation (NEC).

Table 4-3. *Federal Share of Research and Development Funds in the Office, Computing, and Accounting Machines Industry, 1972–84*[a]

Year	Federal Funds as percent of all R&D	Percent of all R&D going to	
		Basic research	Development
1972	n.a.	[1.5]	n.a.
1973	n.a.	[1.4]	n.a.
1974	n.a.	[1.3]	n.a.
1975	21.9 (21.9)	1.2 (1.2) [1.3]	n.a.
1976	21.2 (21.2)	1.6 (1.6)	n.a.
1977	16.4 (19.7)	1.5 (1.6)	n.a.
1978	11.3 (17.6)	n.a.	n.a.
1979[b]	8.0 (17.3)	1.6 (1.5)	87.5
1980	13.3 (18.5)	n.a.	n.a.
1981	13.1[c]	n.a.	81.5
1982	12.9[c]	n.a.	
1983	16.4[c]	n.a.	83.6
1984	15.2[c]	n.a.	84.4

Source: National Science Foundation, *Research and Development in Industry*, various years.
n.a. Not available.
a. Numbers in brackets are prior to 1976 industry reclassification; numbers in parentheses are prior to 1981 industry reclassification of firms in NSF sample.
b. The percentage of federal funding for basic and applied research was (37.0); for development (14.5). The percentage of all R&D for applied research was (11.0).
c. Author's estimate. See appendix C for details.

research and development is evident in the early 1960s for IBM and the late 1960s for Burroughs, Sperry, and Control Data. The decline continues through the late 1970s. By 1980 less than 10 percent of the R&D support came from Defense at most of the major commercial computer firms.[6] Since the start of the military buildup of the early 1980s, however, Defense Department support for research and development has grown more important at most of these firms.

The federal share of R&D funding in the office, computing, and accounting machines industry is displayed in table 4-3. Periodic reclassification of firms' industrial activities has caused sporadic jumps in published data, and the reader is urged to consult appendix C for more details. The trend in the late 1970s is one of continued decline, from 21.9

6. At Sperry the picture is confused by its general role as a major defense contractor on systems other than computers. Only at Honeywell has military research support generally increased over the years. In the 1970s Honeywell shifted toward the military market in selling its computer products.

percent of funding in 1975 to 8 percent in 1979. The federal share rose again to more than 15 percent in the 1980s. But the distribution of federal support across firms was and remains highly uneven. In 1984 the four firms with the largest research programs had about one-fifth of their research and development funding picked up by government contracts, the next sixteen firms with greatest R&D spending none, and the remainder of the industry about 3 percent (see appendix table C-3).

It would be misleading to conclude that the federal role in computer research is of minor importance. Very little of industrial R&D is research; most is concentrated in development. As table 4-3 shows, in the 1970s less than 2 percent of industrial R&D took the form of basic research; perhaps 10 to 15 percent was for applied research, and the remainder was for development.[7] The development-research ratio is about 7 to 1 in industry, and applied research dominates basic research by roughly another 7 to 1.

Perhaps 10 percent of company-funded industrial R&D is for research (basic and applied).[8] Comparing this to figures on federally funded research in math and computer science suggests that government pays about 40 percent of the bill for all computer-related research. Roughly half of this federal research funding has gone into basic research.

The next section examines the funding of the entire computer technology base. It discusses both government and university research and assesses their importance relative to industry.

The Computer Technology Base

Basic research projects undertaken outside of industry have significantly influenced industry. It is precisely in long-term basic research and more technologically radical innovations that government funding is likely to have its most important effects.

To measure the relative influence of federal research spending on the

---

7. Basic research spending is also unevenly distributed across firms. IBM, for example, may spend as much as 5 percent of its R&D budget on basic research, although the industry-wide average is 1.5 to 2 percent. The very rough estimate that perhaps 5 percent of IBM's R&D budget is for basic research comes from an interview with Dr. Glen Bacon, IBM, June 8, 1984.

8. In 1979, the only year for which data were available, research accounted for 9.5 percent of all company-funded R&D. See National Science Foundation, *Research and Development in Industry, 1979,* NSF 81-324 (GPO, 1981), table B-30. For data on federal funding of math and computer science research, see appendix tables C-4 and C-5.

computer industry, it is first necessary to define what R&D spending is relevant to computers. This is not a simple task. It has been argued, for example, that advances in electronic components lie behind much of the continued advance in the industry. Recent National Science Foundation (NSF) data breaking down applied research and development expenditure within the office, computing, and accounting machines sector suggest that roughly half of R&D spending was on products normally classified within other sectors. In 1979 applied R&D on machinery products (including office, computing, and accounting machines as well as other nonelectrical machinery) represented only about 54 percent of total spending within the computer sector.[9]

Nonindustrial research and development funding by the federal government is classified in a totally different way. To measure federal funding, budgetary obligations data must be used in some cases and actual expenditures in others, depending on the data available. While not strictly comparable, these various sources of data will permit some assessment of rough orders of magnitude.

To make a comparison, a relatively narrow definition of computer-relevant research and development is used in this chapter: all research and development within the office, computing, and accounting machines industry, and all activity, using federal or other funds, classified as math and computer science research (but excluding development funds), within universities and colleges and federally funded research and development centers (FFRDCs) administered by universities.[10] Research performed outside of universities and colleges and their FFRDCs, private industry, and industry-administered FFRDCs is excluded. (Examples of such excluded establishments include federal labs, private nonprofit institutions, and other government organizations carrying out relevant research and development.) The overall federal share of R&D funding is almost certainly greater in these institutions than in those that have been included, so the analysis underestimates the true federal role. Also excluded is materials science and electrical engineering R&D in universities. The federal government has given electrical engineering research about twice as much resources as math and computer science research. For materials research and computer science research, federal

9. Ibid., table B-37.
10. FFRDCs administered by private industry are counted in the figures given for the private companies that operate them.

Table 4-4. *Federal Support in Relation to Computer R&D, by Industry, Universities, and FFRDCs, Fiscal Years 1972–84*[a]
Millions of dollars unless otherwise specified

Year	Total R&D — Office, computing, and accounting machines industry	In field of math & computer science — Universities	In field of math & computer science — University FFRDCs	Subtotals for R&D — Industry, FFRDCs, and universities	Subtotals for R&D — Bell Telephone Laboratories[b]	Subtotals for R&D — Industry, FFRDCs, universities, and Bell	Federal R&D funds to — Industry	Federal R&D funds to — Universities	Federal R&D funds to — FFRDCs	Federal funds as percent of all funds — Excluding Bell research	Federal funds as percent of all funds — Including Bell as quasi public
1972	1,456	69	n.a.	n.a.	n.a.	n.a.	n.a.	n.a.	n.a.	n.a.	n.a.
1973	1,733	n.a.	n.a.	n.a.	296	n.a.	n.a.	n.a.	n.a.	n.a.	n.a.
1974	2,103	n.a.	n.a.	n.a.	313	n.a.	n.a.	n.a.	n.a.	n.a.	n.a.
1975	2,220	85	62	2,367	333	2,700	486	65	62	26	35
1976	2,402	87	72	2,561	354	2,915	509	66	72	25	34
1977	2,655	108	79	2,842	389	3,231	435	78	78	21	30
1978	2,883	126	119	3,128	452	3,580	327	85	119	17	27
1979	3,214	176	127	3,517	533	4,050	256	130	127	15	26
1980	3,962	193	162	4,317	640	4,957	526	138	161	19	30
1981	4,428	222	227	4,877	815	5,692	581	161	225	20	31
1982	5,424	245	219	5,888	1,012	6,900	702	179	218	19	31
1983	6,199	278	290	6,767	1,000	7,767	1,017	204	287	22	32
1984	7,280	346	350	7,976	n.a.	n.a.	1,104	253	347	21	n.a.

Sources: NSF, *Research and Development in Industry, 1983*, NSF 85-325 (GPO, 1985), pp. 19, 22; ibid., *1984* (GPO, 1986), pp. 20, 23; NSF, *Academic Science/Engineering: 1972–83: R&D: Funds, Federal Support, Scientists and Engineers, Graduate Enrollment and Support*, NSF 84-322 (GPO, 1984), p. 43; NSF, *Academic Science/Engineering: R&D Funds, Fiscal Year 1983*, NSF 85-308 (GPO, 1985), pp. 8, 9, 130–31; NSF, *Academic Science/Engineering: R&D Funds, Fiscal Year 1982*, NSF 84-308 (GPO, 1984), pp. 8, 9, 129–30; AT&T Bell Telephone Laboratories, *Annual Report*, various years; and A. Michael Noll, "The Impact of Divestiture on Bell System Research and Development Activities," prepared for the NSF under order no. 86-GA-124 (July 20, 1986), p. 34.

n.a. Not available.
a. FFRDCs are federally funded research and development centers (university administered); industry-administered FFRDCs are included in industry category.
b. Half of the total Bell labs' R&D.
c. Author's estimates.

support is about the same size (see appendix table C-4). Government funding for computer and materials research has been heavily weighted toward basic research.[11]

Math and computer science are the academic research areas that are naturally paired with the computer industry; related academic research in other areas is more appropriately paired with the electronics and aerospace industries. To see how the federal role has changed over time, this categorization is the most useful because it approximates the manner in which estimates for the 1950s and 1960s were constructed (as well as the statistics available for other industrial countries).

One key, largely unacknowledged player in U.S. computer research is the Bell Telephone Laboratories. Perhaps half of its research has been related to computers in recent years. Until the 1984 breakup of the Bell system, this research was of a quasi-public nature, funded by the telephone user through a levy on the revenues of the local telephone operating companies. Results of this effort were made available widely and relatively freely. Table 4-4 shows how the breakdown between public and private support for computer research and development would have looked if half of the Bell labs' R&D budget had been included and counted as quasi public.

Even excluding the Bell labs from consideration, the federal role has been significant. This lower bound on the government share of funding (R&D performed in government and nonprofit institutions is excluded) exceeds one-quarter of all R&D in the mid-1970s, sinks to a low of 15 percent in 1979, and then rises well over 20 percent in 1983. When including half of the Bell R&D program as a rough order of magnitude for its computer investments, the share of public and quasi-public funds rises by another 10 to 12 percent of all funding in the area.

In 1965 a study by the Organization for Economic Cooperation and Development (OECD) reported that about half of computer research and development in America was paid for by the U.S. government.[12] A decade later that share had been reduced to one-quarter. After further decline the relative importance of federal funding has bounced back.

11. Basic research in materials and computers has been of roughly equal sizes, but much greater than funds for basic research in electrical engineering.
12. OECD, *Electronic Computers: Gaps in Technology*, Report presented at the Third Ministerial Meeting on Science, March 11 and 12, 1968 (Paris: OECD, 1969), p. 135.

Table 4-5. *The Federal Role in Computer-Related Research,*
Fiscal Years 1967–84[a]
Millions of dollars unless otherwise specified

| Year | Com-pany-funded OCAM research[b] | Math and computer science research | | | Federal math and computer science funds as percent of all re-search funds |
| | | All federal funds | Nonfederal funds | | |
			FFRDCs[c]	Universi-ties	
1967	n.a.	128	n.a.	n.a.	n.a.
1968	n.a.	118	n.a.	n.a.	n.a.
1969	n.a.	108	n.a.	n.a.	n.a.
1970	n.a.	95	n.a.	n.a.	n.a.
1971	n.a.	107	n.a.	n.a.	n.a.
1972	n.a.	121	n.a.	17	43
1973	n.a.	115	n.a.	n.a.	n.a.
1974	n.a.	114	n.a.	n.a.	n.a.
1975	173	125	0	20	39
1976	189	158	0	21	43
1977	222	196	0	30	44
1978	256	216	0	41	42
1979	296	210	0	46	38
1980	344	241	1	55	38
1981	385	279	2	61	38
1982	472	350	1	66	39
1983	518	419	2	74	41
1984	618	440	3	93	38

Sources: NSF, *Research and Development in Industry, 1984*, pp. 20, 23; NSF, *Federal Funds for Research and Development: Federal Obligations for Research by Agency and Detailed Field of Science, Fiscal Years 1967–86* (GPO, 1985), pp. 5, 31; NSF, *Academic Science/Engineering: R&D Funds, Fiscal Year 1982*, NSF 84-308 (GPO, 1984), pp. 129–30; NSF data obtained through computer database; NSF, *Academic Science/Engineering: 1972–83*, pp. 43–44; and NSF, *Academic Science/Engineering: R&D Funds, Fiscal Year 1983*, pp. 16, 130–31.

n.a. Not available.

a. Excludes development expenditure.

b. Assumes 10 percent of all company-funded R&D is research, as was true in 1979. OCAM stands for office, computing, and accounting machines industry.

c. University-administered FFRDCs only; industry-administered FFRDCs are under company-funded research.

Federal Support for Research

As table 4-5 shows, the government's role in computer research appears even greater when development funds are excluded. Roughly 40 percent of all computer research has been paid for by the federal government over the past decade. If only basic research is considered, a reasonable estimate would probably lie in the 60 to 75 percent range (see appendix table C-5). Government research spending is largely concentrated in universities, colleges, and within the government's own labs. It is significantly less important within industry itself, although increasing substantially of late.

In contrast, the U.S. government's share of funding for identifiably computer-related research and development declined from perhaps 75 percent in the early 1950s, to 50 percent in the mid-1960s, to 15 percent in the late 1970s, and then rose over 20 percent in the mid-1980s. If only industrial R&D is considered, the federal share was about one-third of the total in the mid-1960s and 22 percent in the mid-1970s. After slipping to 8 percent in 1979, the federal share had doubled by 1983.

Uncle Sam funded virtually all aspects of computer technology development in the early days. As the technology matured and the commercial industry grew, however, large increases in private research expenditure reduced the federal role in applied research and development, the activities closest to the commercial market. It was only in the higher-risk, longer-term, least commercial basic research projects that the government presence did not shrink to marginal dimensions. Because the fruits of basic research are most difficult to appropriate privately, it is not surprising that federal support has remained preeminent.

Current Trends

Government support for computer R&D within industry ebbed to a low of 8 percent in 1979, but with the military buildup of the 1980s it has since climbed rapidly. In 1984 DARPA began its strategic computing program. Financial support for computer research and development also increased in other Defense Department organizations (particularly the National Security Agency and the Strategic Defense Initiative Office), the Department of Energy, and NASA. Continued expansion of the government's role in supporting industrial research seems quite likely.

Today, however, it is IBM—not the Defense Department—that accounts for the lion's share of research within the U.S. computer industry. Table 4-6 examines IBM's R&D investment in the context of the entire industry. Caution must be used in interpreting these figures because IBM's reported expenditures on research and development include spending in foreign research labs and contract research, both of which are excluded from NSF estimates for U.S. industry. IBM also

Table 4-6. *IBM's R&D in Relation to the U.S. Computer Industry, 1972–84*
Millions of dollars unless otherwise specified

Year	Office, computing, and accounting machines industry		IBM funds only	IBM funds as percent of	
	All R&D funds	Company funds		All R&D funds	Company funds
1972	1,456	n.a.	676	46	n.a.
1973	1,733	n.a.	730	42	n.a.
1974	2,103	n.a.	890	42	n.a.
1975	2,220	1,734	946	43	55
1976	2,402	1,893	1,012	42	53
1977	2,655	2,220	1,142	43	51
1978	2,883	2,556	1,255	44	49
1979	3,214	2,958	1,360	42	46
1980	3,962	3,436	1,520	38	44
1981	4,428[a]	3,847	1,612	36	42
1982	5,424[a]	4,722	2,053	38	43
1983	6,199[a]	5,182	2,514	41	49
1984	7,280[a]	6,176	3,148	43	51

Sources: Industry data from NSF, *Research and Development in Industry, 1983*, pp. 19, 22, and ibid., *1984*, pp. 20, 23; and IBM data from Compustat.
n.a. Not available.
a. Author's estimates.

appears to use a less restrictive definition of R&D in its reports to investors.[13] Despite these problems of definition and measurement, it is clear that IBM leads research and development in the U.S. computer industry.[14] After lagging behind other U.S. computer companies in R&D growth in the late 1970s, IBM greatly increased its R&D budget. Sluggish growth in the 6 to 12 percent per annum range between 1975 and 1981 shot up to 27 percent in 1982, 22 percent in 1983, and 25 percent in 1984. IBM's share of U.S. industry spending topped 50 percent in 1984. The timing of these increases certainly coincides with a perceived challenge in the international marketplace.

13. In 1983, for example, NSF figures show a 10 percent rise in company funds for research and development in the office, computing, and accounting machines industry. IBM's financial reports, on the other hand, show about a 22 percent increase in R&D spending. Because IBM accounts for a large share of all spending in the industry, and other computer firms did not, in the aggregate, hold their research and development roughly constant, IBM presumably must be including in its financial reports considerable spending that is not being reported as R&D to the NSF survey.

14. Although AT&T is a major performer of relevant research, it is not classified in industrial statistics as part of the office, computing, and accounting machines industry.

Procurement

Purchases of computers by the U.S. government have been the second major channel—after R&D expenditures—by which federal policy has influenced the development of the nation's computer industry. At the beginning of the 1950s, the government represented most of the market for industry. Federal agencies used 54 percent of the stock of general purpose computers in 1953. If defense contractors' use of computers to perform federally funded R&D and engineering on cost reimbursement contracts is included, perhaps 70 percent of the computers in use in 1953 were paid for by government users.[15]

As the computer ventured forth in the commercial marketplace in the mid-1950s, this picture changed quite rapidly. By most accounts, 1955 was the year in which use of private computers took a dramatic leap. Less costly computers, particularly the IBM 650, came on the market in large numbers. By the end of 1955 less than 40 percent of the installed U.S. base of computers was used by the government, directly and indirectly. With the delivery of a new generation of business-oriented machines at the end of the decade, the federal share dipped even further. By 1959, 21 percent of the stock of machines was in federal government installations and by 1966, only 10 percent.[16]

If indirect use by military contractors is again considered, the federal share was considerably higher. Moreover, by the late 1950s the size of computers had shrunk to the point where they could be embedded within weapons systems. Thus a more comprehensive estimate that included contractors' computers and weapons systems would probably be closer to 30 percent for the mid-1960s.[17] As late as 1965 more than half of the sales of Control Data, Sperry's ERA division, and other computer firms headquartered in the Minneapolis and St. Paul area went to agencies of the federal government.[18]

A similar story is told by the sales books of major computer producers.

15. See John Varick Wells, "The Origins of the Computer Industry: A Case Study in Radical Technological Change" (Ph.D. dissertation, Yale University, 1978), table 2, p. 199.

16. Ibid., p. 199.

17. See OECD, *Electronic Computers*, pp. 131–34.

18. Kirk Draheim, Richard P. Howell, and Albert Shapero, *The Development of a Potential Defense R & D Complex: A Study of Minneapolis-Saint Paul* (Menlo Park, Calif.: Stanford Research Institute, 1966), p. 128.

Table 4-7. *IBM Sales of Special Products and Services to U.S. Government Agencies, Selected Years, 1956–73*

Year	Percent of IBM's total revenues	Year	Percent of IBM's total revenues
1956	17	1967	4
1961	15	1969	4
1963	7	1971	3
1965	4	1973	3

Source: Montgomery Phister, Jr., *Data Processing Technology and Economics,* 2d ed. (Bedford, Mass.: Digital Press, and Santa Monica Publishing Co., 1979), p. 310.

Table 4-7 shows sales of special products and services to U.S. government customers as a percentage of IBM's revenues through the early 1970s. From the mid-1950s to the mid-1960s, sales dropped sharply from 17 to 4 percent of IBM's revenues, and they continued to decline, although only slightly, through the early 1970s. Because IBM has had a considerably smaller share of the federal government market than is true for the U.S. market as a whole in recent decades, this decline probably overstates the decrease in the government share of sales by other U.S. manufacturers.[19]

During the 1970s the government's share of general purpose computers declined to around 5 percent. Smaller computers used outside the Defense Department and NASA were an important part of the increase in government installations, and a relative shift away from the Defense Department and NASA, particularly toward the Atomic Energy Commission, was an important feature of the changing pattern of government use (see table 4-8). By 1979 defense use of computers, direct as well as indirect (that is, embedded in products purchased by defense users), had shrunk to only 3.6 percent of annual U.S. production.[20] But the defense buildup of the early 1980s reversed that tide. By 1982 defense computer purchases had doubled to 7.1 percent of U.S. output.

The decline in government influence in the U.S. computer market was largely the result of enormous growth in commercial computer sales with expansion into new markets and applications, not of cutbacks in government computer use. At the "high" end of the computer market,

19. See Martha Mulford Gray, *Computer Science and Technology—Federal ADP Equipment: A Compilation of Statistics, 1981,* National Bureau of Standards Special Publication 500-97 (U.S. Department of Commerce, 1982), p. 47. IBM's share of the value of federal central processor units at the end of 1981 was 24 percent.

20. See David K. Henry, "Defense Spending: A Growth Market for Industry," in Department of Commerce, *1983 U.S. Industrial Outlook* (GPO, 1983), p. 42.

Table 4-8. *Distribution of Federal Computers by User Agency, Selected Years, 1966–81*

Year	Department of Energy[a]	National Aeronautics and Space Administration	Department of Defense
1966	9	16	64
1968	10	15	64
1969	12	14	62
1974	20	13	51
1976	24	13	46
1981	26	4	48

Sources: Philip S. Nyborg, Pender M. McCarter, and William Erikson, eds., *Information Processing in the United States: A Quantitative Summary* (American Federation of Information Processing Societies, 1977), p. 28; Martha Mulford Gray, *Federal ADP Equipment: A Compilation of Statistics—1981*, NBS Special Publication 500-97 (GPO, 1982), pp. 66, 71; and U.S. Department of Commerce, National Bureau of Standards, *Computers in the Federal Government: A Compilation of Statistics*, NBS Special Publication 500-7 (GPO, 1977), p. 22.

a. The DOE and the agencies that preceded it before 1977.

in the largest, high-performance computers that defined the state of the art, government purchases continued to be the largest single factor in sales of new, leading-edge machines.

This pattern can be seen, to some extent, in table 4-9, which divides computers into size classes. In 1972, in the most advanced class of computers—International Data Corporation (IDC) Class 7 machines—federal installations were about 40 percent of the total. By 1980 the federal share of Class 7 machines had dipped to 13 percent. This reflects the migration of more commercially oriented computers into the Class 7 category and the lack of a more advanced computer class to define current performance frontiers, rather than a slacking off in the government's role in purchasing leading-edge machines.

If current supercomputers of the epoch are considered—and they are buried in the Class 7 category with more modestly performing systems—a different picture emerges. With the high-performance supercomputer of the early 1970s, the Control Data 7600 (manufactured from 1969 to 1977), roughly 40 percent of the twenty-nine machines produced over its life cycle were purchased by the federal government. The next generation of supercomputers, delivered from 1976 through the mid-1980s, contained two major products: various models of the Cray-1, and the Control Data Cyber 205. As of mid-1983 better than half of these machines had been leased or purchased by the government.[21]

21. See *Supercomputers*, Hearings before the House Committee on Science and Technology, 98 Cong. 1 sess. (GPO, 1984), pp. 429, 434.

Table 4-9. *Federal Computers as a Percentage of U.S. Computer Installations, 1972–80*[a]

Size	1972	1974	1975	1977	1980
Class 2	4.81	3.10	3.09	3.48	4.65
Class 3	8.58	6.89	6.18	4.41	3.33
Class 4	9.36	7.29	6.57	6.81	6.91
Class 5	10.21	8.18	8.68	7.79	7.10
Class 6	13.94	14.53	13.46	12.87	9.41
Class 7	40.17	29.99	24.89	21.83	13.35
All general purpose computers[b]	7.62	5.95	5.64	5.73	5.64
Minicomputers	4.36	3.39	3.04	2.82	2.20

Source: Author's calculations based on Gray, *Federal ADP Equipment*, pp. 66, 71.

a. Size class definitions are those of the International Data Corporation; GSA inventory data on federal computers have been classified according to the IDC classifications; estimates of all U.S. installations are IDC figures.

b. Excludes minicomputers.

Fiscal Assistance

Over the years the U.S. government has tinkered with fiscal measures that are of particular relevance to computer and other technology-intensive firms. Limited amounts of subsidized low-interest capital have been available to defense contractors for facilities of defense interest, including plants in the electronics and computer industries.[22] But by far the most important influence has been the tax system.

Regulations determining depreciation allowances and tax credits on capital investments have directly affected the computer industry. But high-technology industries in general and the computer industry in particular have neither benefited nor suffered systematically, in terms of corporate tax rates, from changes in the tax treatment of their corporate income relative to that of other industries. Effective tax rates on investments in the office, computing, and accounting machines industry

22. Such programs included the "V-loan" program of the Defense Production Act of 1950, which provided Defense Department guarantees on loans contracted by defense producers, direct loans under sections 302 and 303 of the same act, special accelerated depreciation provisions for defense-related facilities, and direct funding of production capacity in products of defense interest. See John E. Tilton, *International Diffusion of Technology: The Case of Semiconductors* (Brookings, 1971), pp. 92–95; and Michael Borrus and James Millstein, "Technological Innovation and Industrial Growth: A Comparative Assessment of Biotechnology and Semiconductors" (University of California at Berkeley, c. 1984), pp. 52–55.

have been very close to the averages for all manufacturing, before and after the changes in the U.S. tax laws instituted in the early 1980s.[23]

From the mid-1960s until 1982, tax laws did favor investment in computers relative to other types of business assets. The effective marginal tax rates on investment in computer equipment were far below those for other assets; indeed, investment was subsidized (with an effective negative tax rate) during some of these years. Furthermore, computing equipment was among the most heavily subsidized of all business assets. Since the relative structure of tax rates remained fairly stable, investment in computer systems appears to have been favorably affected.[24]

This stimulus to demand for computers, relative to other types of capital assets, was abruptly ended by the tax reform passed in 1982. It transformed computing machinery into one of the most heavily taxed forms of capital investment.[25] The positive role that the tax laws played in the tremendous growth in computer use in earlier decades has since been eliminated and even reversed.

Some special features of the U.S. tax system may continue to encourage investment in technology-intensive industries. One is the system of tax advantages given to venture capital companies loaning funds to firms developing new products or processes. Other tax incentives encourage investment in small firms, although these incentives show no particular bias toward technology-intensive start-ups.[26]

23. See Charles R. Hulten and James W. Robertson, "The Taxation of High Technology Industries," *National Tax Journal*, vol. 37 (September 1984), table 2; and Don Fullerton and Andrew B. Lyon, "Does the Tax System Favor Investment in High-Tech or Smoke-Stack Industries?" NBER Working Paper 1600, April 1985, table 3.

24. See Hulten and Robertson, "Taxation of High Technology Industries," table 6 and p. 330; and Fullerton and Lyon, "Does the Tax System Favor Investment," table 1. Hulten and Robertson show office and computing machinery with a 15 percent marginal rate of subsidy in 1965, the least taxed of all equipment and machinery assets, and with a 3 percent marginal tax rate in 1975, trailing only heavy trucks, buses, and aircraft in lightness of tax burden. Fullerton and Lyon in 1985 calculate an effective marginal subsidy of 1.2 percent, exceeded only by the 4 percent subsidy rate on aircraft under the tax law in effect in 1980. The subsidy later increased to 62 percent, the greatest for any type of asset, under the 1981 tax reform.

25. Hulten and Robertson show office and computing machinery with the highest marginal tax rate for any type of machinery or equipment asset after the 1982 reform, as do Fullerton and Lyon (although buildings and structures have higher effective rates).

26. See Edwin Mansfield, "Tax Policy and Innovation: Provisions, Proposals, and Needed Research," in Eileen L. Collins, ed., *Tax Policy and Investment in Innovation*, PRA Report 83-1 (NSF, 1982), pp. 7, 9.

In recent years most discussions of tax incentives have centered on the tax treatment of research and development expenditures. While it may be argued that all R&D spending represents investment in an intangible asset, research and development expenditures in the United States have generally been treated like other current or capital business expenditures: as a current cost if not invested in tangible assets, like other depreciable investment if sunk in a capital good. In the late 1970s the tax expenditure implicit in the deductibility of current R&D expenses amounted to about 4 percent of industrial research and development.[27]

The tax act of 1981 significantly changed established practice by instituting a system of temporary tax credits on incremental R&D investment.[28] Widely differing assessments of the usefulness of such credits have been offered. After considerable public debate the tax law finally passed in 1986 contained an R&D tax credit.[29] The efficacy of R&D tax credits as an instrument of technology policy will certainly inspire further research and debate. Because the experiment is so recent, it will probably be a number of years before empirical research can satisfactorily address these questions.

27. Calculations based on NSF, *Science Indicators, 1980,* table 2-5, app. table 2-5. Treasury Department rules on the allocation of R&D expenses among the foreign affiliates of multinational firms remain an issue of practical importance in allocating taxable income among affiliates and therefore in increasing after-tax earnings. Computer industry executives often raise the issue in public forums. See U.S. Department of Commerce, International Trade Administration, *The Computer Industry* (GPO, 1983), pp. 7, 61.

28. Other features of the 1981 tax act affecting R&D expenditure included more rapid cost recovery for R&D capital equipment investment (judged unlikely to have any great effect on anything) and increased tax deductions for donations of R&D equipment to universities (judged to add a significant incentive to such donations). For these evaluations see Eileen L. Collins, *An Early Assessment of Three R&D Tax Incentives Provided by the Economic Recovery Tax Act of 1981,* PRA Report 83-7 (NSF, 1983).

29. See Richard Corrigan, "The R&D Tax Credit Is the Tax Break That Almost Everybody Seems to Love," *National Journal,* March 16, 1985, pp. 577–79; Anne Swardson, "Verdict Still Out on True Benefits of R&D Tax Credit," *Washington Post,* March 17, 1985; Martin Neil Baily, Robert Z. Lawrence, and Data Resources, Inc., "The Need for a Permanent Tax Credit for Industrial Research and Development," paper commissioned by the Coalition for the Advancement of Industrial Technology, 1985; Robert Eisner, "The R&D Tax Credit: A Flawed Tool," *Issues in Science and Technology,* vol. 1 (Summer 1985), pp. 79–86; and Edwin Mansfield and Lorne Switzer, "The Effects of R&D Tax Credits and Allowances in Canada," *Research Policy,* no. 14 (1985), pp. 97–107.

Market Structure

Government policies regulating market structure have been of great significance to the U.S. computer industry. Vigorous antitrust suits instituted during the 1950s played some role in the rapid diffusion of semiconductor and computer technology from the Bell Telephone Laboratories and IBM, and they may have had an important part in shaping the relatively small influence that patents have exerted over competition in the U.S. market. Antitrust pressure on IBM continued to affect IBM's actions vis-à-vis its competitors in the 1960s and 1970s.[30] In 1981 the Justice Department ended its efforts to press antitrust suits against IBM. This action is widely believed to have prompted IBM's increasingly aggressive legal stance against competitors using technology to which IBM has a patent claim. In early 1985 the Justice Department reviewed the terms of consent decrees signed by IBM in 1935 and 1956 that restricted the corporation's marketing practices.[31]

Under the terms of a 1984 agreement between IBM and the European Community, in effect through 1990, IBM must supply technical interface information on new products within at least four months of the announcement of a new mainframe computer product to firms "directly engaged" in research and development, manufacturing, or marketing in the EC. Although the immediate impact of the measure may not be great, in the long term it clearly circumscribes the actions IBM can take against competitors producing equipment compatible with its computers. The agreement limits the time IBM can deny outsiders access to the technical details of its computer architecture, and because all the significant

30. See Kenneth Flamm, *Creating the Computer: Government, Industry and High Technology* (Brookings, forthcoming), chap. 7. Bob O. Evans, former vice-president for engineering technology at IBM, has described the antitrust litigation as "very costly and stressful" for IBM at the time. The recent end to the government's long-standing suit signals, according to Evans, "that enormous weight has been lifted and we are back to getting on with life." See *The Computer Museum Report*, no. 9 (Summer 1984), p. 18; and ibid., no. 11 (Fall 1984), p. 16.

31. See, for example, John W. Verity and Willie Schatz, "Fast Break in Armonk," *Datamation*, vol. 31 (January 1985), pp. 68–74; Philip H. Dorn, "The Song Remains the Same," *Datamation*, vol. 30 (February 1984), p. 110; and John Marcom, Jr., and Andy Pasztor, "U.S. Is Reviewing Decades-Old IBM Consent Decrees," *Wall Street Journal*, March 5, 1985.

computer firms operate in major markets around the world, the impact of the agreement is international in scope.[32]

Joint Ventures

In 1984 Congress passed the Joint Research and Development Act, perhaps the most important legislation affecting market structure in technology-intensive industry in recent years. The act encourages firms to undertake cooperative research. The law defines joint research and development ventures and asserts that they will not necessarily inhibit competition. If such ventures are disclosed to the Justice Department and approved, possible judgments in private antitrust cases will be limited to actual rather than treble (the usual legal norm) damages.[33]

Japan's announcement in 1981 of its "Fifth Generation" computer research programs provoked the spate of new joint research ventures begun by U.S. firms in 1982 and 1983—ventures that prompted the 1984 law. Because basic research is difficult to appropriate privately, firms will tend to undertake too little on their own. Similarly, some "precompetitive" applied research is frequently duplicated among firms as they develop more applied commercial products. Such duplication cannot be easily captured as a competitive advantage but will reduce the return on a given industry investment in R&D. Reducing duplication and underinvestment in basic and precompetitive research has been the major motivation for experiments with cooperative research ventures.[34]

A direct response to Japanese government policies favoring cooperative research in precompetitive, "generic" technology was the formation of the Microelectronics and Computer Technology Corporation

32. See Andrew Pollack, "Few Dividends Are Seen for Japanese Competitors," *New York Times*, August 6, 1984; David Sanger, "Scoring the Match," *New York Times*, August 3, 1984; Robert T. Gallagher, "IBM-EC Accord: Who Benefits?" *Electronics Week*, August 13, 1984, p. 20; and Paul Tate and John Verity, "Under the Gun," *Datamation*, vol. 30 (September 1, 1984), pp. 42–48.

33. See William F. Baxter, "Antitrust Law and Technological Innovation," *Issues in Science and Technology*, vol. 1 (Winter 1985), pp. 80–91.

34. See William C. Norris, "Cooperative R&D: A Regional Strategy," *Issues in Science and Technology*, vol. 1 (Winter 1985), p. 94; and Lawrence J. White, "Clearing the Legal Path to Cooperative Research," *Technology Review*, vol. 88 (July 1985), pp. 39–44. For a theoretical analysis, see Michael L. Katz, "An Analysis of Cooperative Research and Development," *Rand Journal of Economics*, vol. 17 (Winter 1986), pp. 527–43; and Michael Spence, "Cost Reduction, Competition, and Industry Performance," *Econometrica*, vol. 52 (January 1984), pp. 101–21.

(MCC) in January 1983.[35] MCC has grown rapidly as an experimental test bed for cooperative computer research. By mid-1983 it already counted twelve U.S. companies as participants.[36] Membership shareholders peaked two years later with twenty-one companies and an annual research budget between $60 and $70 million.[37] From a staff of 120 workers in October 1984, MCC raised its head count to 400 by early 1986 and was plunging ahead with a research program focused on four major areas, all directly related to computer products: software technology, computer-aided design of very large scale integrated circuits, packaging and interconnection technologies for computer systems, and advanced computer architecture (the most active of the four areas and reportedly consuming almost half of MCC's resources).[38] MCC research administrators maintain that there is little duplication of their research within the companies, since MCC is oriented toward long-term, fundamental research in contrast to the shorter term work carried out for the most part in the corporate laboratories of participants.[39]

Not surprisingly, cooperative research in a fundamentally competitive

35. To quote William Norris of Control Data, the guiding force behind the conception of MCC: "To retain—and encourage—competitiveness among all participants, cooperative R&D ventures must be confined to the research and advanced technology end of the innovative process. The product and service possibilities that stem from research cooperation must be exploited by individual firms in competitive—rather than cooperative—environments. The Japanese electronics industry has adopted this strategy with great success, and it is a fundamental principle on which MCC is built." Norris, "Cooperative R&D," p. 95. See also Wesley R. Iversen, "Where Joint Ventures Are the Rule," *Electronics,* June 16, 1983, p. 92.

36. Iversen, "Where Joint Ventures are the Rule," p. 92.

37. "MCC: The Past Year's Progress," oral presentation made by John T. Pinkston at the 26th Annual Technical Symposium of the Washington chapter of the Association for Computing Machinery, Gaithersburg, Maryland, June 20, 1985; and David E. Sanger, "Computer Consortium Lags: Rivalries Split U.S. Project," *New York Times,* September 5, 1984. The twenty-one companies were Advanced Micro Devices, Allied Corporation, Bell Communications Research, BMC Industries, Boeing, Control Data, Digital Equipment Corporation, Eastman Kodak, Gould, Harris, Honeywell, Lockheed, Martin Marietta, 3M, Mostek, Motorola, National Semiconductor, NCR, RCA, Rockwell, and Sperry. See Dwight B. Davis, "R&D Consortia: Pooling Industries' Resources," *High Technology,* vol. 5 (October 1985), p. 44. In 1986 Gould dropped out, Mostek sold its share to Hewlett-Packard, and BMC sold its share to Westinghouse. See J. Robert Lineback, "Can MCC Survive the Latest Defections?" *Electronics,* January 22, 1987, p. 30.

38. Sanger, "Computer Consortium Lags"; and Andrew Pollack, "A New Spirit of Cooperation," *New York Times,* January 14, 1986.

39. See Merton J. Peck, "Joint R&D: The Case of Microelectronics and Computer Technology Corporation," *Research Policy,* no. 15 (1986), p. 229.

business environment is problematic. Individual companies reportedly were reluctant initially to dispatch their best researchers to work on the MCC projects, and only intense pressure from the leadership of MCC (first headed by retired Navy admiral and former NSA director Bobby Inman) corrected that situation.[40] Concerns about leaks of proprietary information to competitors in the close confines of the MCC labs are another major issue for participants, and only time will tell if satisfactory controls can be put in place.

In spite of the uncertainties, however, cooperative research is becoming an increasingly important feature on the U.S. research horizon. By the spring of 1985, fourteen joint research ventures had requested approval from the Justice Department.[41] Also in the spring of 1985, the Software Productivity Consortium, fifteen defense contractors interested in developing advanced software tools to reduce computer programming costs, announced the establishment of a research complex in Fairfax County, Virginia. The facility eventually will house about 500 employees.[42] Several other developments are noteworthy. A fiber optics research cooperative is aiming to spend $10 million annually to manufacture technology for optoelectronic devices.[43] The Semiconductor Research Corporation, a nonprofit corporation funded by forty U.S. semiconductor and computer firms, was incorporated in 1982 to increase funding for basic semiconductor research.[44] About $12 million of its $15 million budget went to sponsoring university research in 1984. The

40. Sanger, "Computer Consortium Lags."

41. See "Research Venture Gets U.S. Approval on Computer Work," *Wall Street Journal,* March 5, 1985.

42. See David Stipp, "Eleven Concerns That Develop Software for Defense Mull Joint Research Venture," *Wall Street Journal,* October 9, 1984; and Michael Schrage, "Aerospace Software Consortium to Locate in Fairfax County," *Washington Post,* April 17, 1985, corrected on April 19, 1985. The companies involved include TRW, Boeing, E-Systems, General Dynamics, Ford Aerospace, GTE, Lockheed, McDonnell Douglas, Rockwell, United Technologies, Science Applications International, Vitro, and Northrop. See also "Va. Using $20 Million Carrot to Lure Software Center," *Washington Post,* May 2, 1985.

43. Pollack, "A New Spirit."

44. Members include Advanced Micro Devices, AT&T, Burroughs, Control Data, DEC, DuPont, Eastman Kodak, Eaton, E-Systems, GCA Corporation, GE, General Instrument, General Motors, Goodyear, GTE, Harris, Hewlett-Packard, Honeywell, IBM, Intel, LSI Logic, Monolithic Memories, Monsanto, Motorola, National Semiconductor, Perkin-Elmer, RCA, Rockwell, Silicon Systems, Sperry, Texas Instruments, Union Carbide, Varian Associates, Westinghouse, Xerox, Zilog. See Office of Technology Assessment, *Information Technology R&D: Critical Trends and Issues* (Washington, D.C.: OTA, 1985), p. 190.

organization has also considered establishing "Project Leapfrog," an MCC-style joint research venture in integrated circuit manufacture.[45] Industry, however, has proved reluctant to bear the full cost, and federal assistance has been solicited. A proposal for such a venture—known as Sematech—was formulated by the Semiconductor Industry Association in late 1986, and a 1987 report of the Defense Science Board proposed that the Defense Department fund a similar facility to the tune of $200 million per year.[46]

This surge in cooperative research arrangements has been accompanied by growth in the number of joint industry-university research centers. At the end of World War II, the federal government created a number of federally funded laboratories at universities to pursue basic research deemed to be in the national interest. Project MAC, discussed in chapter 3, was probably the first center to be specifically oriented toward computers. Since then, however, private firms have sometimes taken the initiative in creating university-run research centers working on problems of practical importance to industry. In computer technology, examples of such centers include the Microsystems Industrial Group at MIT, the Microelectronics and Information Sciences Center at the University of Minnesota, the Rensselaer Polytechnic Institute Center for Industrial Innovation, the Center for Integrated Systems at Stanford University, the Microelectronics Center of North Carolina, and the Microelectronics Innovation and Computer Research Opportunities (MICRO) Program at the University of California.[47] The Semiconductor Research Corporation belongs in this category, and MCC—by locating in Austin, Texas, and forming a relationship with the University of Texas—has followed this model to some extent.

45. See Peter Behr, "High-Tech Project Nears Takeoff Point," *Washington Post,* July 8, 1984. One can only wonder whether the participation of IBM in the organization poses a major obstacle for any project to be sanctioned, since the loose guidelines for acceptable cooperative ventures discussed by Justice Department officials seem to involve market share tests.

46. See Richard Bambrick, "Sematech Gets SIA Go-Ahead; Target *Government, Industry* for Funds," *Electronic News,* vol. 32 (November 24, 1986), pp. 1, 10; and Office of the Under Secretary of Defense for Acquisition, *Report of Defense Science Board Task Force on Defense Semiconductor Dependency,* Washington, February 1987, p. 11.

47. See OTA, *Information Technology R&D,* chap. 6; and John Walsh, "New R&D Centers Will Test University Ties," *Science,* vol. 227 (January 11, 1985), pp. 150–52. Similar developments are occurring in biotechnology—examples include the Center for Advanced Research in Biotechnology (CARB) in the Maryland suburbs of Washington, D.C., and the Whitehead Institute for Biological Science at MIT.

Government research agencies have furthered this trend. Examples include the Software Engineering Institute at Carnegie-Mellon University and a group of twenty-five applied research centers being set up by the National Science Foundation as joint industry-government-university programs.[48] All these developments are motivated by the theory that more basic, nonappropriable technology is the social foundation on which successful private product development and competition rest. Driven by accelerating competition with foreign countries that are increasingly the United States' technological peers, U.S. industry is leading the way in sponsoring experiments to improve the yield on investments in basic and precompetitive research.

Are these developments dangerous? Have universities diverted their attention from basic questions, their traditional preserve, to projects of more immediate commercial application? With increasing frequency such concerns have been raised. Basic research creates information that is difficult to commercialize privately. Shifting the gaze of academics to the yardstick of commercial relevance may jeopardize their efforts in areas that are not amenable to immediate commercial spinoffs, but are essential nonetheless to long-run technological progress. Undue emphasis on commercial results could reduce basic research, the traditional strength of the academic sector in the United States. Proprietary restrictions on the results of research also threaten the established norms of open academic and scientific exchange. This, too, may alter the character and direction of academic research.[49]

Standards

Government measures to promote particular computer standards have significantly influenced the ground rules for competition in the industry. Probably the earliest example dates back to the mid-1950s when magnetic tape equipment began to proliferate. Magnetic tape for specific computer systems could not be procured competitively, the many different formats were incompatible, prices remained high in spite of declining costs, and the technical characteristics of tapes could not

48. See Thomas H. Maugh II, "Technology Centers Unite Industry and Academia," *High Technology,* vol. 5 (October 1985), pp. 48–52; and John W. Anderson, "Pushing Ivory-Tower Scientists into the High-Tech Race," *New York Times,* February 15, 1987.
49. See, for example, David E. Sanger, "Computer Work Bends College Secrecy Rules," *New York Times,* October 16, 1984.

be established reliably. The NSA expressed its concern by setting up a million dollar laboratory for testing magnetic tape and establishing standards. By 1963 standardized specifications were published.[50] Tape prices soon began to come down, and in 1967 the tape testing operation was transferred to the National Bureau of Standards, the official arbiter of the standard today.

The Cobol programming language, discussed in chapter 3, is another example of a successful standard promoted by government. The government accounted for a major share of the computer market when these rules were promulgated, but today the relatively small federal share of the market means that such standardization is ordinarily less effective unless backed by industry.

In certain well-defined markets for advanced products, however, government purchasing specifications can still play an important role in setting the rules of the game. This is particularly true in the young but fast-growing computer-assisted design (CAD) industry, where many small firms battle for market share and government users (particularly aerospace firms) represent a major segment of demand. Standardized data formats developed by the Air Force with the National Bureau of Standards have gained wide acceptance by manufacturers because the formats make possible the transfer of information between many disparate pieces of automation-related equipment on the factory floor. Data standards for electronics design information, developed for DARPA's integrated circuit design research program, have become the de facto standard for shipping such designs to "silicon foundries." Standard circuit description languages and libraries developed for the VHSIC program seem likely to become a similar standard. Private firms have increasingly begun to work with the National Bureau of Standards to define standards when they have lacked enough influence to impose their own designs and when the need for a standard has been widely recognized.[51]

50. See Samuel S. Snyder, "Influence of U.S. Cryptological Organizations on the Digital Computer Industry," declassified National Security Agency report released to the National Archives, pp. 15–16.

51. Standardized formats developed by the Air Force are IGES (international graphics exchange standard) for graphics data and PDDI (product data definition interface). The most successful examples of public domain standard formats are CIF (Caltech intermediate form) for mask-level layout, and SDL (Stanford design language) for gate-level descriptions. See A. R. Newton and A. L. Sangiovanni-Vincentelli, "Computer-Aided Design for VLSI Circuits," *Computer,* vol. 19 (April 1986), p. 42. For reference to

Patents

Protection of intellectual property—of which technology is an essential subset—is ultimately a key issue when factors determining industry structure in a technology-intensive product are considered. Strengthening such protection has been the object of U.S. economic policy with increasing frequency. In 1984 the protections of copyright law were extended to the masks used to produce integrated circuits. Under intensive pressure from the United States to follow suit, Japan recently passed a similar law. Copyright protection of computer software has also been advocated. In 1985 the Japanese government, over the objections of the Japanese software industry, passed a bill modeled on U.S. protections.[52]

Government agencies' policies toward patents derived from work on government-financed projects differ: some retain title to the invention but make it available for use by interested parties; others grant title to the contractor but require a nonexclusive royalty-free license for government users.[53] Current statutes and regulations grant considerable flexibility to individual agencies to decide which of these two principles to apply.

The Department of Defense largely sticks to the royalty-free license arrangement (the Navy and Air Force almost exclusively, the Army

---

standard circuit description libraries, see ibid., p. 44; and Ron Waxman, "Hardware Design Languages for Computer Design and Test," *Computer*, vol. 19 (April 1986), p. 92. The Manufacturing Automation Protocol (MAP) is under joint development by General Motors and the National Bureau of Standards. Equipment conforming to the MAP standard, made by a variety of manufacturers, will be able to be hooked together in factory automation systems. MAP is supported by virtually all U.S. firms that have announced factory automation products. MAP and a related office automation standards effort, the Technical and Office Protocol (TOP), recently joined the Corporation for Open Systems (COS), a nonprofit consortium of major vendors and users of computer systems formed to develop nonproprietary standards. See Bob Wallace, "COS, MAP/ TOP Groups Establish Bridge Council," *Network World*, February 9, 1987.

52. See Karen A. Ammer, "The Semiconductor Chip Protection Act of 1984," *Law and Policy in International Business*, vol. 17 (1985), pp. 395–420; "Japan Passes Chip Protection Act," in *Japan Semiconductor Quarterly*, vol. 2 (June 1985), p. 1; Susan Chira, "Japan Plans to Provide Protection for Software," *New York Times*, March 19, 1985; and Stephen Kreider Yoder, "Japan Scuttles Patent Proposal for Software," *Wall Street Journal*, March 19, 1985.

53. For a history of patent policy among federal agencies, see Patrick James Flanagan, "An Analysis of the Evolution of Government Patent Policy in Research and Development Contracts" (Master's thesis, Naval Postgraduate School, Monterey, Calif., 1981).

somewhat less so).[54] Since development costs generally dwarf research costs by a substantial margin, this policy is more likely to lead to commercialization of inventions. Unlike the Defense Department, the Department of Energy (except in areas unrelated to nuclear energy), NASA, NSF, and the National Institutes of Health (NIH) generally retain title to the patent. This policy has the virtue of not granting a competitive advantage at public expense to a particular private firm. The disadvantage is that a firm will rarely spend the money to develop a concept to which it will retain no legal title. Government projects outside of defense (particularly NASA) have had significantly less impact on the commercial development of computer products than have defense programs, but the preponderant role of Defense Department funding makes it difficult to ascribe the differential impact to patent issues alone.

Software

Because applications software is by nature particular to the application for which it is purchased, the federal role in the development of the U.S. software industry is considerably less prominent than for computer hardware. In some areas (for example, operating systems, timesharing, and networks) leading-edge applications sponsored by DARPA have contributed in noticeable ways to the commercialization of new types of general purpose software. But, in general, the bread and butter applications programming used by the average business data processing center is tailored to the specific needs of that business. Except for some well-known scientific and engineering tools developed for advanced government applications (for example, electronics design packages and mathematical software for numerical analysis) federal procurement has influenced American software technology considerably less than hardware technology.

As was true for hardware, federal influence was greatest in the earliest days of the industry. The Air Force's massive SAGE project was particularly important in this regard. In 1955, as the development of the software for this system was begun, the Rand Corporation (placed in charge of the effort and later replaced by a spinoff from its ranks, the

54. See Federal Council for Science and Technology, *Report on Government Patent Policy, Combined December 31, 1973, through September 30, 1976* (GPO, 1976).

Systems Development Corporation) employed twenty-five programmers. Fewer than 200 people in the entire country were capable of writing codes for such complex applications at the time.[55] By 1959 SAGE alone employed 400 programmers. The SAGE operating system was large (over one-quarter of a million instructions), but even larger command and control projects soon followed. The Strategic Air Command Control System (SACCS), one of the largest such systems ever written, ran over a million instructions, and an associated auxiliary message system required another 300,000 lines of code.[56]

These early command and control systems projects transformed the U.S. software industry. By the end of 1960, 3,500 SDC programmers were working on these and other military projects, and another 4,000 "alumni" had left to join private industry. In 1963 there were 4,300 busy programmers at SDC and 6,000 alumni dispersed throughout industry. By the early 1960s numerous contract software houses had sprung up to service the mushrooming military systems market: software firms that had been established to compete for these contracts included the Computer Usage Corporation, Computer Sciences Corporation, and Planning Research Corporation, Computer Applications, Inc., and Informatics. Computer Sciences is now the second largest computer software firm in the world (trailing IBM), and three of the four largest independent American software houses are drawn from this group.[57]

The large and complex applications developed by federal users continue to be a major source of revenues for the U.S. software industry. Because much software is written within firms for their own use, sales figures for products marketed by the U.S. software industry fall far short of total U.S. software production. Within the "merchant" software market, however, the government is the dominant customer. In 1982 roughly $5 billion (about half of U.S. software industry revenues) was

55. See Claude Baum, *The System Builders: The Story of SDC* (Santa Monica, Calif.: SDC, 1981), p. 23. In 1955 an industry directory listed some 1,200 programmers, but fewer than 200 were considered by SDC to be capable of writing these applications.

56. Ibid., pp. 38, 54.

57. Ibid., pp. 47, 66. Those four are Computer Sciences, Informatics, EDS, and Planning Research. This comparison is based on 1983 sales for the twenty largest software firms in the world and excludes divisions of computer manufacturers (like IBM, Burroughs, DEC), foreign firms, and software divisions of large conglomerates (like Arthur Andersen and GE's GEISCO). SDC is now part of Burroughs, the third largest software producer in the world. See U.S. Department of Commerce, Office of Computers and Business Equipment, *A Competitive Assessment of the United States Software Industry* (GPO, 1984), table 10, p. 37.

from packaged custom software and integrated systems, the remainder from standard "off-the-shelf" programs.[58] That year the Department of Defense alone spent roughly $4 billion to $8 billion for custom software, with the bulk of this effort procured from industry.[59]

The largest single customer for the contract software industry, the government has also influenced software technology in recent years by actively participating in an industrywide effort to establish the UNIX operating system as an independent standard. Designed to make software easily portable among the enormous variety of computers manufactured in the United States, UNIX was first developed at the Bell labs in the early 1970s. Then at the University of California, Berkeley, extensive networking and communications functions were added to the basic Bell system. This work was financed by DARPA, which was eager to make it possible for the bewildering array of computer hardware hooked up to its ARPANET to communicate easily with one another and run the same applications.[60] The features of the Berkeley versions of UNIX were incorporated into later versions of the commercial AT&T system. Government contracts are increasingly mandating the use of UNIX in government procurement in support of this movement.[61]

Summary

The federal government has enormously influenced the development of computer hardware and software in the United States at both the micro and macro levels. In research and development its role has shifted from a pervasive, all-encompassing one to focused sponsorship of the most risky, advanced, leading-edge research. In procurement a similar transformation has occurred: from a virtual lock on the market in the early 1950s, government today plays a dominant role only in the most

58. Ibid., p. 34.

59. Benjamin M. Elson, "Software Update Aids Defense Program," *Aviation Week and Space Technology,* March 14, 1983, p. 209.

60. See Donald W. Cragun, "Convergence Effort Combines 4.2 BSD with UNIX System V," *Computer Technology Review,* Fall 1986, pp. 14–23; and interview with John Gage, Sun Microsystems, Inc., January 29, 1987.

61. See Rick Vizachero, "Unix Users Work Toward Standards Set," *Government Computer News,* vol. 6 (February 13, 1987), pp. 1, 5; and Ron Schneiderman, "NBS Will Propose Validation Policy for Unix," *Systems and Software,* January 1986, p. 15, and "Military/Government Users: Moving, But Larger Target," ibid., pp. 24–36.

expensive, high-end products entering the commercial marketplace. (But today's leading-edge product is tomorrow's mundane workhorse in this industry!)

Policies designed to regulate market structure through legal antitrust oversight were largely abandoned in the early 1980s, although the environment in which proprietary rights to new technologies are established may yet reflect the historical legacy of decades of vigorous antitrust actions (as well as the patent licensing policies of government agencies). In the late 1980s the new challenge confronting American industry may be to slow down the diffusion of U.S. technology investments to ever more capable foreign imitators without killing off the freewheeling, loose style of technology diffusion that contributed so greatly to the rapid internal development of the American computer industry.

CHAPTER FIVE

Government and Computers in Japan and Europe

IN THE United States early computer technology had a distinctly military focus and was heavily funded by the government. Japan and Europe pursued rather different technology policies: reducing a substantial lead by U.S. firms in commercial markets was their primary objective. Built into Japanese technology policies devised for their computer industry was a unique blend of cooperation and competition among a diverse group of firms. In Europe, however, all bets usually were placed on a single "national champion," the beneficiary of a steady diet of financial subsidies and preferential procurement policies. As the following history of technology policy in Japan and Europe will show, the competitive approach was more effective.

Technology Policy in Japan

Japan's success in fostering technology-intensive industry has led many to scrutinize the Japanese "model" for clues to help stimulate the U.S. economy. The political air is thick with talk of "targeting," and U.S. managers rush to emulate Japanese management techniques. Yet the historical record seems to show that the Japanese model is more a frame of mind—a willingness to experiment and adapt to changing economic realities, a societal ability to mobilize behind a common social goal—than a rote formula applied year after year to guide economic decisions. The steps taken by the Japanese to foster their computer industry provide a good illustration of this flexibility.

125

There are four major players on the Japanese computer scene, three of them government organizations: the Ministry of Trade and Industry (MITI) and its technical arm, the Electrotechnical Laboratory (ETL); Nippon Telephone and Telegraph (NTT) and its immense laboratories; and the least significant actor from a purely financial viewpoint, the Ministry of Education, which controls activities within the prestigious national universities. In recent years Ministry of Education funding of research and development in Japan's universities and colleges has grown considerably. The fourth player is industry—the corporate research laboratories of Japan's largest industrial firms. The interaction among these groups is an unusual mix of rivalry and cooperation, and the web of relationships constantly changes.

From the early 1950s to 1961 computer development in Japan was mainly carried out within the ETL, NTT, and the University of Tokyo, the flagship of the national university system. Corporate research laboratories scarcely existed, and the first indigenous commercial computers shipped after 1957 were based on designs transferred to industry from these labs. Although the electronics promotion law of 1957 (extended in 1971 and again in 1978) established legal mechanisms for direct assistance to industry, subsidies for research and development on computers were minimal—less than $1 million—until 1961.

Worldwide Explosion in Demand: The Early 1960s

Within the institutions devised to support the development of a computer technology base in Japan, there have been at least three major periods of reorganization. The early 1960s marked the first. Japanese industry began to look at computers with considerably greater interest after IBM was allowed to establish a computer manufacturing base in Japan in 1960. From then on world-class technology was required to stay competitive. Late in 1960 MITI announced a five-year program for national production of electronic computers.[1] Stiff trade barriers were erected in 1961, and the price for foreign admission was access to important technology. After 1962 would-be computer manufacturers forged joint ventures with U.S. computer makers (under the guidance of MITI). The only Japanese company not to depend on imports of foreign

---

1. Tosaku Kimura, "Birth and Development of Computers," *National Sciences and Museums,* vol. 46, no. 3 (1979), Special Issue on Computers (in Japanese).

technology was Fujitsu, the first to establish a corporate computer research lab of any significance.

As a "sweetener," perhaps, for pioneering the path of technological independence, Fujitsu was given the leadership of the very first MITI-funded computer development program, the FONTAC project. Oki Electric and the Nippon Electric Corporation (NEC) joined in the effort, developing peripherals for the main Fujitsu-designed computer. The MITI financial contribution was small—only $1.16 million—from 1962 to 1966, but the project was of great importance to Fujitsu. The FACOM 230-50, the most powerful machine of Fujitsu's computer line, was based on the FONTAC prototype, as was the architecture for Fujitsu's largest family of computers. Perhaps more important, the Electronic Computer Technology Research Association appears to have been the first cooperative research venture to have been established among competing Japanese computer firms.[2]

As the impetus for computer development shifted to more explicitly commercial objectives, MITI's Electrotechnical Laboratory was forced to carve out a new role for itself. The economics of the growing marketplace meant that a standard architecture, and software designed for that standard, were needed. Rather than designing and building its own unique architecture for experimental computers, ETL was instead directed to develop high-performance components that could be used in the existing architecture of Japanese manufacturers.[3] In 1965 the last large computer based on a unique ETL design, the Mark VI, was completed. This high-performance machine, intended to be the Japanese equivalent of the American Stretch and LARC projects and the British Atlas supercomputer, never made the transition from research project to commercial product. Times had changed.

Nurturing Industrial Research: The Mid-1960s

The mid-1960s marked a second major transition. IBM had announced its new System 360 line in 1964, and the Japanese, like other competitors, were in serious danger of being overrun. The System 360 used hybrid

2. The $1.16 million figure was reported in Japan Electronic Computer Corporation (JECC), *EDP in Japan* (Tokyo: JECC, 1975), p. 9.

3. Osamu Ishii, "Research and Development on Information Processing Technology at Electrotechnical Laboratory—A Historical Review," *Bulletin of the Electrotechnical Laboratory,* vol. 45, nos. 7, 8 (1981) (in Japanese).

integrated circuits, less advanced than the monolithic integrated circuits that were then the state of the art. Integrated circuits were already widely available in the United States, although mainly in products built for the military market. Japan lagged in this component technology; NEC did not build the first experimental Japanese integrated circuit until 1962.[4]

Integrated circuit development on a broader front began among Japanese firms in 1964, and digital computer applications led the way (as they did in the United States, where integrated circuits used in military and space guidance computers blazed the trail). MITI awarded the six Japanese companies then producing computers $80,000 to develop specialized integrated circuits for computers. By late 1965 the three largest producers (NEC, Hitachi, Fujitsu) had announced models containing some integrated circuits.[5] Progress was slow, however. NEC did not deliver its machine until 1966, Fujitsu and Hitachi until 1968.[6]

In response to System 360 and a perceived lag in Japanese technology, MITI organized the super high performance electronic computer (SHPEC) program, one of three large-scale national research projects that pooled the resources of government labs and private corporations. This pioneering project began in 1966, ran until 1971, and cost the government about $40 million.[7] Basic research pursued at ETL was later translated into deliverable products developed at cooperating corporations' R&D labs. The first semiconductor memories built in Japan were developed for this

4. John E. Tilton, *International Diffusion of Technology: The Case of Semiconductors* (Brookings, 1971), p. 26.

5. Although the grants were nominally supposed to cover half of the companies' research costs, rarely was more than one-third of actual costs covered. One firm's completed research was to be made available to all other companies involved. See Yasuo Tarui, "Japan Seeks Its Own Route to Improved IC Techniques," *Electronics*, December 13, 1965, pp. 90–93.

6. JECC, *Konputa Noto, 1983* [Computer notes] (Tokyo: JECC, 1983), pp. 539–41. The first commercial Japanese computer containing integrated circuits seems to have been NEC's 2200 Model 500. During the 1960s NEC was the technological leader in the commercial Japanese semiconductor industry. See Tilton, *International Diffusion of Technology*, chap. 6.

7. Estimates of the cost vary widely (perhaps because of fluctuations in exchange rates and different assumptions about the time period): $33.3 million (JECC, *EDP in Japan*, p. 9); $44 million ("Government-Funded Industrial R&D in Japan," JEI Report 42 [Washington, D.C.: Japan Economic Institute, November 6, 1981], p. 3); and $35 million (George E. Lindamood, "The Rise of the Japanese Computer Industry," *ONR Far East Scientific Bulletin*, vol. 7 [October–December 1982], p. 64). The other two projects that initiated the National Research and Development Program were energy-related: magneto-hydrodynamic power generation and desulfurization of industrial fuels. See also Akio Tojo, "National R&D Program on Information Processing Technology in Japan," private memo, n.d.

project, as were high-performance semiconductor logic circuits. Hitachi's large-scale 8700 and 8800 computer models were directly based on the machine developed for this project, and component technology from the program was incorporated by other manufacturers into their computer designs.

NTT, which had played a key role in developing computers using the *parametron* (a unique circuit element invented in Japan), also strengthened its commitment to computer research at about this time. The parametron had proven to be a blind alley, and NTT turned back to semiconductors. By 1963 it had developed its CM-100 transistor computer, which trailed the development of transistor computers by private Japanese industry. (Japanese firms generally had the advantage of direct technical ties to American computer companies.) In 1968, as MITI's SHPEC project was just getting under way, NTT also began a large and well-funded industrial computer development project. The DIPS (Dendenkosha—a Japanese acronym for NTT—information processing system) computer, designed for timesharing and data base management, was complementary to the MITI project. The hardware and software for both systems were quite similar, and the first DIPS computer borrowed high-performance logic technology developed for the MITI machine.[8] The memory integrated circuit developed for the SHPEC program was also used in Nippon Telephone and Telegraph's DIPS machine.[9] The NTT contractors participating in DIPS—NEC, Fujitsu, and Hitachi—were three of the five participants in the big MITI computer project.

Business computer sales' explosive growth in the 1960s, coupled with IBM's System 360 bombshell of 1964, seemed to produce a notable willingness in Europe as well as Japan to experiment with new and unproven formulas. The Electronics Industry Act of 1957 had picked electronics as the core of the future industrial development of Japan. A decade later the act's bold declarations had begun to be translated into significant amounts of cash for research. MITI subsidies for research

8. See National Academy of Sciences, National Academy of Engineering, National Research Council, Computer Science and Engineering Board, "The Computer Industry in Japan and Its Meaning for the United States" (Washington, D.C., 1973), pp. 91–92; Lindamood, "Rise of the Japanese Computer Industry," p. 69; and Morihiro Kurushima, "Diffusion of Results, Patent Management," *Tokyo Kogyo Gijutsu*, vol. 20 (August 1979), translated in *Background Readings on Science, Technology, and Energy R&D in Japan and China*, Committee Print, House Committee on Science and Technology, 97 Cong. 1 sess. (Government Printing Office, 1981), pp. 34–36.

9. Ishii, "Research and Development on Information Processing Technology."

and development authorized under this bill were four times greater in 1967 (as the SHPEC program started) than in 1960.[10]

By the end of this second transition Japan had three basic types of institutional mechanisms to directly funnel public resources into computer R&D efforts within industrial firms. There were two distinct sets of programs run by MITI (conditional loans and consigned payments), as well as significant funds provided by NTT (see table 5-1).

The FONTAC development group was among the first private industrial research associations. It was begun in 1962, the year after passage of the law qualifying cooperative research associations for special government subsidies. Industrial research support in the form of conditional loans from MITI is repayable only if the association makes a profit. In practice, they rarely were repaid. Although barred by law from joint research with private corporations, ETL researchers have often been loaned out in recent years on temporary assignment to direct cooperative research.[11]

The other major form of support, the national R&D projects, was managed directly by ETL, rather than being nominally the responsibility of a research association. Funding for the first projects, such as SHPEC, was dispensed to individual firms as contract research.

A quasi-public agency associated with MITI, the Information Technology Promotion Agency (IPA), administers funding and loan guarantees for software development. The agency's capital draws on funding from both private industry and MITI, while MITI subsidies support its current operating expenses.[12] Since 1976 much of this funding has gone

---

10. Eugene J. Kaplan, *Japan: The Government-Business Relationship, A Guide for the American Businessman* (U.S. Department of Commerce, 1972), p. 92.

11. See Jimmy W. Wheeler, Merit E. Janow, and Thomas Pepper, *Japanese Industrial Development Policies in the 1980s: Implications for U.S. Trade and Investment* (Hudson Institute, 1982), p. 147. Lindamood, "Rise of the Japanese Computer Industry," p. 66, notes that none of the hojokin for the very large scale integrated circuit (VLSI) program had been repaid. Forty-four percent of all MITI hojokin from this period had been paid back by 1982. None of that appears to have been related to the computer projects. See United States International Trade Commission, *Foreign Industrial Targeting and Its Effects on U.S. Industries, Phase I: Japan,* USITC Publication 1437 (Washington, D.C.: USITC, 1983), p. 105. See also Charles L. Cohen, "Japan Pushes IC Research," *Electronics,* September 8, 1983, pp. 94–96. In 1984 MITI formulated proposals that would permit joint ETL research with private corporations, with joint ownership of resulting patents and half of any resulting profits to be received by the government. See Mike Berger, "Japanese Firms Boost Spending for Short-, Long-Term Projects," *Electronics Week,* September 24, 1984, pp. 32–36.

12. See Japan Information Processing Development Center, *Computer White Paper,*

to consigned development of software production technology by a private research association; other funding has gone to the consigned development of specific application programs by other private contractors.

NTT, through its relationships with the NTT "family" of suppliers, supported a considerable amount of research conducted in cooperation with, or under contract to, its technical laboratories. The DIPS project marked NTT's first move into large-scale support for industrial computer development. The development of DIPS has required large sums of research money. The third DIPS computer, the DIPS II, is said to have cost NTT more than $10 million for research and development alone in the early 1970s.[13]

The 1950s style of research support—prototypes designed and constructed within government labs later transferred to private industry—was phased out after the early 1960s. In its place arose a set of institutions stressing joint government-industry cooperation during all phases of research and early development.

Growth of Joint Research: The 1970s

A third major period of change occurred in the early 1970s. The Japanese computer industry faced dual crises. First, upheaval in the U.S. industry precipitated by the introduction of IBM's System 370 rippled out to the foreign associates of IBM's American competitors. As General Electric, RCA, and later Xerox abandoned their faltering mainframe computer product lines, serious problems were transmitted to these firms' Japanese partners. Second, government commitments to open up the Japanese computer market to international trade by 1975 compounded the imminent difficulties faced by Japanese computer producers.

The MITI prescription was radical surgery (the grafting of six independent computer producers into just three groups) followed by intensive care (massive doses of cash for research and product development). Fujitsu and Hitachi combined just long enough (and with the invaluable

1980 edition (Tokyo: JIPDEC, 1981), pp. 44–45; and JECC, *Konputa Noto, 1983,* pp. 104–06.

13. See Carl Louis Coran, "The Role and Significance of MITI in the Economic Development of the Japanese Computer Industry" (M.S. thesis, George Washington University, School of Government and Business Administration, 1976), p. 79.

Table 5-1. *Major MITI Research Programs and Cooperative Research Associations since 1962*

MITI program	Years	Research association	Type of aid[a]
Large national R&D projects			
Super high performance electronic computer (SHPEC)	1966–71	None; tasks assigned to individual firms and joint venture Nippon Software Company (Hitachi, Fujitsu, NEC)	Itakuhi
Pattern information processing system (PIPS)	1971–80	Engineering Research Association (est. 1977)	Itakuhi
Optical measurement and control system (OMCS)	1979–85	Optoelectronics Applied System Research Association (est. 1981)	Itakuhi
Fifth Generation project	1981–91	Institute for New Generation Computer Technology (ICOT)	Itakuhi
New function elements (next generation industry)	1981–90	Research and Development Association for Future Electron Devices	Itakuhi
High-speed computer for science and technology	1981–89	Scientific Computer Research Association	Itakuhi
Interoperable database system	1985–	n.a.	Itakuhi
Industrial research support			
FONTAC project	1962–66	Electronic Computer Technology Research Association	Hojokin
Development of new computer types ("3.5" Generation program)	1972–76	Ultra High Performance Computer Development Group (Fujitsu, Hitachi, Nippon Peripherals Ltd.)	Hojokin
		New Generation Computer Series Development Group (NEC, Toshiba, Japan Business Automation, Japan Data Machine)	Hojokin
		Ultra High Performance Electronic Computer Research Association (Mitsubishi, Oki)	Hojokin
Computer peripheral equipment development	1972–76	Granted to 31 companies	Hojokin
IC development	1973–74	Granted to 8 companies	Hojokin
Very large scale integrated circuit (VLSI) program	1976–79	Super LSI Technology Research Association	Hojokin

Next (fourth) Generation computer basic technology	1979–83	Computer Basic Technology Research Association	Hojokin
Small research projects			
Medical information system, health care network system	1973–	Medical Information System Development Center	n.a.
Visual information system (Hi-Ovis)	1972–79	Visual Information System Development Association	n.a.
Information Technology Promotion Agency (IPA) projects			
Information processing industry promotion	1973–75	Technical research groups on Software Modules for Business Processing (15 companies); Software Modules for Business Management (5 companies); Software Modules in Design Computation (5 companies); Software Modules for Operations Research (8 companies); Software for Automatic Control (4 companies)	IPA support
IPA software development program	1976–	Joint System Development Corporation	Grant to IPA
IPA "Sigma" project	1985–	n.a.	Grant to IPA

Sources: Japan Information Processing Development Center [JIPDEC], *Computer White Paper, 1982* (Tokyo: JIPDEC, 1983), pp. 3–4, *1980*, pp. 6, 34–35, *1976*, pp. 30, 33–34, *1974*, pp. 19–22, 24, *1972*, p. 35; JECC [Japan Electronic Computer Corporation], *Konputa Noto, 1983* [Computer notes] (Tokyo: JECC, 1983), pp. 73, 80–93, 106, 447–49, 460–61; H. J. Welke, *Data Processing in Japan*, Information Research and Resource Reports, vol. 1 (Amsterdam: North Holland, 1982), pp. 22–26, 32, 66; Jimmy W. Wheeler, Merit E. Janow, and Thomas Pepper, *Japanese Development Policies in the 1980's: Implications for U.S. Trade and Investment, Final Report* (Croton-on-Hudson, N.Y.: Hudson Institute, 1982), pp. 147–49, 153; George E. Lindamood, "Current Computer-Related Research and Development Expenditures of the Japanese Government," *Scientific Bulletin*, vol. 8 (July to September 1983), pp. 13–15; George E. Lindamood, "Update on Japan's Fifth Generation System Project," ibid., pp. 16–25; Agency of Industrial Science and Technology and Ministry of International Trade and Industry, *National Research and Development Program (Large-Scale Project), 1985* (Tokyo: Japan Industrial Technology Association, 1985), p. 15; Information Technology Promotion Agency, *An Outline of the SIGMA Project: Toward High Software Productivity and Quality* (Japan: IPA, 1985), p. 1-9; Robert L. Eckelman and Lester A. Davis, "Japanese Industrial Policies and the Development of High-Technology Industries: Computers and Aircraft," staff report, project DTR-16-82 (U.S. Department of Commerce, International Trade Administration, February 1983), p. 16; author's interview with Dr. K. Hakozaki from NEC, April 1984; and Tōsaku Kimura, "Birth and Development of Computers," *Natural Science and Museums*, vol. 46, no. 3 (1979), p. 104.

a. *Hojokin:* conditional loans, interest free; repayment linked to profits on technology. Hojokin usually accounts for 40 to 50 percent of research cost; patents usually belong to the research association, but are sometimes assigned to the government. *Itakuhi:* consigned payments; research done on contract basis for MITI; patents usually belong to the government. *IPA support:* 75 percent of expenses provided by IPA; MITI provides operating cost subsidy and loan guarantees from long-term credit banks to IPA. *Grants to IPA:* all funding provided by MITI; resulting technologies belong to IPA.

help of Amdahl, Fujitsu's new American associate) to unravel the secrets of the IBM computer architecture. They then went their separate competitive ways. Of the other two groups' four participants (NEC, Toshiba, Mitsubishi, Oki), only NEC would survive as a manufacturer of major league, mainframe computers. Coincidentally, the three survivors were all participants—as independent manufacturers—in the design and construction of the DIPS series of timesharing mainframe computers.

Japan's technology policy during this third period of transformation was extremely flexible. It promoted survival of the largest and technologically fittest, not slavish adherence to the MITI game plan. Japan's adjustment to the upheavals in the national and international markets was, therefore, successful. The most useful elements of the experiment were chosen as the basis for the next generation of policy.

During the 1970s the Japanese government vastly increased the overall scale of MITI funding for research as well as emphasized support for cooperative industrial efforts. ETL continued to lead large national research projects in computer technology. But the direct R&D funding delivered to ease liberalization, funneled through private research associations, involved much larger sums.

The best way to track these developments is by examining available statistics on computer research and development in Japan. Fortunately, since the early 1970s reasonably consistent measures exist. Research performers report expenditures on *information research and development,* defined as "research on hardware and software."[14] Note that this information technology R&D excludes considerable sums spent on electronic components and communications technology not specifically earmarked for computer systems (see appendix table D-1). Table 5-2 presents a breakdown by product field and by social objective for fiscal 1983.

The absolute growth rate in Japanese computer research was quite striking: 60 percent in 1973 alone. In 1971 about 98 percent of computer R&D was performed in private corporations (funded by both private and public sources).[15] Just three years later only 40 percent of computer

14. See, for example, Statistics Bureau, Prime Minister's Office, *Report on the Survey of Research and Development, 1982* (Tokyo: Japan Statistical Association, 1983), p. 184. Work on semiconductor devices not specifically intended for use in computer systems appears not to be included in these figures.

15. R&D performed in universities and colleges is excluded in 1971, but it would not have altered this picture much. In 1974, when figures first became available, academia accounted for about 5 percent of the Japanese computer effort.

Table 5-2. *Percent Distribution of Industrial R&D by Product Field and Social Objective, Japan 1983*

Industry	Selected product fields					Social objective, informa- tion technology
	General machinery	Household appli- ances	Communi- cations and electric components	Other electric equip- ment	Electricity and gas	
Electric machinery	6	15	34	29	0	19
Communications equipment and electronic components	7	26	62	7	0	11
Transportation, communications, and public utilities	1	0	61	1	31	8

Source: Statistics Bureau, Management and Coordination Agency, *Report on the Survey of Research and Development, 1984* (Tokyo: Japan Statistical Association, 1985), pp. 126–29.

R&D was taking place inside Japanese companies. As the internal corporate effort declined in importance, R&D in cooperative research associations jumped from less than 1 percent of the total in 1971 to over half in 1974. From 1971 to 1976 Japan's expenditure on computer R&D tripled, with roughly half of the increase being absorbed into external research institutions.

Cooperative research associations blossomed during this period. It appears that they were formally organized as a type of public corporation in 1972 and 1973 and then in 1974 were reorganized as private associations. The reasons are not well documented, but this legal change also occurred in other parts of Japanese industry.[16]

The 1972–76 period marked the era of the "3.5 Generation" program, an effort to catch up to IBM's newly introduced System 370 machines.[17] MITI heavily funded the three computer groups that made up its vision of a restructured Japanese industry. Government funding, matched to private investment, was supposed to have financed roughly half of this

16. In 1973 the Japan Industrial Robot Association switched from *jigyo dentai,* a type of public corporation organized for the promotion of economic and social policies, to *shadan hojin,* a private nonprofit research association. See Leonard Lynn, "Japanese Robotics: Challenge and—Limited—Exemplar," *Annals of the American Academy of Political and Social Science,* vol. 470 (November 1983), p. 19. This was a period of fiscal austerity in Japan. My colleague Ed Lincoln has suggested that this may have been a response to Ministry of Finance pressures to cut down on spending (by forcing the overhead and administrative costs to be absorbed by the private sector instead of the central government). A new Electronics and Machinery Law was passed in 1971, and changes in legal organization may have been helpful in order to qualify for financial subsidies made available from 1972 on.

17. See Kenneth Flamm, *Creating the Computer: Government, Industry, and High Technology* (Brookings, forthcoming), chap. 6.

effort—perhaps 15 to 25 billion yen per year. (Since overhead is not generally funded as part of these programs, somewhat under half of the cooperative expenditure may actually have been covered.) Appendix table D-2 shows major MITI subsidies to computer research programs over the same period, and total subsidies lie in exactly this expected range. Thus the rapid growth of computer R&D, particularly the overnight shift to research performed in research institutions, closely corresponds to the effects of MITI's restructuring of subsidies.

Joint research involved substantial commitments from both government and industry. It was much more than a marginal supplement to industry's own efforts. Computer research performed within corporations actually registered notable declines during some of this five-year period, as research associations stepped up their work. Firms were effectively transferring significant resources out of private, internal efforts and into the joint research associations.

The shift to joint research associations was regarded as an extremely successful experiment. In 1977, more than halfway through the ten-year PIPS project, the contractors were reorganized into a private research association. From then on virtually all MITI funding of computer research in the private sector—including the national R&D projects, which had previously contracted with individual firms—has been dispensed in some form to private cooperative research associations. The Information Technology Promotion Agency channeled much of its resources to another private research association, the Joint Software Development Corporation.

Research in the Public Sector

Within MITI, quite apart from the subsidies administered to outside research laboratories, the Electrotechnical Laboratory has its own scientists doing basic computer research. Although the ETL has received some of the funding from the national research projects, it has additional research resources in its own budget.[18] Most of the computer research

18. In the PIPS program, for example, better than a third of the project's budget was expended within the ETL. See Electrotechnical Laboratory, *Pattern Information Processing System: National Research and Development Program* (Tokyo: ETL, 1978), p. 5. In 1983, in addition to the large-scale national R&D projects, ETL undertook "special research projects" in cryogenic electronics, electronic materials and devices, optoelectronics, intelligent robots, natural language processing, image information

performed within the central government presumably reflects the internal research activity of the ETL. As table 5-3 shows, this has typically ranged from 1.5 to 3.5 percent of all computer R&D in Japan.

For statistical purposes NTT is classified as a corporation, and its research expenditures are buried within the totals for all corporations. The R&D budget of NTT is tabulated separately in appendix table D-1, however. The nearest American analogue to NTT is the Bell Telephone Laboratories, which spent about half of its research resources on computer activities in the 1970s. If one assumes that about one-half of the R&D budget of NTT has gone to computer-related activities, then perhaps one-fifth of Japanese computer R&D has been funded by NTT in recent years.

Unlike Bell labs, NTT has spent a significant portion of its R&D money on research undertaken with, or transferred to, the private firms making up the NTT family. (The Bell labs worked exclusively with AT&T's own internal production arm, Western Electric.) Funds for such joint research seem to be spent within NTT's research laboratories or written into procurement contracts.[19] In recent years NTT appears to

---

processing, computer hardware and software, and information processing in biological systems. See Electrotechnical Laboratory, *Guide to ETL 1983–1984* (Tsukuba: ETL, 1984).

19. Until 1984 NTT was a "special corporation" (like the Japanese National Railways and the Japan Tobacco and Salt Public Corporation). Because these corporations are sometimes put into a separate category in statistics, their R&D expenditure can often be separated from that of other firms. See Statistics Bureau, Management and Coordination Agency, *Report on the Survey of Research and Development, 1984* (Tokyo: Japan Statistical Association, 1985), pp. 9–10. NTT is classified in the "transport, communications, and public utilities" category. In fiscal 1983 all significant firms in that category (with capital of more than 100 million yen) expended 180.3 billion yen for research and development, of which 63 percent (112.9 billion) was spent by the special corporations. See ibid., table 1, pp. 84–85. The seven special corporations that perform research and development and belong to this industry include NTT, the long-distance communications enterprise KDD, the broadcasting firm NHK, the Electric Power Development Company, Japan Airlines, and the Japanese National Railways. But NTT's total R&D expenditure alone for fiscal 1983 claimed 83 percent of the total for the seven. See Nippon Telegraph & Telephone Public Corporation, *1983–84 Annual Report*, p. 31. And R&D in "telecommunications" only by NTT, KDD, and NHK accounted for 91 percent of the total for the special seven. Ministry of Posts and Telecommunications, cited in K. Suzuki and T. Honda, "NTT: Past and Present," February 1987.

The 112.9 billion yen in R&D expenditures for the seven was made up of 114.1 billion in self-financed R&D and 0.7 billion in funds received from outside, less 1.9 billion yen paid for work performed outside. Thus almost no funds could have been paid directly by NTT to outside firms. A similar analysis holds for published data sampled from the early 1970s. NTT's support for outside R&D has either been covered

Table 5-3. *Information Technology R&D in Japan, 1970–84*

Item	1970	1971	1972	1973	1974	1975	1976	1977	1978	1979	1980	1981	1982	1983	1984
Millions of U.S. dollars	83	118	168	301	314	348	398	438	626	725	726	978	1,014	1,230	1,645
Percent performed in							*All expenditures*								
Industry	100	98	65	55	41	51	55	70	67	74	86	78	79	83	88
NTT[a]	28	33	32	21	19	20	18	22	21	19	20	17	16	14	15
Remainder	72	65	33	34	22	31	38	48	46	55	65	61	63	68	73
Central government[b]	n.a.	1	4	3	3	3	2	2	3	4	2	1	2	2	1
Private research institutions[b]	n.a.	*	1	*	51	40	37	23	25	15	8	16	14	10	7
Public research institutions[b]	n.a.	*	31	41	*	*	*	*	*	*	*	*	*	*	*
Universities and colleges[b]	n.a.	n.a.	n.a.	n.a.	5	5	4	5	5	7	5	4	4	4	3
							MITI subsidies								
Millions of U.S. dollars	7	7	24	76	84	74	79	58	75	67	53	58	59	65	59
As percent of information R&D	8	6	14	25	27	21	20	13	12	9	7	6	6	5	4

Source: Data taken from appendix table D-1. Yen are converted to dollars at current exchange rates.
n.a. Not available.
* Positive but less than 0.5 percent.
a. NTT information R&D estimated as one-half of total NTT R&D budget. All information technology R&D performed in "transportation and communications" is assumed to be included in the NTT budget.
b. No data available for universities and colleges in 1970–73, or for government and research institutions in 1970.

have spent much more on computer-related research and development than MITI.[20] While MITI may have received more publicity than NTT for supporting the development of Japan's computer industry, NTT appears to have been considerably more important in supplying resources for technology development.

Universities and colleges have generally accounted for about 4 to 6 percent of Japan's computer effort. The national universities typically account for between two-thirds and four-fifths of this total, the private universities for the remainder.[21] Almost all of this research is funded by government. There have been few direct links between university research and corporate development in recent decades.[22] But as the industrial R&D effort has matured, support for basic research in universities has grown in relative terms, while government aid to private research associations has become proportionately less important.

Figure 5-1 illustrates the importance of various forms of public support for computer R&D in Japan. Since the early 1970s, funds transferred by MITI to the cooperative research associations (assumed to equal 40 percent of their expenditures) have been its major instrument for funding new technology, trailed by R&D within its own labs. NTT's support has vastly exceeded MITI's.

A Fourth Transition?

The overall importance of MITI research support for information technology rose and fell precipitously between 1970 and 1983 (see table 5-3). From under 10 percent of the total in 1970 and 1971, MITI subsidies

---

by procurement contracts or conducted jointly with private firms within NTT itself. See H. J. Welke, *Data Processing in Japan,* Information Research and Resource Reports, vol. 1 (Amsterdam: North Holland, 1982), pp. 44–45.

20. This is based on the assumption that half of NTT's R&D budget (which includes much work on electronic components) is related to computers. If only funds specifically earmarked for information technology (and excluding much component work) are counted, the total is roughly the same size as MITI's spending.

21. In 1983, for example, computing facilities at private universities received a subsidy of about 1.5 billion yen. New computing facilities at public universities accounted for almost 8 billion yen that same year. Because Japanese R&D statistics include capital expenditures (unlike American statistics), these kinds of expenditures may be included in the aggregate computer R&D statistics. See JECC, *Konputa Noto, 1983,* p. 168.

22. In 1983, for example, private universities received 133 billion yen in research funds from government and over 5 billion yen from other sources. See Statistics Bureau, *Report on the Survey of Research and Development, 1984,* p. 162.

Figure 5-1. *Public Support for Information Technology R&D in Japan, 1970–84*[a]

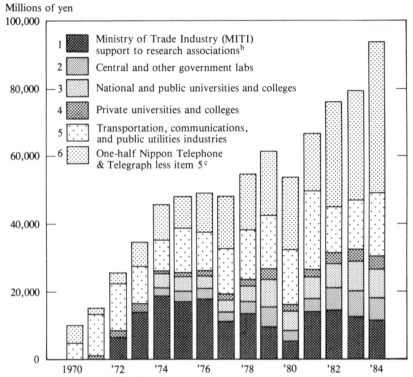

Millions of yen

Legend:
1 — Ministry of Trade Industry (MITI) support to research associations[b]
2 — Central and other government labs
3 — National and public universities and colleges
4 — Private universities and colleges
5 — Transportation, communications, and public utilities industries
6 — One-half Nippon Telephone & Telegraph less item 5[c]

Source: Calculated from appendix table D-1.
a. Except for NTT budget, all figures include only R&D classified as "information technology."
b. Estimated as 40 percent of total R&D in public and private research institutions and associations.
c. In other words, additional funds up to one-half total NTT research and development budget.

climbed to over one-quarter of the total in 1973 and 1974. They hovered at 20 percent in 1976, the last year of the adjustment program. MITI subsidies to private computer research usually run between 40 and 50 percent of the budget of the private research associations. In 1981, for example, 40 percent of the R&D performed in private research institutions (or about 6 percent of information R&D) corresponds almost exactly to a program-by-program inventory of MITI subsidies. MITI funding fell to roughly its 1971 share of the total by 1981.

Computer research in private Japanese firms has soared since 1978, while funding of joint research associations has remained about constant. The figures on MITI funding of computer research in table D-2 portray a similar situation, with current yen funding levels remaining roughly constant through the early 1980s. This has led to computer R&D within private corporations rising from 40 percent of the total, at the peak of the restructuring effort in 1974, to over 80 percent of the total by the mid-1980s. Private research associations, which accounted for more than half of computer R&D in 1974, accounted for only 16 percent of the total in 1981, 7 percent in 1984.

The steep climb in corporate spending on information processing R&D in recent years is evident in table 5-3, as is the declining role of public funding. MITI subsidies accounted for 4 percent of Japanese R&D in 1984, NTT spending (with half of total R&D assumed to relate to computers) another 15 percent. After adding the budgets of government and university research laboratories, roughly 10 percent of all Japanese computer R&D was paid for by direct public funding. With NTT included, the total rises to 25 percent.

The marked rise in the corporate share of Japanese computer R&D is mainly the result of rapidly expanding R&D budgets in the private sector. MITI subsidies remained roughly constant in current yen terms, at around 15 billion yen per year through the early 1980s, and the NTT R&D budget actually declined somewhat during this period. Japanese firms seem to have shifted toward a more research-intensive corporate strategy. In 1984 Fujitsu, Hitachi, and NEC were three of the five large companies in Japan spending over $500 million on research and development, and together they accounted for roughly $2.2 billion in R&D.[23]

As was true in the United States in the late 1950s and early 1960s, the rapid expansion in commercial sales of Japanese computers, rather than cutbacks in R&D subsidies, seems to be the main reason for the overall decline of government's role in pushing the development of computer technology. The bulk of the increased private effort in Japan, as in the United States, went into applied research and development. The Japanese computer industry has matured into a healthy, competitive sector capable of pursuing independent development of its new products.

But MITI, NTT, and the Ministry of Education still seem to be disproportionately important in sponsoring basic research and individual firms in supporting development (see table 5-4).[24] Because the MITI and

23. See Robert Neff, "Japan Polishes Creativity Image," *Electronics,* August 11, 1982, pp. 96–97; and Berger, "Japanese Firms Boost Spending," p. 34. The activities of IBM Japan's research laboratories are included in these figures for Japanese industry.

24. See D. Brandin and others, *JTECH Panel Report on Computer Science in Japan* (La Jolla, Calif.: Science Applications International Corporation, 1984), pp. 1-3, 1-4,

Table 5-4. *Types of Research and Development Performed, by Sector, Fiscal Year 1983*

Sector	Basic research	Applied research	Development
Companies			
Electrical machinery	4	18	79
Communications equipment and			
electronic components	3	20	77
Transportation, communications, and			
public utilities	4	28	67
Special corporations, such as	6	28	66
NTT			
Research institutions and			
associations	13	31	57
Central government	31	39	30
Private	9	31	60
Universities and colleges	56	36	8

Source: Statistics Bureau, *Report on the Survey of Research and Development, 1984*, pp. 119, 148, 160.

NTT research support tends to be skewed toward speculative, long-term research, it is a highly levered commodity. In addition to the dollar or so that is matched with every MITI dollar in the private research associations, firms typically have another one or two dollars invested in related internal projects.[25] The more basic, least appropriable research seems to be what is done cooperatively, while efforts to commercialize these results are pursued internally.

The most visible large-scale national R&D project by MITI in the 1980s was the so-called Fifth Generation project, a ten-year effort begun in 1981 after two years of preliminary studies.[26] Financed, like other national projects, by consigned research grants from MITI, it cost about 7 billion yen per year by the mid-1980s. In a novel approach nine private companies, including the big three computer makers (Fujitsu, Hitachi, and NEC) joined together to finance a private research institution, ICOT (the Institute for New Generation Computer Technology),

3-15, 3-57, 3-58; Edward K. Yasaki, "R&D in Japan," *Datamation*, vol. 29 (July 1983), p. 94; Cohen, "Japan Pushes IC Research"; and Berger, "Japanese Firms Boost Spending."

25. See Brandin and others, *JTECH Panel Report*, p. 1-5; and Miroslav Benda, "Trip Report: Industrial Study Mission to the Fifth Generation Computer Project, Tokyo, November 3–18, 1984" (Boeing Computer Services, 1984), p. 4.

26. See Barry Hilton, "Government Subsidized Computer, Software and Integrated Circuit Research and Development by Japanese Private Companies," *ONR Far East Scientific Bulletin*, vol. 7 (October–December 1982), p. 17.

which is responsible for undertaking the research. ICOT is headed by Kazuhiro Fuchi, who left the Electrotechnical Laboratory to direct the project.

The Fifth Generation project is focused on new computer architectures for symbolic computing and artificial intelligence themes. It builds on the foundations laid by the PIPS project. The public announcement of the Fifth Generation program in 1981 provoked widespread reaction in the United States and Europe. It led to the formulation of the strategic computing program in the United States, the Esprit program in the European Community (EC), and the Alvey program in the United Kingdom. The research agenda for all these projects is quite similar.

Procurement

Japan's promotion of computer technology has extended beyond direct funding of R&D. Measures to promote sales of Japanese computers have played a significant role in developing the Japanese industry. Although Japan has not had the strong military demand for computers that played such a crucial role in the early days of the U.S. industry, the government market has been important nonetheless. Technically not regarded as part of the government, NTT has traditionally directed its large volumes of equipment purchases to the NTT family of qualified Japanese suppliers.

Government procurement represented a considerable share of the market for Japanese computers in the 1960s—probably one-half, with the other half sold internally by computer divisions within their parent corporations.[27] In those early days of the industry, Japanese machines fared poorly in open competition with foreign products.

Computer purchase decisions were largely decentralized in the Japanese government.[28] The "buy Japanese" policy, observed in govern-

---

27. See Joseph C. Berston and Ken Imada, "Computing in Japan," *Datamation,* vol. 10 (September 1964), p. 27.

28. See Julian Gresser, *High Technology and Japanese Industrial Policy: A Strategy for U.S. Policymakers,* Committee Print, Subcommittee on Trade of the House Committee on Ways and Means, 96 Cong. 2 sess. (GPO, 1980), pp. 37–38. MITI has, however, periodically appealed to government organizations to "promote the introduction of domestic computers to foster the domestic computer industry and to expand its share." Such an appeal, for example, was made in 1976 by the MITI minister and later made public. Ibid., p. 68.

ment (and NTT) computer purchases throughout the 1970s, was mainly the result of informal attitudes and practices, not a formal edict issued by some central authority. Japan is a party to the Government Procurement Code of the General Agreement on Tariffs and Trade (GATT), in effect since 1981. Nevertheless, complaints of informal barriers persist among foreign competitors.

Japan's informal procurement policy was highly effective in influencing the purchase of government computers. In September 1975, 93 percent of the value of computers installed in government offices was domestic, as was 96 percent in government-related offices, 88 percent in local public organizations, 68 percent in cooperative societies and miscellaneous organizations, and 90 percent of the value of computers in universities. This compared with an overall average of 56 percent of the value of domestic origin for all Japanese users, 25 percent in financial institutions (perhaps the greatest user of foreign computers), and 23 percent in public utilities.[29] Japanese products continued to hold this favored position in the government market through the late 1970s. Statistics for 1977 show the same or even greater shares for Japanese manufacturers in these markets, while in other, nongovernment markets (financial institutions, for example) their share slipped somewhat.[30]

Quite unlike the case in the United States, the Japanese government's share of the overall computer market has grown over time. In 1968 government agencies accounted for about 5 percent of installed value.[31] As the result of the accelerating computerization of government operations, however, this share kept pace with the private sector. In 1976 installations in government and government agencies stood at 12 percent of the installed computer base; if educational institutions and cooperatives are included, the portion is closer to 20 percent. Roughly the same portion (19 percent) of the value of Japanese installations was accounted for by these same users in 1982.[32] Public authorities in Japan have remained a major force in the general purpose computer market.

Another primary instrument used to stimulate the sales of Japanese computers has been the Japan Electronic Computer Corporation

29. Ibid.

30. Japan Information Processing Center, *Computer Market in Japan* (Tokyo: JIPDEC, 1979), cited in The Futures Group, *The Impact of Foreign Industrial Practices on the U.S. Computer Industry* (Glastonbury, Conn.: The Futures Group, 1985), table 8.2.

31. James K. Imai, "Computers in Japan—1969," *Datamation,* vol. 16 (January 1970), pp. 149–50.

32. See *Japan Electronics Almanac 1983* (Tokyo: Dempa Publications, 1983), p. 39.

(JECC), established back in 1961 when the Japanese computer market was effectively closed to foreign imports and serious promotion of the industry began. JECC has close ties to MITI, which set it up and made key appointments, and to the Japan Development Bank (JDB), which has supplied much capital to the corporation at below-market interest rates.[33]

JECC finances the lease of Japanese computers by Japanese computer users. Participating Japanese computer producers periodically contribute fresh equity capital to the JECC, but subsidized loans from the Japan Development Bank (roughly one-third of its capital) and a pervasive MITI presence effectively make it a quasi-governmental body.

JECC played a very important role in financing computer sales in the early days of the Japanese industry. Its computer purchases accounted for roughly 40 percent of annual installations of computers through most of the late 1960s (see appendix table D-3). But by the mid-1970s JECC's share of the computer market had dropped below 20 percent. These measures are somewhat misleading, however. Japanese computer installations, especially in the 1960s, depended heavily on foreign imports. Japanese computer production statistics include the local operations of IBM Japan (as well as Nippon Univac, Burroughs, and NCR Japan), which represent a major portion of these sales. Products of firms not meeting rigorous domestic content requirements were ineligible for purchase by JECC.

If only "Japanese" computers shipped within the country are considered, JECC played a far more influential role in sealing off a major market for Japanese producers. If deliveries of foreign computers are excluded, JECC generally bought at least half, and it often accounted for as much as 80 or 90 percent of Japanese shipments in the 1960s. If production is considered, JECC accounted for perhaps 40 percent of Japanese output in the mid-1970s.

By late in the decade, however, JECC's share of "Japanese" output slipped to 20 percent of production. Computer purchases by JECC began to level off in the early 1970s, while production continued its steady rise (see figure 5-2).

JECC's access to cheap capital effectively provided a subsidy to Japanese users who purchased Japanese computers. Given comparable prices for machines of roughly equal power, the subsidized leasing terms were an incentive to buy a Japanese machine. As the principal force in

33. See Chalmers Johnson, *MITI and the Japanese Miracle: The Growth of Industrial Policy, 1925–1975* (Stanford University Press, 1982), p. 247.

Figure 5-2. *Computer Purchases and Assets of the Japan Electronic Computer Corporation, Fiscal Years 1961–81*

Billions of yen (logarithmic scale)

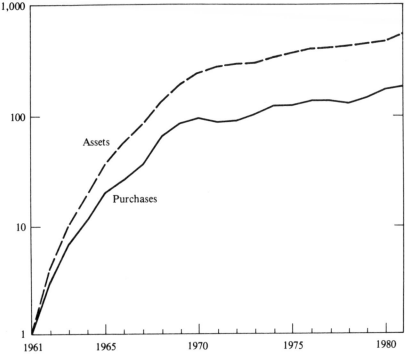

Assets

Purchases

1961   1965   1970   1975   1980

Source: Japan Information Processing Development Center, *Computer White Paper, 1982* (Tokyo: JIPDEC, 1983), p. 17.

the market, JECC had considerable power over prices. Some claim it used this leverage to fix prices at relatively high levels, dampening price competition. Fujitsu and Hitachi, in fact, are said to have increasingly turned to use of their own internal leasing operations in order to offer large customers better prices than those fixed by JECC.[34]

Perhaps the greatest testimonial to JECC's effectiveness in building a market is the establishment in 1980 of JAROL, the Japan Robot Leasing Corporation. JAROL is essentially a JECC for industrial robots.

34. See Leslie Donald Helm, "The Japanese Computer Industry: A Case Study in Industrial Policy" (M.A. thesis, University of California, Berkeley, 1981), p. 31; *High Technology and Industrial Policy*, Committee Print, p. 26; and Ira C. Magaziner and Thomas M. Hout, *Japanese Industrial Policy*, Policy Studies Institute 585 (London: PSI, 1980), p. 85.

Tax and Loan Policies

In addition to funding research and development and promoting the purchase of domestic products, Japan has made explicit and concerted efforts to offer indirect financial support to favored industries, like computers. For example, special tax breaks have been given to computer producers, and favored activities receive low-cost, low-interest financing from government banks. Table 5-5 summarizes two groups of tax breaks for computer producers: those available to all industries and those specifically for producers and consumers of computer hardware and software.

Tax benefits for all producers favor R&D and exports, both key factors in the competitiveness of a high-technology industry. Measures to encourage research include an R&D tax credit, not unlike that implemented in the United States, and accelerated depreciation for R&D capital. Special deductions for expenses related to overseas trade and investment are designed to promote exports.

Similarly, dual objectives are followed in tax breaks focused specifically on computers. Some programs effectively cheapen their cost to users; others favor producers. For example, users enjoy special depreciation deductions applicable to high-performance computer systems and reductions in local taxes on fixed assets. In 1976 over 50 percent of the acquisition cost for a computer could be written off in the year of purchase.[35]

An extensive system of income tax deductions for producers of computer hardware and software increases returns to investment in those favored lines of business. The most significant of the targeted, computer-specific measures is probably the *repurchase reserve allowance,* which allows computer manufacturers to deduct from income a fixed percentage of sales as a reserve against the repurchase of obsolete computers from leasing companies (JECC and others). The rapid decline in JECC's role in the early 1970s, accompanied by sharp decreases in deductible income, lessened the tax benefit of these provisions.

Allocation of financial resources controlled by government authorities has also been a major indirect instrument of national technology policy in Japan. The most important program has been lending by the Japan

35. Japan Information Processing Development Center, *Computer White Paper, 1976* (Tokyo: JIPDEC, 1977), p. 33.

Table 5-5. *Selected Tax Measures Favoring the Japanese Computer Industry*

Years in effect	Measure	Details
General measures		
1967–	R&D tax credit	25 percent of incremental R&D; 20 percent after 1981
n.a.	Accelerated depreciation of R&D capital, hardware	Up to 60 percent deduction in first year
1959–	Deduction for overseas sales of technical services	Part of income deductible
n.a.	Accelerated depreciation of assets used in connection with activities of research associations	100 percent first-year depreciation deduction
1964–	Special reserve for overseas investment	Tax-free reserve of 15 percent income (12 percent, 1980); large firms exempted after 1972
Measures targeting computers		
1961–66	Qualification for special tax treatment law	Partial exemption from income tax
1968–	Computer repurchase reserves	Fixed percent of sales set aside in tax-free reserve (10 percent, 1968; 15 percent, 1970; 20 percent, 1972; 5 percent, 1978; 2.5 percent, 1980)
1972–	Program guarantee reserve	Fixed percent of software sales set aside in tax-free reserve (2.0 percent, 1972; 0.5 percent, 1979; 0.25 percent, 1980)
1979–	General-purpose software package registration system	50 percent of revenues deferred in tax-free fund for four years
1970–78	Special depreciation for large computers	Additional first-year depreciation (20 percent, 1970; 25 percent, 1972; 20 percent, 1976)
1979–	Special depreciation for on-line computer systems	For high-performance systems, additional first-year depreciation deductions (25 percent, 1979; 13 percent, 1980; 10 percent, 1982)
1971–	Reduction of local fixed-asset taxes on computers	Reduction for large computers (33 percent, 1971; 20 percent, 1976)
n.a.	Tax deduction for computer personnel training	20 percent of incremental training expenditure

Sources: Welke, *Data Processing in Japan*, pp. 29, 35; JECC, *Konputa Noto, 1983*, pp. 96–97; JIPDEC, *Computer White Paper, 1982*, p. 4, *1981*, p. 5, *1980*, p. 43, *1976*, p. 33, *1972*, pp. 36, 42; United States International Trade Commission, *Foreign Industrial Targeting and Its Effects on U.S. Industries, Phase I: Japan*, USITC Publication 1437 (Washington: USITC, 1983), pp. 76, 109; Ira C. Magaziner and Thomas M. Hout, *Japanese Industrial Policy*, Policy Studies Institute 585 (London: PSI, 1980), pp. 78, 86; Eugene S. Kaplan, *Japan: The Government-Business Relationship* (U.S. Department of Commerce, Bureau of International Commerce, 1972), pp. 87, 89; and *Corporation Income Tax Treatment of Investment and Innovation Activities in Six Countries*, PRA Research Report 81-1 (Washington: National Science Foundation, 1981), p. 102.

Development Bank to computer manufacturers, mainly through JECC. Significant funds have also been made available through a program of government loan guarantees to Japan's three quasi-public industrial development banks and the government-run Small Business Finance Corporation. Both the JDB and the industrial development banks have subsidized the computer industry to some extent through preferential interest rates and elimination of the compensating balance requirements normally imposed by private banks.[36] Private loans for these same types of products in the 1960s implicitly enjoyed a government guarantee that lowered costs below market rates, some argue. Such "administrative guidance" by government authorities in effect directly rationed cheap capital to favored industries.[37]

Table 5-6 charts the growth of such new lending to the computer industry and estimates the implicit value of the subsidy to the computer industry in the largest group of these loans from the Japan Development Bank. To provide a contrast, estimates of the tax expenditures involved in the most important tax breaks to computer producers are also shown. Since the mid-1970s when data became available, the JDB loan subsidies (mainly to JECC) have amounted to about 3 to 4 billion yen per year or about 2 percent of total computer R&D. Over this same period each of the major tax breaks for producers has been of approximately the same size: 2 to 5 billion yen for the repurchase reserve, about 3.5 billion for the R&D tax breaks (in 1976, the only year for which information was available). Thus from the mid-1970s on, these three items together may have provided an additional 10 billion yen per year in net earnings for producers, perhaps 4 to 8 percent of total computer R&D.

The direct support to computer R&D provided by the large NTT and MITI technology projects was much greater. Interestingly, these fiscal measures may have been considerably larger just before the transition to large-scale government support for research in 1973. The year before, even as the importance of JECC declined, tax expenditures on the

36. See USITC, *Foreign Industrial Targeting . . . Phase 1: Japan,* apps. B and C.
37. See, for example, Comptroller General, *Industrial Policy: Japan's Flexible Approach,* Report to the Chairman, Joint Economic Committee, United States Congress (General Accounting Office, 1982), pp. 8–11, 60–61; Gardner Ackley and Hiromitsu Ishi, "Fiscal, Monetary, and Related Policies," in Hugh Patrick and Henry Rosovsky, eds., *Asia's New Giant: How the Japanese Economy Works* (Brookings, 1976), pp. 203–05; and Yoshio Suzuki, *Money and Banking in Contemporary Japan: The Theoretical Setting and Its Application* (Yale University Press, 1980), pp. 166–81.

Table 5-6. *Fiscal Measures Benefiting the Japanese Computer Industry, 1972–81*
Billions of yen unless otherwise specified

Measures	1972	1973	1974	1975	1976	1977	1978	1979	1980	1981
New lending to computer industry, subsidized loans										
Japan Development Bank (JDB)	15.0	21.5	32.5	46	47	52	56	50	48	46
Long-term credit banks[a]	14.5	13.3	9	12	13	11	8	7	5	n.a.
Small Business Finance Corp.	n.a.	n.a.	n.a.	n.a.	n.a.	n.a.	2.5	3	3	n.a.
Subsidy value of investment and tax measures										
JDB lending	n.a.	n.a.	n.a.	n.a.	n.a.	2.6	2.49	3.13	3.41	4.04
Japan Electronic Computer Corporation (JECC) repurchase reserve	10	6	3	5	5	3	0	3	2	2
R&D tax credit and accelerated depreciation R&D capital	n.a.	n.a.	n.a.	n.a.	3.4	n.a.	n.a.	n.a.	n.a.	n.a.
Chamber of Commerce computer repurchase	n.a.	n.a.	n.a.	n.a.	.04	n.a.	n.a.	n.a.	n.a.	n.a.
R&D as percent of production	13.3	19.1	17.1	20.8	20.5	17.8	16.1	15.8	14.5	16.4
Subsidy as percent of R&D										
JDB lending subsidy	n.a.	n.a.	n.a.	n.a.	n.a.	2.2	1.9	2.0	2.1	1.9
Repurchase reserve	19.6	7.3	3.3	4.8	4.2	2.6	0.0	1.9	1.2	0.9
R&D credit and accelerated depreciation	n.a.	n.a.	n.a.	n.a.	2.89	n.a.	n.a.	n.a.	n.a.	n.a.

Sources: Welke, *Data Processing in Japan*, p. 34; IIPDEC, *Computer White Paper*, 1982, p. 4, 1976, pp. 30, 32; USITC, *Foreign Industrial Targeting: Japan*, pp. 110, 134; and Magaziner and Hout, *Japanese Industrial Policy*, pp. 83, 85–86.
a. Includes the Industrial Credit Bank of Japan, Nippon Credit Bank, and the Long-term Credit Bank.

repurchase reserve amounted to almost 20 percent of computer R&D. Thus the shift away from indirect fiscal and financial subsidies to producers coincided exactly with the increased use of direct payments to promote research and development. Since the early 1970s investment in technology has been selected over investment in other kinds of assets as a social priority.

It is worth noting that the Japanese have used the tax system as an explicit instrument of industrial policy. As table 5-5 makes clear, every two to five years new rates were set under existing tax measures and entirely new menus of benefits created even as old ones were wiped out. This incessant fine tuning of fiscal incentives across industries would be unthinkable in the United States, because of the lack of a political consensus about what sectors to favor and because of the willingness of special interests to use any revision of the tax system as an opportunity to push their narrow sectoral interests.

Market Structure

Joint research, a major element in the rapid development of Japanese computer technology, has created a unique mix of cooperation and competition. In general, Japanese authorities have worked to preserve competition in "downstream" applications and commercialization of new products. But the results of more basic, precompetitive joint research have been shared quite widely to eliminate wasteful duplication and increase productivity of R&D spending.

In the early 1970s under MITI's direction, the three groups of Japanese computer producers (Fujitsu-Hitachi, Mitsubishi-Oki, and NEC-Toshiba) shared costs and product lines but remained in direct competition with other companies. A similar structure was used with the very large scale integrated circuit (VLSI) project of the late 1970s. Fujitsu, Hitachi, and Mitsubishi formed one group, NEC and Toshiba another.

There has been little obvious propensity for these firms to join together to restrain competition. In fact, fierce competition among them has sometimes wrecked experiments in collusion (the disintegration of MITI's plans for the "rationalized" computer industry is an obvious example). But when cooperation has occurred, MITI has generally played an important role in brokering the transaction, usually sweetening it with substantial financial incentives.

Although private cooperative research associations operate under exemptions from Japan's antimonopoly law, they have remained fairly open to public scrutiny. Scientists and research directors, for example, are often posted to the associations from MITI or its laboratories. As noted earlier, ICOT, the institute conducting the Fifth Generation project, is headed by Kazuhiro Fuchi, a former ETL scientist. Research at the Future Electron Device Research Association also has been directed by ETL scientists on leave.[38]

Technology developed under contract from MITI generally belongs to the government and is available under MITI license to all; technology developed in a cooperative research association (even if funded partially by conditional loans from MITI) belongs to the association for license to its members and sale to outsiders. In 1985 IBM signed a widely publicized agreement with MITI that gave it access to the MITI-owned computer patents but *not* to those coming out of research funded by conditional loans.[39] IBM had long had access to computer patents of large computer producers as a result of cross-licensing of its patent portfolio with Japanese companies. The 1985 announcement came at a time of sharp friction between the United States and Japan over trade in high-technology products. Historically, however, patents have had only slight influence on competition in computers.

Trade Policy

Although not strictly a technology policy, trade policy was an essential element in early efforts to foster a Japanese computer industry. Tariffs were first boosted in the early 1960s when the decision to make the computer industry a national priority was made. Perhaps more important, quotas were placed on imports of selected items, including computers and integrated circuits. MITI approval was required on a case-by-case basis to import these items. Foreign investments and technology licensing agreements in the computer industry, like other Japanese industries at the time, were carefully controlled. These restrictions on trade and investment were used as bargaining chips in negotiations with foreign firms over the terms of entry into the Japanese market and to secure Japanese firms' access to foreign technology.

38. See USITC, *Foreign Industrial Targeting . . . Phase I: Japan,* p. 115; Magaziner and Hout, *Japanese Industrial Policy,* p. 41; and Cohen, "Japan Pushes IC Research," p. 96.

39. See Leslie Helm with Alison Leigh Cowan, "IBM Wins the Key to Japan's High-Tech Labs," *Business Week,* August 19, 1985, p. 48.

The decision in the late 1960s to liberalize access to the Japanese economy was the nominal reason for the funding of the 3.5 Generation program. Beginning in 1972 quotas and restrictions on foreign investments and technology transfer were gradually relaxed. By 1976 trade and investment in computers were completely liberalized. Tariff rates were also lowered. Today Japanese computer tariffs are slightly higher than U.S. rates but lower than European rates. Appendix table D-4 portrays the gradual liberalization of Japanese tariff rates on computers and related products since the mid-1960s.

Technology Policy in Europe

European governments have been much less successful than the Japanese and U.S. governments in nurturing national computer industries. One fascinating and absolutely critical difference between Japan and Europe can be seen in their respective responses to the key events of the mid-1960s. The technological lead of America's computer firms, built on its rapid development of integrated circuit technology, widened. At roughly the same time the first IBM System 360 was delivered, and an export license for a Control Data 6600 ordered by the French nuclear program was denied.

In response, European governments in the late 1960s plunged into crash programs to revive the sagging competitive fortunes of domestic computer producers. The Japanese, however, largely relied on technical links between national and foreign producers to keep their producers competitive. The first national computer research project in Japan, begun in 1966, was mainly an exercise in tilling the technological soil. The program developed the technical expertise, particularly in components and circuitry, that allowed national producers to refine and improve their largely imported technology. Not until 1970, when some of these foreign partners began to drop from the scene, did a crisis atmosphere develop. Talk of restructuring began to preoccupy MITI, and expensive crash technology projects were developed.

While the Japanese opted for a program of cooperative research, superimposed on a highly competitive national market, the European governments instead chose to sanction sheltered national favorites. Competition was reduced as government policy chased after size and its perceived advantages. Small firms were encouraged to merge into the state-favored national champions. Scale economies in the use of research, in production, and in marketing were the ultimate objective of these maneuvers. Unfortunately, increased market share did not automatically follow.

Often the sum after merger was less than its parts. The many different lines of incompatible hardware and software absorbed into the resulting champion required many equally incompatible expenditures on product development and support. There was much less opportunity for economies of scale and scope than with a single harmonized product line in a firm of equivalent size. And the multitude of software and hardware products brought under the roof of the national computer champion was an exceedingly ineffective response to the compelling economics favoring an integrated, hardware and software compatible family of computers (the competitive challenge posed by IBM with its System 360 product line).

One might hypothesize that this divergence in strategy was due to market size. Japan's economy, after all, is now considerably larger than any single national European market. This, however, was not true in the late 1960s when the fateful decisions were made. At the beginning of that decade Japan's gross national product was substantially smaller than that of France, Great Britain, or West Germany. Even at the end of the 1960s, national income in Japan and West Germany was of roughly similar size. It was most definitely not the case that three (or six) computer firms could naturally "fit" into the Japanese economy, while only one would exhaust the potential for scale economies in the largest European countries.

By the late 1960s the European champions had been anointed: International Computers Limited (ICL) in Great Britain, Compagnie International pour l'Informatique (CII) in France, Siemens in West Germany. The would-be challengers were then placed on a high-powered diet of protection, procurement preferences, and subsidies. In each of these countries the same basic recipe had different names and subtle variations in flavor. In 1967 France began the initial Plan Calcul and West Germany its first electronic data processing (EDP) program. The following year, Britain nationalized ICL and announced a large injection of public resources into that firm.

Data on how these programs affected computer research and development in Europe are skimpier than the relatively extensive information published by Japan and the United States. Table 5-7 summarizes the

Table 5-7. *Government Subsidies to Computer and Microelectronics Development, Three European Countries, 1967–80*
For France, millions of francs; for West Germany, millions of deutsche marks; for United Kingdom, millions of pounds

France	Grants	*Funds to industry* Computer appli- cations	Edu- cation	CNET[a]	IRIA- CRI[b]	Total	Percent to industry
1967–70, 1st Plan Calcul	600	40					
			420	256	200	2,546	66
1971–75, 2d Plan Calcul	870	160					
1976–80, 3d Plan Calcul							
Government funding of CII-Honeywell- Bull		1,326	...	...	...	...	...
Grants to small firms		112	...	...	...	...	...
1978–81, Plan Circuits Intégrés	600	...	...	...	...	...	...
1977–80, Plan Informa- tisation de la Société	...	400	...	...	...	...	...

West Germany	*Funds to industry* Materials	Applications	Basic research	Education	Total	Percent to industry
1967–70, 1st EDP program	241	57	42	47	387	77
1971–75, 2d EDP program	705	558	227	920	2,410	52
1976–79, 3d EDP program	554	562	195	264	1,575	71

United Kingdom	*Funds to industry* Grants to ICL	Other grants	Other funding	Total	Percent to industry
1969–73	30.9	2.9	13.31	47.1	72

United Kingdom	*Funds to industry* Industrial support	Funding of INMOS	Appli- cations	Edu- cation	Retrain- ing	Total	Percent to industry
1974–79	70–75	50	55	30–40	25	230–45	73–76

Sources: Gareth Locksley, *A Study of the Evolution of Concentration in the UK Data Processing Industry with Some International Comparisons*, Commission of the European Communities Studies Collection, Evolution of Concentration and Competition Series 43 (Luxembourg: Office for Official Publications of the European Communities, 1983), pp. 44, 48–49, 52; Giovanni Dosi, *Industrial Adjustment and Policy: II; Technical Change and Survival: Europe's Semiconductor Industry*, Sussex European Papers 9 (Brighton, U.K.: Sussex European Research Center, 1981), pp. 29, 82–83; Jean-Hervé Lorenzi and Eric Le Boucher, *Mémoires Volées* (Paris: Editions Ramsay, 1979), pp. 109, 140–44; and The Futures Group, *The Impact of Foreign Industrial Practices on the U.S. Computer Industry* (Glastonbury, Conn.: The Futures Group, 1985), p. 5.32.

a. Centre Nationale d'Etudes des Telecommunications.
b. Institut de Recherche d'Informatique et d'Automatique–Comité de Recherche en Informatique.

major computer and microelectronics support programs undertaken in France, West Germany, and the United Kingdom during the late 1960s and 1970s.

France

The first two installments of France's Plan Calcul lasted through the mid-1970s. Roughly 60 percent of the funding associated with the program, mainly research support, went to industry, most of the remainder to government research institutions. When CII and Honeywell-Bull were merged in 1975, with a controlling interest held by the French government, another shift in policy occurred. The new CII-HB was promised 1,200 million francs in government subsidies from 1976 to 1980, hundreds of millions in additional funds to cover the old CII's losses, and 4 billion francs guaranteed public procurement during the remainder of the decade. Smaller producers in the industry were promised a 112 million franc subsidy over the 1976–79 period.[40] Since CII-HB was now essentially a state enterprise, subsidies no longer were structured as part of a coordinated sectoral research program. Instead they were incorporated into the firm's budget as unrestricted government aid.

Attention shifted to building up the French semiconductor industry. The major sectoral programs of the late 1970s involved large amounts of research funding to French integrated circuit producers, who were only marginally involved in computers. Significant funding for novel uses and applications of computers was granted by the French government, however, as part of the "Informatization of Society" program.[41]

In 1981 most of Honeywell's interest in CII-HB was purchased by the newly elected government of French president François Mitterrand. The suitably renamed CII-Bull became a key participant in the 1982 "Plan Filière Electronique," which called for state investments of 55 billion

40. Jean-Hervé Lorenzi and Eric Le Boucher, *Mémoires Volées* (Paris: Editions Ramsay, 1979), p. 109.
41. Ibid., pp. 140–46; and Giovanni Dosi, *Industrial Adjustment and Policy: II, Technical Change and Survival: Europe's Semiconductor Industry*, Sussex European papers 9 (Sussex, U.K.: University of Sussex, Sussex European Research Centre, 1981), p. 29. The widely read report entitled *The Computerization of Society*, prepared by Nora and Minc, two career civil servants associated with the French economic planning apparatus, suggested that investments in new information technologies would have wide-ranging effects. See Simon Nora and Alain Minc, *The Computerization of Society: A Report to the President of France* (MIT Press, 1981).

francs in a series of national projects in electronics and computers (along with 85 billion francs in private sector investments) over five years.[42]

In technology-intensive French industries, much of the subsidies and support received from the state have come from the military. Some of the failures of French industrial policies in electronics have been blamed on inherent conflicts between the objectives of building an industrial base oriented toward military requirements and the dissimilar nature of the commercial market.[43] Certainly, some of the initial stimulus for developing a national technology base arose when French military activities were denied access to sensitive American computer technology. And the French military played an important role in internal discussions of computer policy.[44] But France's subsidy programs have not been controlled or administered by the military. In 1975, for example, some 90 percent of the public funding for computer research in industry came from the Ministry of Industry, only 10 percent from the military.[45] Commercial triumphs, rather than military systems, were the prime objectives.

West Germany

German policymakers at first pursued a strategy nearly identical to that of their French neighbors. The largest computer producer, Siemens, along with AEG Telefunken received a very large share of the funds dispensed as part of the first German EDP program. The support provided by this program involved a joint effort by two different government agencies. The Ministry of Economics supplied long-term, interest-free loans for new product development, production, and marketing (technically repayable when a profit was made); the Ministry of Research and Technology provided grants for basic research and advanced development. Both funding efforts covered no more than 50 percent of the costs

42. United States International Trade Commission, *Foreign Industrial Targeting and Its Effects on U.S. Industries, Phase II: The European Community and Member States,* USITC Publication 1517 (USITC, 1984), p. 51.
43. See John Zysman, *Political Strategies for Industrial Order: State Market and Industry in France* (University of California Press, 1977), pp. 144–50.
44. See Jean-Michel Quatrepoint and Jacques Jublin, *French Ordinateurs* (Paris: Editions Alain Moreau, 1976), pp. 19, 29–30.
45. Ministère de l'Industrie, Service du Traitement de l'Information et des Statistiques Industrielles (STISI), *La Recherche Développement dans les Entreprises Industrielles en 1975* (Paris: Imprimerie Nationale for STISI, 1978), table 7.

of chosen projects.[46] As table 5-7 shows, almost 80 percent of the funding went to development of products and applications in industry.

Siemens, at the center of this strategy, was allied technologically with RCA in the 1960s. Rather than spend huge amounts to design and manufacture computers, Siemens had built a sales and distribution network, while mainly relying on links to RCA for its technology. Unfortunately, near the end of the first EDP program, RCA decided to cut its steady losses and get out of the computer business. As had also been the case in Japan, the erstwhile foreign partners of U.S. firms exiting from the industry were left with a serious problem.

Like Japan, Germany responded by investing large amounts in building up the technological capacity of national firms. The second EDP program, covering the first half of the 1970s, increased funding sixfold over the levels of the first. Furthermore, significant changes were made in the structure of the program. For one thing, a large share of the funding in the second program was invested in building up basic technological infrastructure. Roughly half of the assistance provided went to basic research and education, mainly in universities and research institutions.

Even as Siemens floundered, Nixdorf, the first serious European minicomputer producer, flourished with virtually no assistance from the German government. The late 1960s had witnessed the birth and rapid growth of Nixdorf, one of the few genuine success stories on the European computer scene.[47] The company had targeted a developing market niche largely overlooked by the major state-backed European computer producers, which were for the most part obsessed with producing large mainframe computers to compete against IBM. The second EDP program veered away from the national champion model and opted for a more diverse menu of assistance to producers. Some called the new priorities a dual champion model, with Nixdorf and Siemens sharing government funding for industrial research and development.[48] The

46. See the submissions of the U.K. Department of Trade and Industry (app. 19) and International Computers Limited (app. 29) in House of Commons, *The Prospects for the United Kingdom Computer Industry in the 1970s,* Fourth Report from the Select Committee on Science and Technology, Session 1970–71, vol. III, Appendices (London: Her Majesty's Stationery Office, 1971).

47. Another—later but similar—was Norwegian producer Norsk Data. It also focused on a specialized niche—very high performance minicomputers (superminis).

48. See Nicholas Jécquier, ''Computers,'' in Raymond Vernon, ed., *Big Business and the State: Changing Relations in Western Europe* (Harvard University Press, 1974), p. 218.

policy represented a middle way between the French strategy of placing all bets on a single national producer and the Japanese policy of supporting investment in a common generic research base to be incorporated into the products of a number of highly competitive national producers.

It was during the second German program that the first abortive attempts to create a single computer market in Europe took place. Efforts to create Unidata, uniting CII, Siemens, and Philips (in the Netherlands) in a single integrated computer line, collapsed in a cloud of bitter recriminations. Siemens was then forced to look elsewhere for outside technology. Since the mid-1970s Siemens has marketed under its label Fujitsu's IBM-compatible mainframe computers. Ties with outside foreign firms have continued to play an important role in Siemens's investments in technology. Recent examples include joint ventures with ICL and Philips to develop computer systems oriented toward artificial intelligence applications, with Philips to develop high-density integrated circuits, and with Toshiba to acquire its technology for megabit memory chips.[49]

Some elements of the second German EDP program attracted little support. The third program, begun in 1976, scaled back funding to education considerably, although support for industrial research and development and basic research was continued at comparable levels. This also proved unsatisfactory as the gap between academic research and industrial practice widened.[50]

United Kingdom

The British government began support for the development of computer technology at the end of World War II. The sums expended were relatively small, however. In 1950 British computer technology matched or surpassed that of the United States in many respects. Within a decade, lacking needed financial and technical resources, British producers had slid into decline. The fragmented computer industry disintegrated in the early 1960s. With government assistance, numerous small British firms were merged into larger entities. This policy culminated in the creation in 1968 of International Computers, Limited, the only British computer

49. See Laura Raun and Peter Bruce, "Europe's Risky Dash to Catch Up in Microchips," *Financial Times*, March 14, 1986.

50. See John Gosch, "Germany Spends for Its High-Tech Future," *Electronics*, May 17, 1984, p. 103.

company from this period that has survived. As other European governments began to funnel large infusions of resources into their national champions in the mid-1960s, the British felt compelled to pursue a similar course. Very little cash was actually invested in this effort at first: perhaps 9 million pounds per year in the early 1970s.

By the mid-1970s, however, the British computer industry—in the very early days a world leader, later a European leader—was in extremis. It was steadily losing market share even in its own home market. Large sums, about 40 million pounds per year, were spent in the late 1970s to revive the industry. ICL and a government-backed semiconductor producer, Inmos, were the major recipients of this aid. Perhaps three-quarters of government spending went into industrial research and computer applications.

Like Siemens, ICL turned to Japanese suppliers for technology. Although it sold Fujitsu computers under its label for a while, ICL has been primarily interested in obtaining high-performance semiconductors, unavailable in Britain, for use in products of its own design. Its current line of computers uses semiconductors built by Fujitsu to ICL-supplied specifications in ICL's own computer architecture.[51]

Government Funding of R&D

Government subsidy of computer research in Europe has been just as important to national firms in recent years as in the United States and Japan (see table 5-8). Before the Plan Calcul days of the mid-1960s, public funds paid for about 12 percent of industrial R&D in the computer industry in France. A decade later, as the second Plan Calcul was winding down, that share increased to around one-third, and during the third Plan Calcul it dropped to around one-quarter. The small visible share of public funds in French research and development in the late 1970s and 1980s is somewhat deceptive: public support now comes in the form of a general budget subsidy for a public enterprise, not as funding explicitly restricted to particular R&D projects and thus labeled as money for R&D.

In Britain, a similar change to general budgetary support occurred. The amount of computer R&D in industry financed by government

51. See Kevin Smith, "ICL Banks on Networks and Japanese Chips," *Electronics Week,* May 6, 1985, pp. 24–25.

Table 5-8. *Business Expenditure on Research and Development in the Office and Computing Machines Industry, Three European Countries, Selected Years, 1965–81*
Funds in millions of dollars

Country and year	Percent of funds[a]			Total funds[b]
	Public	Private	Other	
France				
1965	12	88		24.0
1975	33	52	14	191.8
1975[c]	32	44	24	194.5
1976	13	60	27	183.9
1977	26	60	14	213.0
1978	12	88		264.9
1979	4	70	26	322.4
West Germany[d]				
Machinery industry, except instruments				
1967	39	63		217.0
1969	18	82		164.1
1971	9	90		358.4
1973	21	78		571.7
1975	20	79		747.9
1977	10	89		1,016.9
1979	10	89		2,107.5
Mechanical engineering, 1977	15	85		760.4
Electrical engineering, 1977	19	81		1,921.4
United Kingdom				
1967	13	64	23	35.7
1968	12	71	17	45.5
1969	26	54	20	55.0
1972	33	66	2	68.3
1975	15	59	25	112.4
1978	16	53	31	274.0
1981	21	79		319.2

Sources: Organization for Economic Cooperation and Development, *Science and Technology Indicators; Basic Statistical Series—Volume D: Research and Development in the Business Enterprise Sector, 1963–1979* (Paris: OECD, 1983), pp. 158, 160, 162, 169–77, 313–21. For the exchange rate, International Monetary Fund, *International Financial Statistics: Yearbook 1986* (Washington: IMF, 1986), pp. 332–33, line af; pp. 344–45, line af; pp. 682–83, line ah. For France 1965, OECD, *Electronic Computers: Gaps in Technology,* report presented at the Third Ministerial Meeting on Science of OECD Countries, 11–12 March, 1968 (Paris: OECD, 1969), p. 135; for France 1975[c], Ministère de l'Industrie, STISI—Service du Traitement de l'Information et des Statistiques Industrielles, *La Recherche Développement dans les Entreprises Industrielles en 1975* (Paris: Imprimerie Nationale en 1975 (Paris: Imprimerie Nationale, 1978), p. 52; for France 1976, STISI, *Recherche et Développement dans les Entreprises: 1976* (Imprimerie Nationale, 1978), p. 46; for France 1978, STISI, *Les Firmes Industrielles et la Recherche Développement* (Imprimerie Nationale, 1982), p. 83. For West Germany 1977, United States International Trade Commission, *Foreign Industrial Targeting and Its Effects on U.S. Industries, Phase II: The European Community and Member States,* USITC Publication 1517 (Washington: USITC, 1984), p. 85. For United Kingdom 1981, U.K. Department of Trade and Industry, *Annual Review of Government Funded R&D: 1984* (London: Her Majesty's Stationery Office), pp. 32–34.

a. "Other" includes funds received from abroad. Inconsistencies in treatment of foreign funds are presumed to account for occasional jumps in private and other funding shares; for example, United Kingdom 1972.

b. At current exchange rate.

c. May classify CII-Honeywell-Bull differently from the rest of the French series.

d. The German series usually refer to the OECD definition of machinery industry, which includes computing and office machinery. Specialized computer firms, such as Nixdorf, are classified in mechanical engineering, whereas Siemens is probably classified in electrical engineering (in 1984 data processing accounted for only 17 percent of its revenues). *Datamation,* vol. 31 (June 1, 1985), p. 64.

Table 5-9. *Average Annual Expenditure on Computer
and Microelectronics Programs in France, West Germany,
and the United Kingdom, 1967–80*
Francs for France; deutsche marks for West Germany; pounds for United Kingdom

Country	National currency (millions)	U.S. dollars (millions)
France		
1967–75	283	57
1976–81	406	87
West Germany		
1967–70	97	25
1971–75	482	167
1976–79	394	189
United Kingdom		
1969–73	9.4	23
1974–79	38.3–40.8	78–83

Source: IMF, *International Financial Statistics: Yearbook 1986*, pp. 332–33, line af; pp. 344–45, line af; pp. 682–83, line ah. Rates averaged over given years.

shifted from 10 to 15 percent in the mid-1960s, to one-quarter with the creation of ICL in 1968, to one-third in the early seventies, down to about 15 percent in the late 1970s, and back up to 20 percent in the early 1980s.

Comparable data unfortunately do not exist in Germany, where statistics on computer producers are buried in statistics on broader industrial sectors such as electrical engineering and mechanical engineering. For the machinery industry as a whole, however, a familiar pattern prevails. From a peak of 40 percent during the heady investments of the late 1960s, the government-funded share of research and development dropped into the 10 to 20 percent range in the 1970s. Computers absorbed a disproportionate share of this funding. A more detailed disaggregation for 1977 suggests that a figure in excess of 15 or even 20 percent might be appropriate.

Table 5-9 shows that Britain at first invested considerably less money in R&D relevant to the computer industry than did France and Germany. Germany invested relatively little until the crisis years of the early 1970s, when it stepped up its outlays and greatly outstripped both Britain and France. By the late 1970s Germany was investing resources in its computer industry that nearly amounted to the efforts of Britain and France (roughly comparable in size) combined. In the mid-1970s the

German computer industry was (along with ICL) one of the two strongest European competitors,[52] and at the close of the decade the German computer industry was regarded as perhaps the strongest in Europe.

Thus in France, West Germany, and the United Kingdom government support for industrial computer R&D rose steeply during the crisis years of the early 1970s. The overall growth of the market outpaced public support, however. As table 5-8 shows, the portion of industrial R&D accounted for by public subsidy seems to have slipped from more than a third in the early 1970s to the 15 to 20 percent range in the late 1970s.

Of course, considerable public money was invested outside of industry in research labs and educational institutions. Therefore, these figures understate the importance of public funding for computer research as a whole. In the early years when government funded more than one-third of industrial research, perhaps 35 to 45 percent of all European computer research was paid for by government funds. As the portion of industrial R&D paid for by public subsidy slipped into the 15 to 20 percent range, the overall share of public investment in computer research probably declined to the 15 to 25 percent range.[53]

The data for France and Britain clearly point to another important phenomenon, the internationalization of research activity. Between one-fifth and one-third of the industrial research carried out in their computer industries in recent years has been funded from abroad. Local research labs established by foreign firms have become increasingly common, as a way of tapping into national research efforts and as an economic means of using local research talent in a global development effort.

---

52. U.S. Department of Commerce, *The American Computer Industry in Its International Competitive Environment* (GPO, 1976), p. 35.

53. These conclusions follow from the following logic: assume as a reasonable approximation that all computer funding can be assigned to one of three categories—government-funded industrial research, privately funded industrial research, and government-funded nonindustrial research. Let A be the portion of all government funding of computer research going to industry, B the share of government funding in all industry research. Rough magnitudes for A (ranging from 0.5 to 0.8) can be found in table 5-7, rough estimates of B (ranging from about 0.15 to 0.30) in table 5-8. Then the share of government funds in all computer research, G, is given by $B/(B + A - AB)$, and possible values are

A: 0.5 0.6 0.7 0.8   0.5 0.6 0.7 0.8   0.5 0.6 0.7 0.8
B: 0.1 0.1 0.1 0.1   0.2 0.2 0.2 0.2   0.3 0.3 0.3 0.3
G: 0.18 0.16 0.14 0.12   0.33 0.29 0.26 0.24   0.46 0.42 0.38 0.35.

The Boom of the 1980s

In Europe a new cycle of accelerated public investment in industrial technology, particularly semiconductors and computers, began after Japan's announcement in 1981 of its Fifth Generation program. To create a European technology base and a single European market, national efforts are being coordinated with international cooperative projects. The most visible program specifically targeting computers is the European Strategic Program for Research and Development in Information Technologies (Esprit), which will spend roughly $1.5 billion over the five-year period that began in 1984. The European Community will pay roughly half of the funding; the remainder will be paid by the firms undertaking the research. Large projects will be eligible for a subsidy of up to 50 percent of cost, smaller projects for 25 percent funding.[54] Numerous European firms are participating on a cooperative basis in what is explicitly labeled precompetitive research.

In 1985 the EC announced a similar program, dubbed RACE (for research and development in advanced communications technologies for Europe), to cover the closely related area of telecommunications.[55] The EC also funds cooperative research projects in narrower information-related areas such as computer-aided design (CAD) and very large scale integrated circuits.[56]

Other pan-European efforts have been negotiated between individual firms, often with government support. In 1984 ICL, Bull, and Siemens jointly established a center in Bavaria for artificial intelligence and advanced computer research.[57] Philips in the Netherlands and Siemens began their so-called Megaproject in 1985, a five-year research program to develop megabit RAMs (random access memories with the capacity to store millions of "bits" of information). The two firms are paying most of the costs of their joint research; roughly one-sixth of the funding is coming from the Dutch and German governments.

In the fall of 1985 eighteen European governments approved yet

54. See USITC, *Foreign Industrial Targeting . . . Phase II: The European Community*, pp. 35–40.

55. John Gosch, "Europe Ready to Start R&D on Compatible Telecom Net," *Electronics*, August 19, 1985, pp. 28–29.

56. "Europe Embarks on Large Joint Effort in Telecom Chips," *Electronics*, February 9, 1984, p. 71.

57. See *Datamation*, vol. 29 (October 10, 1983), p. 104.

another set of cooperative research programs heavily tilted toward information processing. Of ten pilot projects approved for the European "Eureka" program (designed as a technological response to the United States' Strategic Defense Initiative), five involve computer systems or components.[58]

National as well as international computer development programs have been created recently in Europe. Britain's Alvey program was announced in 1982 in response to the Fifth Generation announcement the year before and the presumption that the United States would accelerate its support for research.[59] The Alvey program was slated to spend about $525 million on research programs from 1983 to 1988, with $315 million coming from the Department of Trade and Industry, the Ministry of Defense, and the Department of Education and Science, and the remainder coming from industry. The British government covered 50 percent of the cost of projects in which industry invested.

In France the Filière Electronique R&D program, a much larger effort, was announced by the Mitterrand government in 1982. This program was scheduled to funnel into the French electronics industry about $18 billion (about 40 percent coming from the government) over a five-year period. The faltering pace of economic growth in France, however, has cast serious doubt on whether these goals will be met.

Germany announced an equally substantial program in early 1984. The Ministry of Research and Technology plans to administer a five-year government investment of $1.2 billion in research and development related to information technologies. Up to 50 percent of the cost of industrial projects is to be paid for out of these monies. Roughly half of the money is to be invested in components and the remainder in computers, automation, and robotics. Much larger sums in electronics procurement by military and other government users are expected to follow. Unlike previous German efforts, this program is geared toward strengthening university-industry ties and supporting projects in small,

58. See John Tagliabue, "Europeans Approve High-Technology Plan," *New York Times*, November 7, 1985; and "Pushing the State of the Art," *Datamation*, vol. 31 (October 1, 1985), p. 72. One of these projects is the joint development of a supercomputer by Matra of France and Norsk Data of Norway.

59. See Department of Industry, Her Majesty's Stationery Office, "A Programme for Advanced Information Technology, The Report of the Alvey Committee," in Office of Technology Assessment, *Information Technology R&D: Critical Trends and Issues* (OTA, 1985), pp. 265–66.

entrepreneurial firms rather than the large established producers. Co-operative, joint research is to receive special emphasis.[60]

The recent boom in cooperative projects among European computer producers has not been limited to research. Common standards for hardware and software are being established by joint agreements with increasing frequency. In 1985 the UNIX operating system was adopted as the standard for minicomputers to be built by Bull, ICL, Siemens, Olivetti, Philips, and Nixdorf. Similar moves have been announced by Japanese and American computer firms. Seven European and two American computer companies formed the X/Open group in 1986 to establish a standard version of the UNIX operating system for use in European markets.[61] Twelve European firms and five U.S. computer makers are participating in discussions on implementation of the open system interconnection (OSI) standard. This standard is designed to permit communications among computers and office and industrial automation equipment of different makes.[62]

Government Procurement and Fiscal Measures

In other respects policies to support the computer industry have been fairly similar in France, Britain, and Germany. Many studies have described how government procurement was systematically used to provide markets for the national champion's output.[63] In spite of such policies, however, national producers fared much less successfully in these sheltered markets in Europe than in Japan, where more than 90 percent of the value of government users' installations was Japanese

60. See Gosch, "Germany Spends for Its High-Tech Future"; and "Bonn's Late Push in the High-Tech Race," *Business Week,* April 9, 1984, pp. 43–46.

61. George Anders and Richard L. Hudson, "Six European Computer Makers Reach Accord Aimed at Competing with IBM," *Wall Street Journal,* February 19, 1985; "European Software Agreement," *New York Times,* February 19, 1985; and Robert T. Gallagher, "Europeans Are Counting on UNIX to Fight IBM," *Electronics,* July 10, 1986, pp. 121–22.

62. See, for example, Paul Betts, "Computer Groups Seek Common Standards to Counter IBM," *Financial Times,* December 31, 1984; and Robert T. Gallagher, "Europe Finally Gets Moving on Standards Making," *Electronics,* April 28, 1986, pp. 48–49.

63. See House of Commons, *Prospects for the United Kingdom Computer Industry*; Angeline Pantages, Nancy Foy, and Andrew Lloyd, "Western Europe's Computer Industry," *Datamation,* vol. 22 (September 1976), pp. 63–76; and Jécquier, "Computers," pp. 221–23.

equipment. In 1972 CII held only 25 percent of the French government market, and even today, years after CII's merger with a much larger and healthier Honeywell-Bull, only two-thirds of the civil service's computer base are French machines.[64] The same is true in Britain: in 1970, 71 percent of public computer installations were British brands; by 1974 that fraction had fallen to 56 percent.[65] During the early 1970s the German government reportedly ordered that IBM's share of central government purchases be reduced from 80 to 60 percent, mainly to benefit Siemens. By 1975 over half of the value of computers sold to the public sector in Germany were German machines.[66]

The contrast with the 90 percent share of Japanese computers in government markets is striking. The dismal performance by national firms in these protected markets is evidence perhaps of serious deficiencies in technology and product line. Even the enforced loyalty of government users was insufficient to staunch sales by foreign competitors. Although all three countries signed the 1981 GATT Procurement Code, use of procurement to favor national firms continues to be an important instrument of national technology policy.[67]

European markets were also sheltered by important barriers to trade. Fixed at 7 percent in the early 1970s, European tariff rates are now only marginally higher than U.S. rates (4.9 percent and 3.9 percent, respectively).[68]

A variety of fiscal measures favors computer producers. France,

64. U.S. Department of Commerce, *Global Market Survey: Computers and Related Equipment* (GPO, 1973), p. 44; and Department of Commerce, International Trade Administration, *The Computer Industry* (GPO, 1983), p. 32.

65. Calculated from the figures given in Paul Stoneman, *Technological Diffusion and the Computer Revolution: The UK Experience* (Cambridge University Press, 1976), table 2.3; and Alan Peacock, *Structural Economic Policies in West Germany and the United Kingdom* (London: Anglo-German Foundation for the Study of Industrial Society, 1980), p. 76.

66. House of Commons, *Prospects for the United Kingdom Computer Industry,* app. 29; and Peacock, *Structural Economic Policies,* table 5.15.

67. See USITC, *Foreign Industrial Targeting . . . Phase II: European Community,* pp. 52–53, 71, 98–99. Billions in government procurement, for example, are a key feature of the latest German sectoral program in computers.

68. Before Britain's entry into the Common Market, British tariffs on computers were a rather stiff 14 percent. Upon entry these were reduced to EC rates of 7 percent on central processing units, 4 to 10.5 percent for peripherals and parts. See Department of Commerce, *Global Market Survey,* p. 122.

West Germany, and the United Kingdom have general tax incentives encouraging R&D investments.[69] All allow the current deduction of expenses for R&D investments. France and Britain have special depreciation allowances for investments in R&D-related assets. West Germany has a graduated system of R&D tax credits for incremental investments in R&D, and France in 1985 announced that it, too, would establish an R&D tax credit.[70]

Cheap, subsidized capital has been available to computer producers from government sources. The mechanisms vary: direct regulation of bank loan portfolios and interest rates in France; use of state-controlled investment banks in Germany; equity, loan guarantees, and low-interest loans provided by government organizations in Britain. These are not industry-specific programs, however. They are available to any firms that meet criteria for government interest. Germany and Britain also have programs to encourage the use of new, technology-intensive equipment produced by specific sectors, including computers. In Germany small sums are spent to subsidize the use of computer software and microelectronics. In Britain limited government funds subsidize the use of new equipment incorporating computers in selected applications.[71]

In Europe, where the national champion model was selected early on, antitrust has generally not been an important issue in computers. Its main application, in fact, has been against foreign competitors. The Commission of the European Community has brought various actions against IBM to limit its market power. As a result IBM agreed in 1984 to disclose technical details of new products, shortly after announcing them, to Common Market firms.

Summary

"Targeting" policies that funnel public resources into private industry to create a competitive advantage have been widely used to favor national computer producers. Table 5-10 attempts to summarize some

69. See National Science Foundation, Division of Policy Research and Analysis, *Corporation Income Tax Treatment of Investment and Innovation Activities in Six Countries*, PRA Research Report 81-1 (NSF, 1981), pp. 46–49, 69–72, 121–25.

70. David Dickson, "New French Law Boosts Industrial R&D," *Science*, May 31, 1985, p. 1071.

71. USITC, *Foreign Industrial Targeting . . . Phase II: European Community*, pp. 59–64, 73–82, 87–89, 100–12.

Table 5-10. *International Comparison of Industrial R&D in Computers, Selected Years, 1965–83*[a]
Millions of 1982 dollars

| | United States | | Japan | | | |
| | Includes Bell Telephone Laboratories | Excludes Bell Telephone Laboratories | Includes Nippon Telephone and Telegraph | Excludes Nippon Telephone and Telegraph | | United |
Year					France	Kingdom
1965	n.a.	>1,391(32)	n.a.	n.a.	>75(12)	99(13)[b]
1972	n.a.	3,131(n.a.)	257(67)	135(20)	n.a.	147(33)
1975	4,305(32)	3,744(22)	353(72)	225(36)	323(33)	190(15)
1979	4,767(21)	4,089(8)	794(36)	593(11)	410(4)	380(16)[c]
1981	5,578(27)	4,711(13)	894(29)	701(7)	n.a.	340(21)
1983	6,929(28)	5,966(16)	1,110(23)	920(6)	n.a.	n.a.

Sources: Tables 4-3, 4-4, 5-3, 5-8; and OECD, *Electronic Computers*, p. 135. Figures are converted to 1982 dollars by using the GNP deflator in *Economic Report of the President, January 1987*, p. 248. Industrial R&D in Japan includes information R&D performed in industry and research associations; public funds are approximated by MITI computer subsidies (and NTT funds when included).
a. Numbers in parentheses are the percentage of public funds.
b. For 1967.
c. For 1978.

of the data on research in computers presented in this and earlier chapters in a consistent and comparable way. The data on research in industry are available for the United States, Japan, France, and Great Britain.

The figures for the United States and Europe refer to research and development expenditure in the computer industry; those for Japan include R&D on computer hardware and software (since most Japanese computer production is in integrated industrial conglomerates) plus private research institutions (since most of the public funding of industrial computer research has gone to cooperative research associations). Because the Japanese figures include the large research program of NTT, an attempt to separate out the NTT expenditure (half of the budget of NTT is assumed to be computer related) has been made for purposes of comparison. Similarly, because NTT's American counterpart, the Bell Telephone Laboratories, has been a major force in U.S. computer technology, half of its R&D budget has been added to the U.S. figures for purposes of cross-country comparisons.

A popular view is that Japanese industry is the most dominated by government targeting, European industry somewhat less so. The United States is seen as the least interventionist of the major industrial countries. But even in terms of industry R&D, the United States is *not* notably less inclined to fund industrial investment in technology directly out of the public coffers. With the enormous growth of the commercial market in the United States from the mid-1960s to the late 1970s, government influence lessened considerably, reaching its nadir in 1979. The rhythm of support picked up in the early 1980s, and U.S. government funding of industrial computer R&D now assumes only a little less prominent role than in Europe and a considerably greater role than in Japan.

If the picture is widened to include R&D outside of industry, the government influence is even more important. In all the countries examined in this chapter, basic research is largely performed outside of industry. In the United States, academic institutions are the primary locus for this activity; in Japan and France, the national laboratories, although Japan has been increasingly supportive of academic research in recent years. West Germany and Great Britain are at intermediate points on this scale, splitting their basic research between public research institutions and academia. This is not particularly surprising. Basic research is perhaps the least appropriable and therefore the most in need of public funding.

The ups and downs of national targeting efforts reflect a cycle of action and reaction. A widening U.S. lead in computer technology in the 1960s stimulated the first government interventions in Europe and Japan. The upheaval in the U.S. computer industry in the early 1970s provoked a major escalation abroad, as countries debated how to replace the fallen U.S. partners upon which their companies had depended for crucial infusions of new technology. Expenditures in Europe and Japan zoomed, as efforts were made to create an indigenous technological base. The budgetary distractions of Vietnam coupled with a wide American lead in computer technology reduced U.S. investments in research. It was not until the late 1970s, when Japanese research investments noticeably began to pay off in narrowing the U.S. lead, that the United States again invested heavily in new computer technology. The 1981 announcement of the Japanese Fifth Generation program fanned the smoldering embers of worry into a raging blaze. Both the U.S. government and industry reacted with heavy new research investments in the early 1980s. In Europe the Japanese announcement, and perhaps equally important the U.S. response, also accelerated research spending.

The perception of Japan's success by foreign competitors acted not only as a catalyst for overall increases in their expenditure but also as an incentive to reexamine the structure and organization of their research programs. As table 5-10 makes evident, Japan's success cannot be attributed to the sheer magnitude of the resources that nation has invested in developing computer technology. The United States spends vastly more, and certainly the combined R&D spending of Great Britain, France, and West Germany exceeds that of Japan. The good health of the Japanese computer industry must be attributed instead to other factors: the careful maintenance of competition in the domestic market, the joint nature of national industrial research projects, the emphasis on viewing national industry in the framework of an international market. Japan's subsidies for computer research are not unique; conditional loans and grants have been used in Europe since the 1960s. But the focus on joint, precompetitive "generic" research is. U.S. and European research programs' new emphasis in the 1980s on cooperation and sharing in basic research represents a radical departure from past practice. By implication, much of Japan's success is attributed to the way in which it has rationalized its subsidy to R&D and encouraged shared use of the more fundamental elements of industrial technology.

There are other noticeable international differences in the policy instruments used to target computers. Tax incentives to stimulate investment within the favored industry and to expand use of computers in other sectors have played a much more important role in Japan than in other countries. Nearly every year tax measures to accomplish these ends have been modified. Such incessant tinkering would be almost unthinkable in a different political system. Infusions of subsidized capital into the industry have been important in Europe and Japan but not in the United States, where intervention in capital markets is, with few exceptions (notably housing), not viewed as an acceptable instrument of economic policy.

Semiconductors are the cornerstone in the technological base upon which computers rest. Recent efforts by European firms to develop state-of-the-art semiconductors emphasize this critical role. Development of integrated circuits, the top priority in Japan in the 1970s, was absolutely essential to the emergence of Japanese firms as serious competitors in computers. Realization of this fact led to major investments in integrated circuit research in France in the late 1970s, the founding of Inmos with government assistance at roughly the same time in Great Britain, and heavy new investments in West Germany. Roughly half of Britain's Alvey program investments have gone to develop integrated circuit technology.[72] The United States' lead in this area has

72. See "Chips Take Lion's Share of Alvey Cash," *Financial Times*, June 26, 1985.

slipped, prompting renewed American investments in new component technologies. Wafer-scale integration, exotic (nonsilicon) materials, rapid turn-around "silicon foundries" and associated design tools, and the very high speed integrated circuit (VHSIC) program are all areas in which large new public investments are being made with an eye leveled on the foreign competition.

CHAPTER SIX

National Technology Policy: Past, Present, and Future

THE DEVELOPMENT of the electronic digital computer is a useful case study in the development of modern high-technology industry. The computer was born during the second world war, a product of powerful and pervasive institutional change that reshaped the American economy. It ranks among the most research-intensive goods, and development of computer technology requires complex interactions among the interests of the state, private business, and the public welfare. Determining the contours of investment in technology is one of the most important economic choices that societies make.

The computer emerged in an arena that was international in scope right from the start, where it was impossible to separate competition at home from rivalry abroad. Firmly connected to the United States' national security, economic and military, the computer was guaranteed a special status by the willingness of the military services to push its development when civil authorities seemed to lack the interest, the will, or the resources.

The Past: A Summary

At first the economic significance of computers went unnoticed; military need, not the economic imagination, propelled the technology forward. A few far-sighted visionaries saw the computer's commercial potential, but had it not been for the military's interest in powerful information processing capacity, its development would certainly have been delayed by years, perhaps even decades.

Throughout the 1950s the links between commercial and military technology remained strong. Many of the American computers built were government-financed machines adapted to the commercial marketplace. The differences between the United States and the other industrialized countries during this decade are particularly striking. The scale and scope of funding for computer development in the United States dwarfed efforts abroad. The Air Force's SAGE project alone accounted for billions of dollars in development funds, compared with tens of millions, perhaps, invested abroad. Great Britain, initially a credible technological rival to America in computers, slipped further and further behind. Close to one hundred firms entered the computer business in the United States in the 1950s compared with fewer than ten in England. When business demand for computers exploded in the early 1960s, the scientifically oriented machines built by British firms were overrun by business-oriented American computers, and the long, sad decline of the British computer industry quickened. France, Japan, and West Germany trailed far behind the United States in the infancy of computer development. They each had a few small, primitive machines not far removed from experimental research prototypes. Other European countries dropped out of the competition altogether, and their researchers staffed the first multinational laboratories, the early outposts of an increasingly internationalized industry.

The American market decisively shifted away from government customers toward commercial business users in the late 1950s. The rapid growth of the market was largely driven by technological advance: continuous, accelerated declines in the cost of computing power opened up new applications. Use of information processing machines had become economic. But the technological base from which these cost declines flowed, including electronic components, continued to benefit from a steady diet of government funding.

As the market for business computers opened wide in the early 1960s the technological lead of U.S. firms translated into solid profits. Dependence on the United States for what was becoming an essential capital good increased. U.S. export controls on shipments of high-performance computers to France dramatized that the so-called strategic argument for having an autonomous technology base was more than a thinly veiled appeal for protection of an infant industry. Interruption of the supply of products embodying state-of-the-art technology could have potentially crippling effects, not just on military preparedness, but also on the increasing number of user industries.

France, then West Germany, and then Great Britain embarked on crash programs to build up their national base in computer technology. The basic formula was generous R&D funding, government procurement preferences, and protection from foreign imports. The latter policy, as it turned out, served mainly to increase U.S. computer firms' European investments.

Analysts at the time emphasized the advantages of market size in reducing the per unit development costs for new products. Consolidating all computer production into one favored "national champion" was a popular solution. The hope was that by creating a smaller, national, "scale model" of IBM, the European markets dominated by IBM would be recaptured. It was an inward looking strategy that overlooked the economic logic for tapping into global markets in technology-intensive goods. And it was a losing strategy in Europe for precisely the same reasons that facing off with IBM in established markets was a losing strategy in the United States. Worse yet, no support was given to new entrants in a position to go after new markets in the manner that was to prove successful in the United States.

Of the European countries only West Germany reconsidered its initial strategy. This change of heart came after Nixdorf, with absolutely no help from the state, bested the performance of the chosen national champion by pioneering the European minicomputer market. This more diverse style of support has been relatively effective. Today the German computer industry is generally regarded as the strongest in Europe. Although computer research in Britain is quite highly regarded, its commercial industry remains weak. And France's two decades of protective nurture for a single national champion has had little apparent impact on its ability to prevail against its rivals in open competition.

Japan took a rather different tack. By carefully controlling access to the Japanese market, Japan's Ministry of Trade and Industry (MITI) attempted to induce U.S. computer producers to transfer computer technology to Japanese manufacturers. At the same time it promoted research and development within Japanese industry. The development of the underlying technological infrastructure took place under the technical leadership of Nippon Telephone and Telegraph (NTT) and MITI's Electrotechnical Laboratory. In the early 1970s this infrastructure was seriously shaken when many of the American firms with arranged marriages to Japanese producers dropped out of the battle for computer markets.

A new focus on support for national R&D efforts, with heavy reliance on MITI-brokered cooperative industrial research, was begun. In entirely unforeseen ways this strategy proved effective. The key development in international competition in computers in recent years has been the steady and rapid advance of Japanese computer technology. Japan now has achieved parity with the United States in many commercial products. Japan's announcement in 1981 that it intended to become a leader in frontier research areas (the oft-mentioned Fifth Generation project) prompted considerable reaction around the world.

The bold technical goals of this ambitious project reflect a shrewd assessment of economic realities. After all, if advanced parallel computers or new types of software products render existing technology truly obsolete, whole new methods of programming will be needed. Then the existing stock of software—the basis for much of IBM's advantage in global markets—will gradually be replaced. A new generation of fundamentally different types of advanced products will open up a vast new market—a market where past hegemony will provide minimal advantage.

The Role of Government

The role of government in stimulating the development of computer technology in the United States, unlike Europe and Japan, became considerably less visible during the 1960s. As the commercial market mushroomed, the general influence of government sales and R&D funding steadily declined. Nevertheless, the most sophisticated and most advanced hardware and applications continued to be funded by federal users.

The military services have always provided the bulk of government funding for U.S. computer research. For a while, the military share of computer research support declined, but the host of new military programs to sponsor computer technology announced in the early 1980s, in apparent reaction to the eroding American lead in commercial markets, suggests that this trend has been reversed. Civilian funding for computer research, particularly for applied research and engineering projects, has also increased dramatically in the United States in the last several years.

Military dominance of U.S. computer research contrasts sharply with the situation in Europe and Japan. The sources of funding have primarily been commercial even in France, where access to supercomputers needed for military research was a catalyst to the program of support for computer technology begun in the mid-1960s. In West Germany and Japan, ministries charged with supervision of industrial development and scientific research, not the military, have been the big spenders on computer development.

In the United States, spin-offs into the industrial sector have been a major objective of military support for computer technology. The promise of significant "fallout" motivated programs begun by the Defense Advanced Research Projects Agency (DARPA) in the early 1960s as well as its recent grand effort, the strategic computing program. By upgrading the technology that the military can procure from industry, the military, as a computer user, benefits. Needless to say, industry and the commercial computer user also benefit, and the social returns reaped from commercial use (which certainly overwhelm those from military use in sheer numeric terms) have probably far outweighed the gains from reduced cost and increased capabilities of military systems. In fact, technological megaprojects like the SAGE air defense system—expensive white elephants from a strictly military point of view—gave rise to important new commercial technology. They are remembered with pride and affection as great successes rather than as costly and failed attempts at buying a technological national security fix.

Attempts to quantify the extent of government involvement in financing computer research turn some popular myths about "targeting" policies on their heads. While it is true that Japanese authorities heavily subsidized computer development in the 1970s, these efforts have never approached the relative share of all R&D funds supplied by the U.S. government in the 1950s and 1960s. The proportion of computer R&D performed in MITI-organized cooperative computer research projects in the mid-1970s—the peak—was about half of the total, and only one-quarter of all funds were supplied by government. This fraction is just a little more than the share of all distinctly identifiable computer research paid for by the U.S. government in the early 1980s. Moreover, the Japanese government's relative role in financing computer research declined significantly in the late 1970s. Today government directly funds *less* of Japan's industrial computer research and development than is the case in the United States or Europe.

There are other means of supporting a research-intensive industry, and historically they have been important. In Japan during the 1960s and early 1970s, tax measures favored computer producers and users. But in the mid-1970s policy shifted to favor investment in particular technologies over other, more general subsidies to investment, and tax subsidies shrank in significance. Emphasis was redirected to research and development. Overall, there is little evidence that such tax preferences are a major factor in competitiveness today. (But one unusual, and perhaps irreproducible, feature of Japanese tax policies favoring high technology is the frequency with which incentives have been set, adjusted, and revised.) In Europe policy shifted in the opposite direction, and general subsidies to cover the losses of the ailing British and French national champions increasingly replaced the more targeted support for research and development that was typical of earlier years.

There is also little evidence that the subsidies inherent in the provision of low-cost loans from state-controlled financial institutions have been very important in recent years in Europe (with the possible exception of France's aid to Bull) or Japan. Direct support for research seems to be the targeting weapon of choice, and general subsidy the medicine of need for truly desperate financial ailments.

Procurement preferences by government users have been a powerful instrument of policy in Europe and Japan. By far the highest proportion of government markets has gone to national producers in Japan. European procurement has also favored national firms but to a lesser extent, perhaps in part because the products offered by European producers have not matched those of Japanese manufacturers in quality and breadth.

In the United States federal procurement of foreign hardware has never been much of an issue, presumably because of the superiority of American technology. But now Japanese producers are offering supercomputers that are competitive with American products (with the added fillip of some degree of compatibility with IBM machines).[1] It remains to be seen whether the United States' open procurement policies will continue. None of the new supercomputing centers sponsored by the National Science Foundation (NSF) will use Japanese equipment. The

---

1. Benchmark tests run on Cray X-MP/2, Fujitsu VP-200, and Hitachi S810/20 supercomputers in 1984 and 1985 showed the Cray and Fujitsu machines roughly comparable in performance for typical workloads from the Los Alamos National Laboratory and the Hitachi machine somewhat slower. See Olaf Lubeck, James Moore, and Raul Mendez, "A Benchmark Comparison of Three Supercomputers: Fujitsu VP-200, Hitachi S810/20, and Cray X-MP/2," *Computer,* vol. 18 (December 1985), pp. 10–24.

moment of truth may yet come when one of the U.S. national laboratories or universities considers buying a Japanese supercomputer.[2]

The structural aspects of Japan's support for research, not just the billions of yen invested, explain its successful record in catching up to the United States in state-of-the-art commercial computer technology. Japan clearly pioneered the concept of joint industrial research. Together and in parallel, industry and government invest in a generic, precompetitive, technology base, which is then further developed into commercial products within individual firms. Such arrangements reduce duplication of the least appropriable elements of investment in technology, which, although critical to further progress, are not particularly rewarding to the company that shoulders their financial burden. Cooperative research also effectively shares the risk in more speculative, long-term research investments. The best testimony to the perceived success of these policies is the extent to which they have recently been imitated in the United States and Europe, in many cases as the result of private initiatives.

Perhaps the most fascinating aspect of these nations' technology policies is the cycle of action and reaction stimulated through competition in the international marketplace. Pushed by the desire to stay competitive with foreign producers, governments have repeatedly altered their policies in reaction to developments abroad. The United States' superiority in a rapidly expanding market pushed Europe and Japan to large-scale intervention in their industries in the mid-1960s.

As a direct consequence of the financial demands of the Vietnam War, the U.S. government's support for computer technology, insulated from international competition by the lead it enjoyed at the time, declined. It was the visible return on Japan's technology investments in the late

2. C. Gordon Bell, the NSF administrator charged with oversight of its supercomputer program, recently noted that it was "NSF's intent to fund the five national centers such that they can all have the leading-edge computers manufactured by our *domestic* industry" (emphasis added). Willie Schatz, "Render unto Caesar," *Datamation*, vol. 33 (March 1, 1987), p. 22. In fact, the heavily discounted sale of an NEC supercomputer to the Houston Area Research Consortium (HARC) in March 1986 provoked a considerable outcry. And the award of a procurement contract to Honeywell, involving the sale of its largest mainframe computer model, sparked some public furor in the fall of 1986. The reason for the episode was that the Honeywell computer was actually manufactured by Japan's NEC Corp. See Richard Gibson, "Honeywell to Sell Pentagon a Computer Designed in Japan; Competitor Cries Foul," *Wall Street Journal*, October 17, 1986; and Karen Gullo and Robert Poe, "Where There's Smoke, There's Fire," *Datamation*, vol. 33 (March 1, 1987), p. 18.

1970s that awakened American industry and government from their complacent slumber. And it was the direct challenge of Japan's Fifth Generation program that provoked a massive new wave of American (and European) R&D investment in the mid-1980s.

Ironically, domination of the international marketplace is in many respects the least significant reason for a society to invest in computer technology. The social rate of return to this investment has been quite high. With rather conservative assumptions, an economic rate of return on the order of 50 to 70 percent is produced for society; more realistic assumptions would push the calculations even higher. Private returns, on the other hand, are considerably lower because of the pressures of competition from other high-tech firms and the relatively short time during which private firms have an exclusive monopoly over the fruits of their R&D investments. The social benefits of R&D investment may last forever, but the private profits produced, while sweet, are short lived.

The bulk of the social return is mainly reaped by domestic consumers in lower prices, and it far outweighs any technological rents derived from domestic and foreign sales. Yet, because foreign sales are a large portion of private revenues (typically 40 to 50 percent for U.S. firms), rents derived from foreign operations are a major source of private return on U.S. investments in computer technology. Without them, marginal projects would not be undertaken, and the pace of technological advance would slow considerably.

The Directions of Technical Advance

The economic rationale for a continuing government role in computer development is closely tied to the degree to which private firms can capture the results of R&D investments. No matter how great its payoff, basic research is more difficult to appropriate privately and therefore less likely to be undertaken by private firms. Private firms also are less likely to undertake radical innovations (as opposed to incremental advances) because much of the uncertainty in moving far beyond existing demand curves can be resolved only by actually developing and marketing a highly innovative good. Prospecting for profitable innovations on the technological frontier yields information about the nature of demand that is as easily grabbed by claim jumpers as by the risk-taking explorer.

Therefore, private firms have a considerable incentive to hold back and not hazard their own capital in removing these uncertainties.

Over time government support has assumed its greatest role in exactly these two areas: the most basic research and the most radically innovative projects. In the very beginning of the computer industry, government dominated all aspects of the technology, from financing development to buying production. But as computers evolved and diverged technologically, government became more important in some aspects of technology development, much less important in others.

The growth of the U.S. market is instructive. Around 1950 the government (defense contractors included) was the only significant customer and funder of research. The technological directions that were being explored were aimed at improving all dimensions of computer performance. Around the mid-1950s small start-up firms began to deliver machines that were smaller and offered lower performance but were much, much cheaper. Their designers took established technologies and invented clever ways to cut cost without proportionate losses in performance. Government users remained the initial customer for many of these machines, but they played little direct role in their design.

In countries with less-developed computer industries, such as Japan and France, the market for smaller machines was the niche into which their early computers fit. Because of the emphasis in this market on clever designs using already developed component technologies, and on settling for lower performance, a recent entrant has some chance of becoming competitive without spending enormous amounts on research and development. U.S. government research support, on the other hand, clustered around the high-performance, large-scale, scientific end of the computer spectrum. Government users began to purchase commercial, business-oriented machines for their ordinary data processing needs, and federal support for research and development was reserved for technologies that pushed the limits of speed and size and therefore favored developments most applicable to the very largest, high-end, scientific machines.

When the commercial market began to really take off in the mid-1950s, government sales became considerably less important to U.S. vendors of small- and medium-sized scientific computers and business-oriented machines of all sizes. Government purchases rapidly shifted toward more commercial types of applications. Even before private

Figure 6-1. *Public versus Private Investments in Technology*

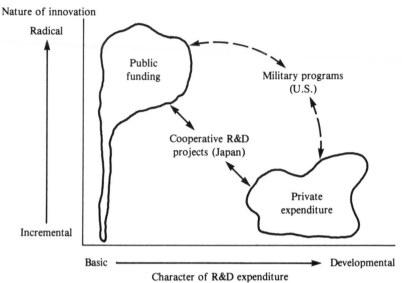

Nature of innovation

Radical

Public
funding

Military programs
(U.S.)

Cooperative R&D
projects (Japan)

Private
expenditure

Incremental

Basic ⟶ Developmental

Character of R&D expenditure

business, government had begun to automate and computerize its record-handling and data management functions.[3]

Thus as the U.S. industry matured, the government's role in stimulating research and sales grew quantitatively smaller. Federal research support was concentrated in leading-edge, high-performance machines. However, since the most advanced technology ultimately diffused into the mainstream of commercial computing, the impact of this support was considerably more influential than the numbers might indicate. The results of these efforts were transferred to industry through the publication of research and, more important, through the mobility of engineers. Then and now it is the most advanced, risky, and speculative technologies that benefit the most from government research expenditure.

Figure 6-1 portrays one way of viewing the distribution of potential R&D projects. On one axis, projects are sorted by the mix of R&D effort required, from most basic to most applied and developmental. On the

3. Government users pioneered the commercial uses of computers in the early 1950s. The first computers sold for commercial-type applications were used in the military. (UNIVAC number 2, for example, went to the Air Force in 1952, for use in inventory management and logistics applications.)

other axis, projects are distributed by the extent of their departure from current practice, from marginal, incremental improvements on current technology to truly radical leaps into the unknown.

By definition, basic research is undertaken with no concrete application in mind, but rather to add to the general stock of knowledge. Ultimately, of course, basic research may influence both incremental and radical commercial innovations. The results of the most basic research might be scattered somewhat randomly along the "nature-of-innovation" axis. Applied research and development, by contrast, are focused on particular results, and the objectives of the organization undertaking the project play a much greater role in determining the outcome of the effort. For that reason, innovations resulting from applied research and development projects are depicted in this figure as clustered along particular areas of the nature-of-innovation axis that are related to the interests of the R&D sponsors.

Commercial projects tend to be concentrated in the lower right quadrant of the diagram. Conversely, public support grows proportionately more important as more basic, radical projects are considered, moving up and to the left in the diagram. The results of pure basic research will tend to be scattered along the entire nature-of-innovation axis. But, as more applied research is considered, it will be the most "far-out," radical projects unlikely to attract the interest of private sponsors where public resources will make a difference in determining whether or not the project is undertaken.

Such radical "blue sky" projects may have relatively little existing stock of trained manpower to draw upon. Whole new sets of skills and expertise may have to be created. The people who embody the fruits of this very costly investment can easily pull up stakes and migrate elsewhere. Thus in precisely the most radical, costly, and risky projects, the difficulties of capturing the payoff may be the greatest.

If one considers technology policy as a tool for joining public support for more basic research to the less radical, developmental effort most profitable for private interests, the varying character of national technology policies might be sketched in figure 6-1. In Japan the government-sponsored cooperative R&D projects are a direct bridge of sorts between upper left and lower right, between government-funded basic effort and privately sponsored development projects.

In the United States the link between government-sponsored basic research undertaken in universities and private development has been less direct. If military interests in research and development are located in the upper right quadrant (that is, the development of radical new weapons systems yielding qualitative strategic advantage), then participation by both industry and academia on such projects has provided an indirect link between the public radical/basic and private incremental/ development orientations.

Public investment in the basic and radical has always been linked to private investment in development of the practical. When far-out government research projects and starry-eyed university research have begun to pan out, commercial firms have frequently "bought in" to the concepts by hiring the persons involved. On a more mundane daily basis, by recruiting graduate students trained in more exotic academic research funded out of the public coffers, commercial firms have maintained a continuous inflow of good, basic, new ideas without much of the large and relatively unprofitable (from a single firm's perspective) investment that would otherwise have been required.[4]

It is at the most daring leading edge that government research support continues to play its crucial role. These projects are too risky, too long-term, and too little of their results can be kept within the firm, for companies to be much interested in investing in them. *Basic, pre-competitive, radical, long-term*—these are the adjectives that describe the types of research where public support can be most important in supporting a social investment that otherwise might not be made or made at a considerably slower rate.[5]

---

4. There is a growing body of literature on the statistical relationship between federal contract research and development performed in the private sector and both productivity and private R&D effort. Such studies have generally found small but significant direct effects on private productivity and a considerably more important indirect effect in stimulating private R&D. See David M. Levy and Nestor E. Terleckyj, "Effects of Government R&D on Private R&D Investment and Productivity: A Macroeconomic Analysis," *Bell Journal of Economics,* vol. 14 (Autumn 1983), pp. 551–61; Edwin Mansfield, "R&D and Innovation: Some Empirical Findings," in Zvi Griliches, ed., *R&D, Patents, and Productivity* (University of Chicago Press, 1984), pp. 127–48; and Zvi Griliches, "Productivity, R&D, and Basic Research at the Firm Level in the 1970s," *American Economic Review,* vol. 76 (March 1986), pp. 141–61. For an alternative analysis, see Frank R. Lichtenberg, "The Relationship Between Federal Contract R&D and Company R&D," *American Economic Review,* vol. 74 (May 1984, *Papers and Proceedings, 1983*), pp. 73–78.

5. Several researchers have found that a general slowdown in basic industrial R&D coincided with the decline of federal R&D support in the 1970s. See, for example, Edwin Mansfield, "Basic Research and Productivity Increase in Manufacturing," *American Economic Review,* vol. 70 (December 1980), pp. 863–73; and Griliches, "Productivity, R&D, and Basic Research."

The Present: Probing the Technological Frontier

Computers are a thriving industry in the late 1980s; shipments amount to almost 1½ percent of the U.S. gross national product.[6] Sustained and continuous technological innovation explains the dynamism of this sector, and—despite a temporary setback dealt by the economic slow-down of the mid-1980s—continued long-term growth near historical rates is probable well into the indefinite future.

Amid this prosperity and growth, are government policies to support innovation superfluous? After all, the U.S. computer industry is con-stantly turning out new and more powerful products. Why should government fund research and development when the competitive pressures in private industry already seem so effective in generating this constant stream of innovation?

The answer is not simple. American industry certainly continues to be effective in introducing new, technology-based products. Much of this innovation, however, takes the form of marginal, incremental improvements on established technologies. The fundamental aspects of a bread-and-butter business computer of 1985 were not terribly different from the designs of 1965. Some marginal architectural improvements were made, and enormous improvements in component cost and per-formance were achieved, but essentially the designs represent a much improved embodiment of concepts that have been floating around for decades. When one looks carefully at the most radical, truly revolution-ary concepts that are still quite experimental in nature and just beginning to come to market, a rather different impression emerges.

"New wave" computer products include high-speed communications networks linking multiple computers (or even multiple processors within a single computer), systems and languages using artificial intelligence (AI) concepts, special computers designed to run this AI programming efficiently, and ever more powerful supercomputers. All these products draw heavily on a continuing legacy of government-funded research support, and many of the first commercial sales continue to be made to government users.

A November 1986 advertisement by Texas Instruments (TI) in *Sci-entific American* makes this linkage explicit:

At the heart of Knowledge Technologies [Texas Instruments' new

6. See table 2-2.

line of high-performance AI computers] lies the development of a pioneering semiconductor chip. We developed it under contract to the U.S. Government for use in aerospace and defense, but its impact will be felt in all areas. One of its first commercial applications will be to enhance the power and performance of the TI Explorer computer, already one of the world's most advanced AI development tools. Also, it will add new members to the Explorer family of products.[7]

Even today, public support primes the pump of tomorrow's commercial technology.

Issues for a National Technology Policy

Currently economic theory does not go much beyond explaining why public policies to increase investments in some types of research (particularly long-term, basic research) might be socially useful. Empirical studies (including this one) have repeatedly suggested that fairly dramatic underinvestment in R&D is often the outcome of laissez faire. In many respects, it is not very useful to debate this point. Economic, political, and social forces have made government support for high technology a given of the political economy of an advanced industrial country in the late twentieth century. Discussion, then, must necessarily focus on the details of how governments support technology.

FOCUSED SUPPORT FOR RESEARCH. The economic arguments for public support for R&D primarily revolve around three issues: the inability of firms to totally capture all returns on technology investments, economies of scale in the use of new technology and their consequences, and the difficulties of capital markets in dealing with very risky and costly projects.[8] Policies to correct the imperfections of real-world markets

7. Advertisement run in *Scientific American,* vol. 255 (November 1986). Other key elements of the Explorer computer's design are licensed from MIT, where they were developed with DARPA support.

8. One such difficulty involves the issue of moral hazard, first raised in Arrow's classic 1962 article. Kenneth J. Arrow, "Economic Welfare and the Allocation of Resources for Invention," in National Bureau of Economic Research, *The Rate and Direction of Inventive Activity: Economic and Social Factors* (Princeton University Press, 1962). If an inventor is able to completely shift the risk of an R&D project by selling all the equity in his venture in competitive capital markets, he will also shed the incentive to perform the R&D in the most efficient possible fashion. On the other hand, if constrained to retain some minimum equity share in the venture, suboptimal allocation of capital may result.

should address the concrete details of these three problems. If the purpose of public support for research and development is to ensure that socially worthwhile R&D investments are made that otherwise might not be, then public resources should be directed to the areas where appropriability problems are greatest (that is, basic, high-risk research and radically innovative, leading-edge projects).

Such considerations argue against using an R&D tax credit as the sole instrument of a technology policy. The strength of the R&D tax credit is that it marries market forces to public tax expenditures. But this strength is also a weakness since an objective of public support ought to be to direct resources into worthwhile areas that the market does not find privately profitable. The R&D tax credit is a relatively blunt instrument. It tends to produce overinvestment (from the social viewpoint) in projects where returns are most easily captured and continued underinvestment in projects that are most difficult to appropriate privately.[9] Sufficient resources can be directed into the hard-to-capture areas only by vastly overinvesting in easily captured research and development, if a tax credit were to be used as the sole instrument of policy.

This is not to say that some R&D tax credit may not be valuable. For most kinds of R&D—basic, applied, and development—there is a general tendency for social return to exceed private return. Some level of tax credit is a useful measure to correct for this fact. But a tax subsidy can direct resources into the areas with large differences between private

9. This argument is easily made in a more rigorous fashion. Let the total social return to development expenditures, E_D, be given by $R_D (E_D)$; the social return to basic research be given by $R_B (E_B)$. Let the per unit cost of R&D effort be r. Also, let R'_D, $R'_B > 0$; R''_D, $R''_B < 0$ (diminishing marginal returns to R&D effort). It is assumed that fraction c_D of the social return to development investment cannot be captured privately, fraction c_B of basic research, and that $1 \geq c_B > c_D \geq 0$. Let a rate of subsidy of s be granted to all private R&D expenditure. Then profit maximization implies investment in R&D up to the point where

$$R'_D = \frac{(1 - s)}{(1 - c_D)} r \quad \text{and} \quad R'_B = \frac{(1 - s)}{(1 - c_B)} r.$$

Social optimality argues for sufficient investment such that the left-hand side, in both cases, is equated to r. Thus, because c_D and c_B are different, setting s such that just the right amount of D takes place implies continued underinvestment in B, while sufficient B is undertaken at the cost of excessive D. If c_D and c_B are very different (that is, c_D close to 0 and c_B close to 1), the problem will be especially great. In principle, different values of s could be applied to the two categories of expenditure, but this would be impractical given the impossibility of defining or enforcing a rigorous separation between research and development.

and social returns—particularly basic and risky, far-out projects—only by pulling far too many resources into the easy, already profitable types of projects. Public policy ought to be designed to favor research in general, as well as those specific types and areas of R&D activity where both the payoff and the obstacles to private capture of that return seem greatest.

The large social rate of return reaped from all U.S. investments in computer technology, while not unheard of, appears to be greater than the returns available in certain other sectors. Because there is no market mechanism that necessarily directs resources into research areas with the greatest social returns and because social return on investment in a technology may be quite different from private return, large disparities between the social returns on alternative research expenditures may exist. Therefore, some form of targeting is inevitable when actions are based on assessments of relative social return. Those with government research dollars to dispense well realize that they are charged with putting that money where, in their judgment, it will do the most good. Their professional assessment is what plays a key role in approving projects. In practice, targeting decisions of sorts are made routinely on a daily basis.

THE COOPERATION-COMPETITION MIX. An effective technology policy may seek to encourage a mixture of cooperation and competition among private firms and between industry and academia. By encouraging cooperation on the least appropriable, basic elements of technology, more long-range research with a potential broad economic impact on industry may be undertaken. Joint research involving industry and universities can focus on commercially important (but difficult to capture for private advantage) themes that firms would otherwise neglect.

Yet a competitive market has always been essential in increasing the pace of computer innovation. A sheltered monopoly has less incentive to innovate than a firm feeling the hot breath of competition on its neck. The best evidence of the desirability of maintaining a competitive market for downstream products, even when firms share considerable research, is the history of otherwise superficially similar technology policies in Europe and Japan.

MULTIPLE SOURCES OF R&D SUPPORT. Diversity in funding sources and in research has a positive value. The history of support for technology in the United States and Japan, where different supporters of high technology have pursued distinctly different research agendas, is one of good and not-so-good decisions being made by each group. In the United States if one group had been the supreme arbiter of research policy, ENIAC, UNIVAC (universal automatic computer), Whirlwind, and other significant technology projects might never have been undertaken. Even within a single large and closely managed organization like IBM, various forms of competition in research have been carefully used to reduce the probability that any single erroneous decision will have a lasting impact on the fortunes of the organization. Because research is such a small part of the total expenditure required to develop a new product, funding multiple approaches in the research stage is a cheap way to reduce the risks involved in innovation.

MILITARY VERSUS CIVILIAN CONTROL OF RESEARCH INVESTMENT. After the first great wave of investment in technology during World War II, voices within the U.S. government argued for continuing federal support for technology but with a focus on helping industry to develop useful commercial applications. For a brief time the experiment flourished: the first fully operational computer in the United States came out of this effort.

At the time the economic arguments for investing public resources in technology had yet to be articulated. Scarcely a glimmer of the full glory of the harvest to be reaped from the unprecedented wartime effort was then visible. To powerful critics, this experiment represented a needless meddling with market forces. The effort was publicly crushed, and since then—except for basic research in universities and health research—federal support for technology has had to be justified in terms of some well-defined mission of the federal government. Defense, a cure for cancer, and putting a man on the moon are objectives deemed appropriate by Uncle Sam. But helping to build the technological infrastructure needed for a competitive American industry has not traditionally been on his list.

Since the mid-1950s, the only politically acceptable way to support the technological development of U.S. industry has been to declare it militarily strategic. Rather intricate contortions have sometimes been required to justify military expenditures that are fundamentally intended to build up the general level of industrial and scientific capacity in the U.S. economy. Unfortunately, such "frills" are often among the first casualties during military budget cutting. From the perspective of military planners, technology investments, like other items in the defense budget, are judged in terms of concrete, deliverable results and performance. The general benefits to the economy are counted only insofar as they show up in the cost and performance of other military budget items. Thus for the military, like private industry, the widespread diffusion of new technology into industry is best enjoyed if someone else's technology dollar has paid for the show.

Cyclically, almost predictably, years of budget plenty end and lean years begin. Ax in hand, military cost cutters go after items of least immediate operational relevance, and military-sponsored research programs defensively must show near-term results. DARPA, for example, has weathered several of these cycles: tolerance for visionary research projects with only indirect military relevance has been followed by budgetary distress and renewed emphasis on immediate applications, engineering, and working hardware.

Pressures to focus defense R&D on specific military missions are a constant of the political process. Even today, when economic competition with Japan is high on the agenda of projects like DARPA's strategic computing program, military research expenditure is constantly forced to define itself in terms of concrete military applications. Strategic computing, for example, must channel a significant portion of its funds to traditional military contractors, and evidence of production of concrete military applications—deliverables—must be presented to justify continued funding. For DARPA the pendulum has swung back toward applications and development.[10] These constraints in all likelihood make for a less effective policy in support of the long-term, industrial technology base.

Even in good times it is not always clear that the talk of "fallout" and economic benefits is well founded. The problem with using such appeals to justify military investments is that they cloud the issues on which judgments are to be made. If the investment were justifiable on purely military grounds, no such appeal would be required. If it were justifiable on purely economic grounds, then a rationale replete with numbers and bottom lines would have to be constructed. By moving in the no-man's-land between strategic and economic benefit, a project can slip past the snares of both economists and tough-minded generals.

Is there any way to evaluate the effectiveness of a policy that explicitly

10. See Tim Carrington, "Pentagon's Research Agency Will Shift Emphasis to Building Arms Prototypes," *Wall Street Journal*, September 16, 1986; and George Leopold, "Will Shifts at DARPA Weaken Basic Research?" *Electronics*, December 9, 1985, p. 47.

seeks out technology with long-range commercial value (rather than relying on the incidental spillover from military projects) in giving American industry a competitive edge? This is the heart of the matter, and unfortunately there are no easy answers.

One of the continuing preoccupations of scholars studying the relationships between research and development activity and technological advance has been to characterize the differential effects of different types of R&D activity on productivity and innovation. There have been two broad types of studies—*statistical analyses,* which examine correlations between different categories of expenditure and measures of innovation, given some assumed web of causation; and *case studies,* which attempt to trace the links between particular advances and the concrete research programs from which they resulted.

Each type of study has major limitations. The statistical studies have been hampered by the limited amount, poor quality, and high level of aggregation of data on research and development expenditure. If all the major linkages among the different types of R&D expenditure, product sales, and innovation were examined, a very detailed breakdown of research funded as well as performed by government, industry, and universities would be needed. The segmentation of research and development by funders reflects the fact that a funder's objectives in all likelihood influence the outcome of an R&D project. Because of economically significant differences in private appropriability, research and development probably should be broken down further into basic, applied, and development expenditure. But because of limited data, even the best statistical studies rarely attempt to do more than disaggregate between basic research and applied and development activity or, as an alternative, between all privately and publicly financed research and development within industry.

University-based research is generally not even considered when studies unravel these relationships within industry, although—as the development of computer technology makes strikingly clear—major outputs from government-funded R&D programs have repeatedly been transferred from universities to industry with few dollars changing hands and little in the way of a paper trail. A 1986 study of industrial research and development that distinguishes between military and nonmilitary funding roils these troubled waters more. Frank Lichtenberg argues that military R&D expenditures, by stimulating contract-seeking research and development on the part of private firms expecting future procurement contracts, substantially undercount the true magnitude of resources drawn into the military R&D effort.[11]

A broad survey of the origins of key elements of computer hardware reveals significant links between major concepts and pioneering government-supported projects. The innovations cover a variety of technical areas. Many important companies repeatedly declined even subsidized opportunities to explore these new technologies in the early years, and if the federal government had not stepped in, private interest alone would certainly have generated much slower development of the technology.

Spinoffs from military computer projects continue to have a profound impact on the development of commercial computer technology. But it is far from clear that channeling such funding through military programs maximizes commercial spinoffs. Funneling R&D funding through military sponsors may even impede commercial applications in some respects. For example, compilations of patent statistics show that research and development connected to military sponsors yields considerably fewer patents of commercial interest than do equivalent expenditures by other government agencies.[12]

The Case for Civilian Objectives

A highly trained and motivated civilian agency, if given the mandate of cooperating with American industry and academia to improve the

11. Frank R. Lichtenberg, "Private Investment in R&D to Signal Ability to Perform Government Contracts" (draft, Columbia University, Graduate School of Business, 1986). See also Mansfield, "Basic Research and Productivity Increase in Manufacturing"; Griliches, "Productivity, R&D, and Basic Research"; and E. Wolff and M. I. Nadiri, "Interindustry Effects and the Return to R and D in Manufacturing," 1984, and "Linkage Structure and Research and Development," 1984, as cited in M. Ishaq Nadiri, "Economics of R and D Investment," *NBER Reporter* (Summer 1985).

12. In 1976 only 1 percent of the unexpired patents owned and available for licensing from the Air Force were actually licensed, as were 1 percent for the Navy, 3 percent for the Army, and 4 percent for NASA. This compared with 11 percent for the Energy Research and Development Administration (now the Energy Department), 13 percent for Interior, 15 percent for Commerce, 10 percent for Agriculture, and 23 percent for the Department of Health, Education, and Welfare. See Federal Council for Science and Technology, *Report on Government Patent Policy, Combined December 31, 1973, through September 30, 1976* (Government Printing Office, 1976), pp. 440–41.

However, since the practice of Defense and NASA has generally been to grant to contractors patent rights when requested, this may merely mean that the best inventions are harvested by contractors, leaving the chaff for the government sponsor. This is consistent with the fact that the Army and NASA, which show higher percentages of their patents actually licensed, give away their rights somewhat less frequently. See chapter 4.

long-term technological future of the American economy, ought to be able to get at least as big a commercial bang for the federal research buck as a Pentagon planner looking for an economic hook to pull in additional support for a new weapons system. If the streamlined efficiency of defense programs was an unassailable article of faith, Pentagon budget administrators might be the best that could be, and the secondary importance of commercial objectives to many such projects might be offset by the superior performance of Defense Department administrators on technology investments. But this is not the case.

Support for industrial technology ought to be decoupled from a volatile military budget. Military perceptions of the size and nature of the external military threat change. The needs of American industry do not necessarily march in harmony with the rhythm of international military competition. Military objectives, like commercial objectives, revolve around concrete goals, like delivering weapons systems on schedule, on target, and on budget. Inevitably, the long-term, the basic, the not immediately tangible are given short shrift when funding shrinks and purely military objectives are used for triage among wounded programs.

Moreover, military and commercial objectives can conflict. Research on weapons systems, by nature, imposes a curtain of secrecy over developments that might have beneficial consequences for industry if widely diffused. During the 1940s and 1950s, scientists running military programs actively worked to propagate the new technology as widely as possible among American industry. This played a major role in the rapid development of American industrial muscle in computers. Conversely, more recent attempts to control the export of information across national boundaries may directly limit the distribution and application of useful results within those boundaries.

On occasion, control can prove indirectly counterproductive to economic interest. America's attempt to deny the French nuclear program access to a supercomputer in the mid-1960s (a futile attempt) sparked crash development programs and ultimately reduced American computer sales in foreign markets in later years.

Important military systems requirements may sometimes have small commercial value. Resistance to radiation and electromagnetic pulse, for example, yield a relatively small return in commercial markets but are a central focus in products aimed at military markets.

Military specifications and test procedures sometimes drive technology in the wrong direction—that is, away from the most important commercial markets. For many years military testing and "burn-in" requirements may have been an obstacle to adoption of statistical quality-control techniques in the American electronics industry.[13] Military testing requirements for electronics packages emphasize extreme and rapid changes in temperature—relevant perhaps to aircraft, but not normally encountered in most natural environments. On the other hand, the test most relevant to commercial products—simulating the stress of switching power on and off—is not included in military specifications.[14]

The American armed forces have strongly supported research on manufacturing technology. They generally fund programs that reduce the cost of military weapons systems, which, like other highly specialized capital goods, are usually produced in small lots or batches. They have not focused on reducing costs in large-scale mass production, as is typical in consumer markets. Some have argued that similar focus has affected the type of semiconductor research supported by military programs and has made such spending less useful to commercial industry.[15]

Finally, government subsidy to industrial computer research (which largely comes out of U.S. military budgets) is distributed in a highly uneven fashion. The firms that receive assistance are not always the ones most able to successfully introduce new innovations commercially. DARPA funding for the strategic computing program, for example, has departed from past practice and placed a heavy emphasis on supporting research in the large, specialized defense systems contractors. These firms, had they the inclination, may not have the ability to rapidly commercialize new technology in the marketplace. The skills needed to compete effectively in the military market may be quite different from the ones needed to succeed in the commercial market, and programs that channel research resources to more heavily defense-oriented contractors may yield proportionately less commercial return.

13. See Kenneth Flamm, "Internationalization in the Semiconductor Industry," in Joseph Grunwald and Kenneth Flamm, *The Global Factory: Foreign Assembly in International Trade* (Brookings, 1985), p. 122.

14. Tobias Naegele, "Englemeier: 'Mil Specs Drive People in the Wrong Direction,' " *Electronics*, October 28, 1985, p. 57.

15. The case is made in Leslie Brueckner with Michael Borrus, "Assessing the Commercial Impact of the VHSIC (Very High Speed Integrated Circuit) Program," Roundtable on the International Economy (University of California at Berkeley, 1984); and Jay Stowsky, "Competing with the Pentagon," *World Policy Journal*, vol. 3 (Fall 1986), pp. 697–72. The semiconductor manufacturer Intel is reported to have opposed VHSIC on similar grounds. Glen R. Fong, "The Potential for Industrial Policy: Lessons from the Very High Speed Integrated Circuit Program," *Journal of Policy Analysis and Management*, vol. 5 (Winter 1986), p. 277.

A Missing Link

Outside of the military research agencies (and, to a lesser extent, the National Aeronautics and Space Administration and the Department of Energy), the government organization that spends the most research cash in the national interest has been the National Science Foundation. Recently the NSF has shifted a larger share of its budget into more applied, engineering programs with a distinct emphasis on cooperation with industry. This shift clearly reflects its (and the government's) growing preoccupation with maintaining industrial competitiveness in an increasingly challenging international marketplace.

Supporting industrial technology, however, is not what the NSF was set up to do. Its first and most outspoken proponent, Vannevar Bush, believed that basic research divorced from the immediate needs of commercial industry was the essential foundation for applied forms of technological progress. This conviction prompted his call for the establishment of the NSF. Forging direct links between university research and applied industrial objectives is far from the foundation's original charter of supporting basic scientific knowledge, unfettered by any requirement that it show industrial relevance. To quote Bush, "basic research is essentially noncommercial in nature. It will not receive the attention it requires if left to industry."[16] The whole decisionmaking structure of the NSF was set up around academics making judgments about the academic research projects of their peers based purely on scientific merit: profitability and potential industrial application were of secondary concern if any.

In the late 1960s the NSF began to edge toward other priorities. Applying technology to solve social problems emerged as an objective appropriate to the times, and Congress in 1968 amended the NSF's charter to include applied research among the agency's concerns. Much of this thrust fizzled out in the late 1970s.[17] By the 1980s the challenge of newly felt international competition sparked a new emphasis on economic relevance, and the shift began toward engineering, particularly the NSF's Engineering Research Center program, which has been the focus for recent growth in agency funding.

A wholesale shift in NSF priorities toward applied research, engi-

16. Vannevar Bush, *Science: The Endless Frontier,* Report to the President on a Program for Postwar Scientific Research (GPO, 1945), p. 17.
17. See NSF Advisory Committee on Merit Review, *Final Report,* NSF 86-93 (Washington: NSF, 1986), pp. 11–12.

neering, and advanced development projects represents a major change in course for the NSF. If one agrees with Bush that basic research deserves its own organization, then NSF's new focus on industrial technology fills one space by emptying another. Judging what areas of applied industrial research merit long-term support is a very different type of judgment—in part an economic one—than the pure consideration of intellectual merit around which NSF procedures are organized.

A vacuum now surrounds an important social purpose: to support applied research and early development of the new technologies required to keep America's industries economically fit. The industrial technology base is no one agency's explicit target. All responsible public servants in the various research-funding bodies, of course, realize that the technology base is a fundamental national interest, even if it is not explicitly written down in the *Federal Handbook*. So the missions and charters of the various agencies are stretched whenever a particularly worthwhile investment comes along.

The Future: New Technology for American Industry

How can national policy better serve the common national interest in expanding and improving American society's investment in technology? For decades this question was rarely asked. The United States' lead with respect to other countries' technologies was so great, its economic muscle so strong, that the unforeseen fallout from its huge investments in military R&D was quite sufficient to keep the nation's industrial technology second to none. Today, however, competitors have caught up to the United States in important areas and may even have passed it in others. They are investing sums comparable in magnitude to U.S. military R&D programs in commercially oriented research ventures.

As chapter 2 made clear, public investments in computer technology are justifiable on purely economic grounds. The wisest investments are in the most basic research and high-risk, radically innovative projects. To plant technological seed corn that industry can harvest later, the areas of research with the greatest commercial and industrial potential should be selected. And the selection mechanism should be workable in the institutional context of American industry.

What is the simplest national policy to achieve these objectives? It is to use public resources to partially offset the costs of joint industrial investment in basic and "generic" technology development. The policy is clearly workable. Concerns about increased international competition have already prompted American business to form cooperative, joint research associations in unprecedented numbers. Today support for joint, precompetitive, generic R&D is quite widespread. Influential figures within even that most entrepreneurial of American high-technology sectors, the beleaguered American semiconductor industry, are now calling for a massive new cooperative research program to tackle the technological roots of its current distress.[18] With little publicity, powerful bureaucrats are taking steps on their own to fund such programs.[19] Never has the moment seemed better to explore a new direction, an experiment in policy, and never have the stakes seemed higher.

Underwriting some portion of these ventures with federal funds or tax expenditures would pull more resources into the applied research and generic technology development undertaken by these organizations, as well as raise the overall level of R&D investment. Moreover, such a policy would guide public funds into areas that industry believes to be productive, but where the benefits are difficult to capture and individual, private efforts therefore unlikely to succeed.

If, say, 40 percent of the investment is offset through the tax system or direct funding, firms will still be providing the remaining 60 percent of the funding by risking their own resources. The resources so invested will then be funneled to the projects thought to have the highest payoff for the industry as a whole. A funding mechanism that shares costs and risks creates built-in incentives for allocating resources efficiently.

And, of course, jointly pooled resources will be directed into precisely those areas—basic, and generic, precompetitive research—that are least likely to be appropriated (and hence funded) by individual firms. Perhaps the most eloquent testimony to the effectiveness of these arrangements is the extent to which their use grew in Japan, where they were first

18. See "Editor's Overview," and Harvey Brooks, "National Science Policy and Technology Innovation," in Ralph Landau and Nathan Rosenberg, eds., *The Positive Sun Strategy: Harnessing Technology for Economic Growth* (National Academy Press, 1986), pp. 15, 156–57; and Richard R. Nelson, *High-Technology Policies: A Five-Nation Comparison*, American Enterprise Institute Studies in Economic Policy (Washington, D.C.: AEI, 1984), p. 73. See also Richard Bambrick, "Sematech Gets SIA Go-Ahead; Target Gov't, Ind. for Funds," *Electronic News*, November 24, 1986.

19. Administrators in the Department of Defense and the National Science Foundation, for example, recently budgeted contributions of $1.1 and $0.1 million dollars respectively to the nonprofit Semiconductor Research Corporation for precisely these reasons.

devised and tested, and is now being emulated in Europe and the United States.

The institutional mechanisms required to establish such a program, in some sense, already exist. The Stevenson-Wydler Technology Innovation Act of 1980 called for the establishment of a cooperative generic technology program, new organizations within the executive branch to study and stimulate the development of technology applicable to industrial needs, and the organization of centers for the development of industrial technology at universities and other nonprofit institutions. The Commerce Department was empowered to fund up to three-quarters of project costs at the centers for industrial technology, which were eventually intended to become self-supporting.[20]

The Commerce Department, however, never implemented most of the provisions of this law. This was a political decision. But the fragmented and sprawling bureaucracy of the Commerce Department may not be the best organization to implement such a program. It already wears too many hats: protector of declining American industries, champion for small business, forecaster of the weather, compiler of economic and demographic statistics, promoter of American exports, registrar of patents, traffic cop for the radio spectrum, extoller of the virtues of tourism in the United States. Although the Commerce Department does have isolated centers of technological expertise—particularly the National Bureau of Standards—overall it has not displayed a solid understanding of, or informed interest in, important technological issues. A more effective steward of America's technological edge in world markets might be a smaller, totally dedicated organization.

The National Technology Office

The purpose of this National Technology Office (NTO) would be to monitor the international competitiveness of American products both on the market and under development, report on its observations for public debate, facilitate the formation of joint research ventures within American industry, and serve as custodian of the public interest in those associations formed to carry out joint industrial research. The organi-

20. See Office of Technology Assessment, *Information Technology R&D: Critical Trends and Issues* (Washington, D.C.: OTA, 1985), pp. 32–33; and J. A. Alic, "The Federal Role in Commercial Technology Development," *Technovation*, vol. 4 (1986), pp. 266–67.

zation might resemble a civilian DARPA, charged with stimulating long-term investment in key industrial technologies. The private sector could define areas for investment by forming joint research associations with particular objectives and then seeking partial federal financial support. The role of the NTO would be to approve the bona fides of the group seeking partial support—something like approving the tax exemption of a nonprofit organization—and to certify that the project involved the kind of activity that the program was intended to assist—namely, generic, precommercial technology development.

The precise method of backing private investments, be it tax credits for eligible R&D or direct grants in important but imperfectly appropriable technology projects, is less important than the principle. Business and society must be partners if needed investment in America's future are to be made. They must share the risks and rewards of their long-term technology investments. Each must contribute if they are to jointly prosper.

As a clearinghouse for joint research, the NTO could eliminate obvious duplication and aid the flow of nonproprietary information within industry and between industry and academia. And it would be in an invaluable position to mobilize American industry in the face of new technological challenges. It could constantly scan the technological horizon, identify important new developments, sound the alarm, or propose an initiative when necessary. And it would safeguard the public interest in the collusive arrangements that cooperative research must, by definition, involve. Joint industrial research programs generally require some form of antitrust exemption. The National Technology Office might offer cooperatives antitrust relief, in addition to partial matching of funding on eligible projects, as a quid pro quo for a public representative (perhaps drawn from its ranks) on their boards to keep an eye on the public interest. That interest would include the responsible expenditure of public funds and the guarantee of adequate downstream competition in products developed privately using this research base. To ensure equality of opportunity and absence of political bias, such ventures would be open on equal terms to all firms willing to meet whatever transparent and nondiscriminatory financial and participatory requirements were established.

Setting up the NTO would require skilled personnel able to develop useful working relationships with industry. Technically knowledgeable specialists would mix with economic and financial analysts within the organization. To keep its technical skills at the cutting edge of innovation, it might have an internal research capacity, not unlike MITI's relationship with its internal industrial science laboratories.

Fortunately, there already exists within the federal government a small but competent band of technical specialists that has extensive experience working with industry on joint research projects. That group, of course, is the National Bureau of Standards, the same NBS that back in the 1950s built the first fully operational stored program computer in the United States. Today it is deeply involved in applied research on manufacturing technologies, computers, and robotics.

Standards issues are reshaping commercial markets and technology. With General Motors, the NBS is testing an architecture for future automated manufacturing systems as part of the program to develop the Manufacturing Automation Protocol (MAP). With the cooperation of other firms, the NBS is working on computerized manufacturing and design standards such as the integrated graphics exchange standard (IGES) and the product data definition interchange (PDDI) standard. In addition, it is doing work under contract to DARPA as part of the strategic computing program.[21]

One simple solution, then, would be to take part of the technical core of the NBS, transplant it to a new organization, and greatly expand the scope of the work those specialists currently direct. This technical staff and trained economic and financial analysts would make up a small hybrid organization—something like a cross between the current NBS, Arthur D. Little, the Congressional Budget Office, and the Office of Technology Assessment. The charter of the new organization would be to monitor the technological health of American industry, keep abreast of developments abroad, issue periodic reports, and formulate long-range proposals for accelerating the advanced research and development needed to maintain the quality of America's industrial technology base.

The President's Commission on Industrial Competitiveness released a report in 1985 that advocated more radical changes. It favored the creation of a "superagency" to preside as czar over *all* nonmilitary research.[22] The National Technology Office, however, would have as its

21. NBS is doing research on speech coarticulation as part of the speech understanding segment of the program. See Defense Advanced Research Projects Agency, *Strategic Computing: First Annual Report* (Arlington, VA.: DARPA, 1985), p. 9.

22. See President's Commission on Industrial Competitiveness, *Global Competition: The New Reality*, vol. 1: *Report of the President's Commission on Industrial Competitiveness* (GPO, 1985), pp. 22–23, 51.

only concern the state of American industrial technology. Although the only group in government with this specific charge, it would be one of many influences in the government's research policy community. The NTO would supplement, not replace, the voices of DARPA, the NSF, and NASA. These agencies could get back to performing the missions for which they were designed. No longer would they be involved in the contorted justifications required to deal with unmet social needs outside their charters.

How might the NTO mobilize the collective efforts of American industry in the face of technological challenges from abroad? The following scenario describes one set of circumstances in which the NTO might function as a catalytic agent for joint industrial research.

Synchrotrons and Other Developments

The NTO might play a vital role in the development of high-intensity X-ray lithography apparatus to etch microelectronic devices with very fine, dense features. Such devices are essential for future generations of high-performance semiconductors in general, and computer circuitry in particular. The technology is still experimental, and a practical system awaits the development of a compact, superconducting, synchrotron storage ring. (Developing this equipment might dovetail nicely with applied research on newly discovered superconducting materials.) This equipment, once developed, may be quite expensive—perhaps $10 million for a synchrotron X-ray source and the capacity to etch six to ten semiconductor wafers at once.[23] Although most semiconductor and computer firms are interested in the technology, few can afford to risk the large investments required by such a costly and highly speculative project.

As of mid-1986 this technology was being explored on a large scale with government support in West Germany and Japan but not in the United States.[24] IBM has been cooperating with the Brookhaven National Laboratories of the Department of Energy in the development of

23. The cost estimate was given in a presentation by Peter Rose of the Eaton Corporation at the National Research Council Seminar on "Advanced Processing of Electronic Materials in the United States and Japan: A State of the Art Review and Its Policy Implications," Washington, D.C., June 4, 1986.

24. See National Research Council, *State of the Art Reviews: Advanced Processing of Electronic Materials in the United States and Japan* (Washington, D.C.: National Academy Press, 1986), p. 24.

a synchrotron-based etching system, but this appears to be a modest effort falling well short of the large investment required to develop a practical prototype machine.

In the summer of 1986 MITI formed a cooperative research venture company, K. K. Sortec, to develop compact, synchrotron-based X-ray etching systems. This effort was part of the Japan Key Technology Center, a new organization founded in the fall of 1985 and authorized to fund up to 70 percent of the cost of private research ventures. Seventy percent of the funding for the ten-year venture, with a budget now pushing $5 million, is coming from the government, the remainder from a consortium of thirteen Japanese firms.[25] Another synchrotron project is under way within NTT.

Many U.S. electronics specialists (including those of the National Research Council) believe synchrotrons merit further exploration, but no major private venture in this costly and speculative area had been announced in the United States as of early spring 1987. An alert, disciplined, and well-motivated organization like the NTO—even with less government support (say a 30 percent share)—could quickly take the lead in mobilizing U.S. firms in ventures similar to those of the Japanese.

Other areas where support for joint industrial research might improve the competitiveness of American industry abound. In early 1987 American electronics producers appealed to the government for support for a joint venture to develop advanced semiconductor manufacturing technology. This is another logical entry point for an NTO-type program. Why not have industry organize a Stevenson-Wydler-style joint venture to direct such an R&D effort, with perhaps half of the expense shared with the federal government? Industry, rather than Pentagon planners, could select the most commercially promising areas and direct its collective efforts there.

Other frontier technologies that might usefully be explored in this fashion for the collective benefit of American high-tech industry include new and exotic materials (high-temperature superconductors, ceramics, diamond films), optical switches and transmission, experimental software production systems, and molecular engineering methods. The

25. The companies include computer producers NEC, Hitachi, and Fujitsu. Other members are Matsushita, Mitsubishi, Sanyo, Sharp, Sony, Oki Electric, Sumitomo, Toshiba, Nikon, and Canon. See Charles L. Cohen, "Japan Kicks Off X-Ray Fab Project," *Electronics*, August 7, 1986, p. 44.

ultimate authority on the wisdom of particular choices would be American industry. It would have its own cash at risk—a powerful incentive to choose what will prove the most commercially successful.

In the final analysis the question may be whether the United States is willing to change the way it does research. For forty years it has avoided difficult questions about the role of government in the development of technology by relying on the military services as the custodians of the nation's economic future. The military option is workable within the context of U.S. institutions, but it fails the other tests of a good technology policy. The cyclical feast and famine of the military budget process inevitably directs research and development away from long-term projects of only indirect military interest when the crunch eventually comes. Worse yet, economic judgments about long-term commercial promise are not part of these budget choices. In fact, appeals to commercial fallout are generally the sign of a military project that cannot be justified on its security merits, just as appeals to defense applications are the sure sign of a commercial project that isn't making it as a business proposition. We are left with a muddle—too little accountability and too much pork barrel.

The military option kept the United States moving along nicely in an era when it was the king of a one-lane road, but it needs revision as the country turns onto a four-lane superhighway crowded with other drivers jockeying for position. Panels of respected American scientists and engineers have recently published a virtual blizzard of reports that warn of dangers on the technological frontier in a number of important areas.[26]

Opening Markets in High-Technology Products

To meet the challenge of the competitive international environment, the United States must keep open global markets for its technology-intensive products. This should be the country's first priority. The protectionist backlash that is unleashed in the United States by foreign

26. National Academy of Sciences, National Research Council, *High-Technology Ceramics in Japan* (Washington, D.C.: National Academy Press, 1984); J. Nevins and others, *JTECH Panel Report on Mechatronics in Japan* (La Jolla, Calif.: Science Applications International Corporation, 1985); H. Wieder and others, *JTECH Panel Report on Opto- & Microelectronics* (La Jolla, Calif.: Science Applications International Corporation, 1985); and G. Turin and others, *JTECH Panel Report on Telecommunications Technology in Japan* (La Jolla, Calif.: Science Applications International Corporation, 1986).

targeting policies, and more blatant moves around the world to favor national firms in national markets for advanced products, is a short-sighted reaction that works against the United States' long-term objectives. A recent trend toward erecting protectionist barriers around high-technology sectors in the United States (in semiconductors and advanced machine tools, for example) may work against the long-term interests of American high tech by setting dangerous precedents for the nation's trading partners and competitors.

What may be needed is a set of agreed upon principles of nondiscrimination on the basis of national origin analogous to those ruling trade in conventional goods, as in the GATT. At a minimum, the United States should continue to work for a reciprocal opening of markets in technology-intensive goods that would explicitly strengthen provisions related to government-controlled procurement. Exceptions based on national security considerations should be few and well defined.

Attempts to eliminate subsidies to research and development from international trade in high-tech products—given the compelling economic arguments for, and history of, government involvement in fostering technology development—seem fruitless. A more useful approach might be to open up programs to fund the development of technologies used in internationally traded products, on a reciprocal basis, with the United States' major industrial trade partners. Indeed, bilateral initiatives of this sort have already been discussed publicly. In 1978 some elements in the military and the Department of State favored a bilateral accord permitting Japanese participation in the Defense Department's VHSIC (very high speed integrated circuit) program in exchange for U.S. participation in MITI's VLSI (very large scale integrated circuit) program. Opposition within the Defense Department ultimately killed this exchange, but the proposal demonstrated that serious interest in such accords exists.[27]

Opening up U.S. research programs to industrial competitors on a reciprocal basis would be particularly advantageous in the computer field. All the major industrialized economies are currently funding computer technology programs of comparable sizes. Making the results of these programs available across national boundaries would improve the efficiency of global expenditures on computer research and devel-

27. See Jill Hills, "Foreign Policy and Technology: The Japan–US Japan–Britain and Japan–EEC Technology Agreements," *Political Studies*, vol. 31 (June 1983), pp. 212–15.

opment by reducing duplication, help others avoid blind alleys, and generally improve the flow of basic, precompetitive information.

The Japanese have edged in this direction by seeking international academic participation in their Fifth Generation program, as have the Europeans by accepting IBM and the Digital Equipment Corporation as participants in the Esprit projects of the European Community. In a sense, the United States already has, too, by training in its universities so many of the world's computer scientists. If all current computer support programs in industrialized countries were opened to firms from the other countries active in the field, each country (including the United States) would gain access to research with funding exceeding that of its own national program.

This piecemeal approach toward reducing the impact of any single nation's public R&D support on the competitive position of its firms in international markets seems a useful step toward rationalizing global R&D and improving the potential welfare of all. But the risk of international competition in high-tech products heating up into open trade war, with individual countries closing off their research and markets from competitors, will still exist.

Ultimately, all would lose with such a balkanization of national markets for high-tech goods. Policies designed to slow the international diffusion of technology may well inhibit advance within domestic industry, and by limiting foreign sales reduce the incentive to invest in the development of new technology and the competitiveness of the industries involved. Rather than attempting to erect a fortress around existing national technologies in a futile attempt to preserve some static advantage, international competition could more fruitfully focus on developing new technology as quickly as possible, in order to stay one step ahead in the game.

The most reasonable outcome might be a gradual series of small, partial, and perhaps bilateral steps that liberalize participation in and access to research programs in some equitable fashion. For example, the Japanese government might be asked to permit American firms to participate in its synchrotron research in exchange for entry by Japanese companies into American joint venture research in another high-risk, exploratory area of semiconductor manufacturing technology.[28] The

---

28. The United States retains a lead in key areas of exploratory research on microelectronic manufacturing technology, including ion implantation, thin-film epitaxy,

exact outlines of a finished package remain unclear, but it is time to start thinking about what sorts of experiments will lead policy down a productive path.

The challenge for an increasingly technology-intensive American economy will be to steer itself away from the worst, and toward the best, of all possible high-tech worlds. In the worst case—fractious international discord over trade in advanced products—a heavy lid would be slammed over free access to information, U.S. borders would be sealed against the entry of new foreign products, and, overall, use of new technology and the rate of technological progress would slow measurably.

In the best case, international economic rivalry would be channeled into competition based on innovation and differentiation; an ever greater variety of useful products would become available to all people. The greatest fruits from continued growth would then flow to those countries that were best able to nurture innovation and to meet the demands of a wide and sophisticated global marketplace for quality, reliability, and utility. In such a world, basic scientific information would flow freely, international cooperation on fundamental research would be the rule rather than the exception, and competition would focus on the socially beneficial provision of variety and quality.

The choice of futures is America's to make. The only certainty is that the global economy in the next few decades will be tied to technology on a scale never seen before. The development of the computer will perhaps be remembered as the first large step down this road.

---

and film deposition and etching. See National Research Council, *State of the Art Reviews: Advanced Processing of Electronic Materials*, pp. 10, 16, 20.

Modeling the Cost of Information Processing Capacity

THIS APPENDIX uses an approach based on production theory to assess the magnitude of improvements in the price and performance of computer systems. Computers are viewed as durable capital goods producing a flow of information processing services, whose utility as an input to the production of other goods and services can be characterized by a single, scalar value. (The flow of services is assumed to be proportional to this index of information processing capacity, IP.)

From a simplified, stylized model of a computer (see figure 2-1) an expression that links system performance to the performance of its component parts may be derived.[1] The single most important parameter affecting the performance of a computer system is the speed of its various component subsystems.[2] The speed of an information processing device

---

1. This approach is based on the work of the respected computer scientist David J. Kuck. See "Computer System Capacity," section 2.5, in David J. Kuck, *The Structure of Computers and Computations,* vol. 1 (John Wiley and Sons, 1978), pp. 155–69. More complex performance models view a computer system as a network of queues and evaluate its behavior using either analytic methods or numerical simulation models. For a useful overview of the use of such models at IBM, see Yonathan Bard and Charles H. Sauer, "IBM Contributions to Computer Performance Modeling," *IBM Journal of Research and Development,* vol. 25 (September 1981), pp. 562–70.

2. See Harold S. Stone and others, "Hardware Systems," in Bruce W. Arden, ed., *What Can Be Automated?* (Cambridge: MIT Press, 1980), pp. 404–09; C. Gordon Bell and Allen Newell, *Computer Structures: Readings and Examples* (McGraw-Hill, 1971), pp. 49–52; Daniel P. Siewiorek, C. Gordon Bell, and Allen Newell, *Computer Structures: Principles and Examples* (McGraw-Hill, 1982), pp. 42–61; and C. Gordon Bell, J. Craig Mudge, and John E. McNamara, *Computer Engineering: A DEC View of Hardware Systems Design* (Bedford, Mass.: Digital Press, 1978), app. 3.

is measured by its *bandwidth*, the number of bits of information passing through it per second.

The performance of an entire computer system can also be measured in terms of bandwidth. To obtain the maximum bandwidth of a network of computer systems operating in parallel, one could take this performance measure for each computer system in the complex and add them together. In other words, for identical computer systems multiply the quantity of computers by the information processing capacity per computer.

A similar analysis might compute the maximum information processing capacity of a single computer system in terms of the bandwidth of each of its subsystems. In a modern computer a control unit generally overlaps the operations of processor, memory, and input and output units. Thus maximum system bandwidth may be taken as the sum of these individual component bandwidths.[3]

In Kuck's model the *effective* bandwidth of the entire computer system depends on the bandwidths of the individual components and on the requirements of the particular application. The maximum bandwidth of the system is attained when the bandwidth of each of the components is fully used. Particular applications, however, make vastly different demands on bandwidth for distinct system components. Some problems are *processor bound*, others are *memory bound*, still others are *disk* (or *input-output*) *bound*.

Kuck defines *utilized system bandwidth* as the sum of the utilized bandwidth of each of the system components.[4] The bandwidth of each of the components is assumed to be used in an application-specific fixed proportion.

For example, in the case of a simple problem in a rudimentary system with only two kinds of components (a processor and main memory), utilized system capacity is expressed by Kuck as

(A-1) $$I_s^u = \left[min \left(\frac{I_p}{\beta_p}, \frac{I_m}{\beta_m} \right) \right] (\beta_p + \beta_m),$$

where

3. Kuck, *Structure of Computers and Computations*, pp. 163–64.
4. Kuck assumes that each of the system components operates entirely in parallel. The considerable parallelism in the design of modern computer systems does allow the operations of individual components to overlap. However, the earliest computers were serial in design with each component processing a bit while the others waited for its actions to terminate. Ibid.

I_s^u = utilized system capacity

β_p = processor bandwidth used per unit utilized system capacity

β_m = memory bandwidth used per unit utilized system capacity

I_p = processor bandwidth installed

I_m = memory bandwidth installed.

The β's are specific to the particular application chosen.

Given prices for memory and processor bandwidth, what processor and memory configuration minimizes the cost of utilized system bandwidth? In this simple example the answer is to configure a computer system using the same fixed proportions of the two components as are required by the application.

If the system were to run an assortment of tasks, the cost minimization problem would be more complex. The composition of the bundle of tasks, the component bandwidth requirements for each application in the bundle, and the relative prices of component bandwidth would jointly determine the least costly configuration through a straightforward application of linear programming techniques. This assumes that there are no indivisibilities or other economies of scale in the provision of system bandwidth.

With an arbitrary number of different system components, the cost per unit of utilized system bandwidth on a particular problem will be minimized by a system configuration optimized for that particular problem. This is an important rationale for the product differentiation actually observed in the computer industry. Yet the relative fixity of the development costs for a computer system and resulting economies of scale, as well as economies of scope in the use of software, provide economic incentives for the design of a "general purpose" computer.[5] Such a machine comes close to attaining the minimum cost per unit of utilized system bandwidth on a group of problems typical of the business computing workload.

Kuck's assumption that the relative use of bandwidth of different system components is absolutely fixed on a particular type of problem is probably somewhat unrealistic. The history of computer design is replete with examples of cheap components being substituted for expensive ones through ingenious designs or programming ingenuity motivated precisely by the economic concerns described here.

5. See Kenneth Flamm, *Creating the Computer: Government, Industry and High Technology* (Brookings, forthcoming), chap. 7.

To permit greater substitution between components, an average information processing capacity for a computer system (averaged from utilized system bandwidth with representative workload weights that reflect typical mixes of tasks run on computers) is approximated as

(A-2) $I = f (I_p, I_m, I_d, I_t, I_l, I_c)$.

Function f is assumed to be a twice continuously differentiable, positive function. The other values are as follows:

I_p = installed information processing capacity (bandwidth) of the central processing unit

I_m = installed main memory capacity

I_d = installed capacity of moving-head disk files

I_t = installed capacity of magnetic tape units

I_l = capacity of line printers

I_c = capacity of punched card equipment.

Configurers of computer systems produce their products by rearranging the technologies embedded in these subsystems to meet specific user requirements. Few large computer systems are exactly alike, and even in seemingly standard "boxes"—the central processing unit (CPU) and main memory packaged in a central unit—there are often subtle differences due to minor customization by the manufacturer to meet the special needs of users.

It is assumed that actual information processing capacity is assembled so as to minimize the cost of system bandwidth on average. In other words, given the current price of bandwidth for the various system components, the cost of some I, as expressed in A-2, is minimized. Actual installed systems are assumed to be close to the current minimum cost configurations, but not exactly so, since design decisions based on prices from previous years may be reversed as the costs of different components change. Compared with most capital goods, computer systems have a notoriously short life span during which they are often retrofitted and upgraded, so this is not an unreasonable approximation.[6]

The function f in A-1, giving average computer system bandwidth as a function of component subsystem capacities, is taken to be relatively

6. Phister calculates that average life for a general purpose computer fluctuated between 4.5 years and 7.7 years over the period 1956–74. See Montgomery Phister, Jr., *Data Processing Technology and Economics*, 2d ed. (Bedford, Mass.: Digital Press, 1979), p. 255.

stable over time. Function f will be assumed to display constant returns to scale; doubling the inputs of all subsystems doubles aggregate system capacity. Many commercial data processing tasks can be divided up and run in smaller pieces on a number of identical computers in the way implied by this assumption.

To measure the effective bandwidth of each class of system components, multiply the bandwidth per component times the number of components. Processor bandwidth is just the speed of an individual processor, since in a computer of the standard Von Neumann design there is only one processor. In the experimental "parallel" computer architecture now appearing on the commercial market, one might wish to multiply number of processors by individual processor bandwidth.

For main memory the question is somewhat more complex. If all bits of memory could be accessed simultaneously, main memory bandwidth would equal total amount of memory times the bandwidth of any particular memory element. In practice, however, the external connection between the central processor and memory can handle only a limited number of bits at once (that is, the data path has a limited width). Because main memory typically is accessed much more slowly than the internal clock speed of the processor, this limitation is finessed by introducing a series of additional buffers, or very fast *cache memory*, into the processor itself. Breaking main memory into a number of individual units accessed in parallel, or adding extra circuitry to read the much slower main memory into cache independently of the central processing unit are alternative solutions.

The net effect is to introduce considerable parallelism into the use of main memory, since quite a large amount of main memory can then be accessed in the same time required to access any single bit.[7] The degree of main memory parallelism depends upon a computer's architecture. To estimate improvements in computer performance, it is assumed that parallelism has increased roughly in proportion to memory size. Usable memory bandwidth is equal to some constant fraction of total main memory per CPU times bandwidth per memory element:

(A-3)   *main memory bandwidth/CPU* $\propto$

$$amount\ of\ memory/CPU \cdot \frac{1}{access\ time}.$$

7. For an extensive discussion of main memory organization see Kuck, *Structure of Computers and Computations*, chap. 5.

Note that access time (seconds per bit) is the inverse of bandwidth.

For magnetic disk files (and secondary memory in general), it is tempting to use the data transfer rate per unit as a measure of bandwidth. The capacity (size) of the storage media installed on the disk drive, however, can take on an important dimension in determining the total effective bandwidth of the drive on certain types of data-intensive applications. If, for example, low-capacity disk packs must be changed frequently on a drive, or additional data transferred to or from the drive from slower magnetic tape, the effective bandwidth delivered by a drive can be much less than the theoretical rate.

Therefore, two bounds on effective bandwidth are proposed: the data rate per drive unit and the product of data rate per unit and data capacity per unit. The latter, more optimistic measure assumes that the effective data rate in certain data-intensive applications depends on disk capacity as well as on raw data transfer rates. Disk capacities on drives have increased considerably faster than transfer rates over time. In short,

(A-4)   *disk memory bandwith/CPU* $\propto$
number disk drives/CPU • data rate per drive • (capacity per drive)$^\delta$

will be measured. The range $0 \leq \delta \leq 1$ is used to mark possible bounds for effective bandwidth. The restriction that $\delta \leq 1$ reflects an assumption that the marginal payoff from greater capacity, in terms of effective bandwidth, eventually declines.

Exactly the same principles are applied to measuring the effective bandwidth of tape drives, with

(A-5)   *tape drive bandwidth/CPU* $\propto$
number tape drives/CPU • data rate per drive • (tape capacity per drive)$^\delta$.

As before, $0 \leq \delta \leq 1$ marks the upper and lower bounds of effective bandwidth.

For input and output peripherals the measurement of bandwidth is straightforward. On line printers and card readers and punches, the characters processed per minute times total number of units is an adequate measure of information processing capacity.

Assume cost minimizing behavior on the part of those who configure computer systems and standard assumptions about function f. A unit cost function c, which gives the unit cost of information processing capacity (system bandwidth) in terms of the prices of a unit of capacity of the various system components, may be derived from A-2 and can be expressed as

(A-6) $P_{IP} = c(P_p, P_m, P_d, P_t, P_l, P_c).$

Function c will be approximated by the generalized Leontieff functional form, which is exactly measured by the Fisher "ideal" price index,[8]

$$(A\text{-}7) \qquad \frac{c^1}{c^0} = \frac{\sqrt{\sum_j (p_j^0 q_j^0 / \sum_k p_k^0 q_k^0)(p_j^1 / p_j^0)}}{\sqrt{\sum_j (p_j^1 q_j^1 / \sum_k p_k^1 q_k^1)(p_j^0 / p_j^1)}}$$

with superscripts 1 and 0 referring to time periods, subscripts j and k indexing inputs, and p and q referring to prices and quantities.

The most important data required to calculate this index of information processing capacity cost are the cost of bandwidth for each of the major categories of system components.

Processor capacity can be measured by millions of operations per second (MOPS), millions of instructions per second (MIPS), or millions of floating-point operations per second (megaflops). Megaflops are customarily used to measure high-performance computers for scientific and engineering work requiring large amounts of precise numerical mathematics. Operations other than floating-point arithmetic are regarded as "overhead" for the computational work.[9]

Because such execution rates vary dramatically according to the mix of instructions and tasks in the program, the performance statistics quoted by manufacturers are probably close to the theoretical peak

8. The generalized Leontieff functional form may be regarded as a second-order approximation to an arbitrary function, and the price index a so-called "superlative" index of the cost of system bandwidth. See W. E. Diewert, "Exact and Superlative Index Numbers," *Journal of Econometrics,* vol. 4 (1976), pp. 115–45; W. E. Diewert, "Superlative Index Numbers and Consistency in Aggregation," *Econometrica,* vol. 46 (July 1978); and Lawrence J. Lau, "On Exact Index Numbers," *Review of Economics and Statistics,* vol. 61 (February 1979), pp. 73–82.

9. Some argue that MOPS are preferable to MIPS since instruction sets vary widely from machine to machine, and even on a single machine instruction lengths and operand size can show enormous variation. Because operations are defined at a higher and more standardized level of conceptualization than machine instructions, MOPS might be the better measure. See Kuck, *Structure of Computers and Computations,* p. 158; and Stone and others, "Hardware Systems," p. 405.

speed at which the simplest operation can be performed, assuming near optimal conditions. Nonetheless, quoted execution rates remain the best available measure of performance over a wide range of machines and an extended period of time.

Analogous measurements for the bandwidth of other components in a computer system would include characters accessed for retrieval or storage per second for memory devices, and characters that can be read or written per second for input and output devices.

To construct such a measure for internal memory, multiply the amount of available memory by the inverse of the average access time for a character held in memory (that is, characters per second equals the inverse of seconds per character). As mentioned earlier, this measure of bandwidth assumes parallelism in memory organization has increased in rough proportion to memory size.

For moving-head files and tape drives the rate at which characters can be sent to the processor is multiplied by the data storage capacity of the device as an upper bound on effective bandwidth by one in the more conservative measure. On moving-head disk drives the data rate is taken as the inverse of the average access time for the device.[10] On tape drives the maximum data transfer rate is used. Unit cost for a drive (including the cost of both the controllers and the drives attached to them) is divided by one of these alternative measures of bandwidth to get the cost of bandwidth. A mean cost series is also constructed for disk and tape memory, as the geometric mean of the high and low bounds for the cost of bandwidth in these devices.

For line printers and card readers and punches, the rate at which characters can be written or read is used to measure bandwidth. Average cost for one of these machines is again divided by bandwidth to get the price of bandwidth.

Table A-1 presents average market prices per unit of installed U.S.

10. The actual rate at which data is transferred between the processor and a moving-head magnetic storage device reflects three factors: the average seek time (movement of read and write heads), the rotational latency (time to rotate the magnetic media into position at the beginning of the desired data), and the rate at which data can be transferred once the heads are in the correct position on the media (the data rate). See Phister, *Data Processing Technology*, p. 546. If a very large, physically contiguous block of data is read, the average transfer rate is approximated by the data rate. This should be interpreted as a maximum rate. In this appendix the inverse of Phister's calculation of average access (seek plus latency) time, which would be appropriate for the transfer of a very small block of data, is used.

Table A-1. *Average Price of Computer System Components,*
1955–78[a]
Thousands of dollars unless otherwise indicated

Year	Central processing unit	Main memory byte (dollars)	Magnetic tape unit[b]	Moving-head file unit[b]	Line printer unit[c]	Card punch unit
1955	612.50	4.00	...	...	105	40
1956	295.71	4.20	25.00	...	108	40
1957	234.13	4.55	25.71	50.00	110	40
1958	199.52	4.76	26.67	50.00	113	40
1959	176.53	4.98	25.86	50.00	114	40
1960	143.18	5.19	29.03	50.38	112	38
1961	145.37	5.27	30.61	51.92	98	36
1962	170.00	4.89	31.92	52.86	76	33
1963	125.81	5.17	32.24	54.83	61	31
1964	88.08	5.43	32.72	55.41	60	30
1965	88.47	4.98	32.82	53.91	59	30
1966	69.78	3.61	32.68	49.63	57	30
1967	105.68	2.48	32.25	42.41	55	30
1968	120.84	1.95	32.42	38.02	51	30
1969	157.68	1.73	32.64	36.04	46	30
1970	168.83	1.57	32.55	34.49	43	30
1971	164.98	1.31	31.69	34.11	45	29
1972	137.59	1.06	29.58	34.59	48	28
1973	129.57	0.83	27.38	34.50	51	26
1974	152.65	0.67	25.44	34.08	55	24
1975	200.81	0.58	24.57	31.86	58	23
1976	259.03	0.52	25.43	31.83	60	22
1977	339.57	0.39	26.53	30.87	62	22
1978	410.18	0.29	27.45	30.45	63	22

Source: Montgomery Phister, Jr., *Data Processing Technology and Economics,* 2d ed. (Bedford, Mass.: Digital Press, and Santa Monica Publishing Company, 1979), pp. 251, 257, 259, 261, 266, 600–05, 607.
a. Prices apply only to general purpose computers, a constantly changing, rough category that excludes minicomputers and other small systems.
b. Price includes associated controllers.
c. Price is the average for one system, consisting of a line printer and its associated controller.

capacity for six computer components.[11] Table A-2 presents measures of performance for these components. Costs will be converted to a dollar per characters (or bits) per second basis, which defines the average cost of bandwidth. The first column estimates the total installed processor bandwidth for the U.S. general purpose computer stock, measured in

11. Estimates of the value of the stock of all computer subsystems except central processor units are usually an estimate of current market value, using prices based on current rental values or purchase prices. Central processor value is calculated as a residual by deducting the value of the stock of all other subsystems from the "installed value" of all computer systems. The installed value of computer systems estimates are largely based on annual computer censuses published by the magazines *Computers and Automation* and *EDP Industry Report* and continued by the International Data Corpo-

Table A-2. Measures of Component Performance, 1955–78[a]

| Year | Central processing unit (CPU)[b] | | Internal memory[c] (access time (milliseconds per byte)) | Moving-head files[d] | | Magnetic tape units[e] | | Line printers (lines per minute)[f] | Card readers and punches (characters per second)[g] |
	Total installed MOPS	KOPS per CPU		Access time (milliseconds)	Capacity (megabytes per unit)	Maximum data rate (bits per second)	Capacity (millibytes per unit)		
1955	0.12	0.50	17.00	500.00	…	15.00	…	195.00	0.33
1956	0.45	0.64	15.90	426.40	…	28.34	5.00	208.00	0.53
1957	0.88	0.70	14.80	352.80	6.67	41.67	4.29	221.00	0.73
1958	1.79	0.85	13.70	279.20	6.25	52.09	5.33	234.00	0.93
1959	3.31	1.06	12.60	205.60	6.11	62.50	5.17	247.00	1.13
1960	7.48	1.70	11.50	132.00	6.15	116.25	8.71	260.00	1.33
1961	14.80	2.41	9.60	123.10	6.92	170.00	10.70	352.00	1.36
1962	25.10	3.10	7.70	114.20	8.29	172.50	11.86	444.00	1.38
1963	47.40	4.05	5.80	105.30	9.14	175.00	12.40	536.00	1.40
1964	108.60	6.50	3.90	96.40	9.59	177.50	12.72	628.00	1.42
1965	213.00	9.86	2.00	87.50	9.60	180.00	13.26	720.00	1.44
1966	542.00	20.00	1.75	77.66	9.07	226.67	14.39	699.33	1.47

1967	1023.00	33.00	1.51	67.82	11.44	273.33	15.58	678.67	1.49
1968	1698.00	45.89	1.26	57.98	15.18	320.00	16.50	658.00	1.51
1969	2000.00	50.00	1.02	48.14	18.44	475.00	17.00	637.34	1.53
1970	2194.00	52.36	0.77	38.30	21.33	630.00	17.47	616.67	1.56
1971	3200.00	71.11	0.78	37.66	25.31	785.00	18.45	722.48	1.58
1972	4657.00	92.77	0.78	37.02	33.42	940.00	18.58	828.28	1.60
1973	5600.00	96.05	0.79	36.38	43.23	1095.00	19.59	934.09	1.60
1974	6925.00	112.60	0.79	35.74	59.25	1250.00	20.63	1039.89	1.60
1975	8500.00	136.88	0.80	35.10	71.51	1250.00	21.67	1145.70	1.60
1976	10258.00	172.11	0.60	34.20	90.80	1250.00	23.67	1251.50	1.60
1977	13000.00	223.37	0.41	33.30	107.30	1250.00	25.71	1357.31	1.60
1978	26064.00	449.69	0.41	31.70	132.24	1250.00	27.70	1463.11	1.60

Source: Phister, *Data Processing Technology*, pp. 257, 259–60, 262, 335, 339, 367, 372, 377, 384–85, 602–04, 629, 631, 640.

a. For technologies used in internal memory, mass memory, and card punches, this table takes data for models selected as representative technologies in a given year and estimates other years by linear interpolation.

b. Millions of operations per second (MOPS) capacity of installed stock of general purpose computers; thousands of operations per second (KOPS).

c. IBM models 705 (1955); 1401 (1960); 360/30 (1965); 370/135 (1970); IC memory in 370/125 (1975); 370/148 (1977).

d. IBM 350-3 (1955); 1301-1 (1960); 2314-1 (1965); 3330-1 (1970); 3340-B2 (1975); 3350 (1977); 3370 (1979).

e. Maximum tape speed measured in 1,000 characters per second. IBM 727 (1955); 729-2 (1957); 729-4 (1959); 7340-1 (1961); 2401-6 (1965); 2420-7 (1968); 3420-8 (1974).

f. In 1955, 1960, 1965, 1970, and 1976, Phister's estimates of distribution by speed were used to estimate an average speed; linear interpolation was used for intervening years.

g. IBM 711-2 (1955); 1402-N1 (1960); 3505-B2 (1972).

Table A-3. *Price (Adjusted for Performance) per Unit Bandwidth, System Components, 1957–78*[a]
Current dollars; 1972 = 1.00

Year	Central processing unit	Internal memory	Moving-head files			Magnetic tape units			Line printers	Card readers and punches
			Upper bound	Lower bound	Geometric mean	Upper bound	Lower bound	Geometric mean		
1957	225.51	94.77	94.59	18.87	42.25	158.28	36.51	76.02	8.59	6.67
1958	158.27	92.73	86.05	16.09	37.21	69.83	20.04	37.41	8.33	4.17
1959	111.83	90.93	72.81	13.32	31.14	47.48	13.22	25.05	7.96	3.03
1960	56.79	87.11	57.66	10.62	24.75	25.32	11.87	17.34	7.43	2.26
1961	40.73	81.36	38.90	8.06	17.70	18.11	10.43	13.75	4.80	1.77
1962	36.99	68.90	21.24	5.27	10.58	9.16	5.85	7.32	2.95	1.38
1963	20.94	60.81	18.63	5.09	9.74	6.05	4.04	4.94	1.96	1.27
1964	9.13	51.23	16.64	4.78	8.92	5.90	4.04	4.88	1.65	1.21
1965	6.05	35.39	14.91	4.29	7.99	5.60	3.99	4.73	1.41	1.19
1966	2.35	17.25	13.31	3.61	6.93	5.06	3.92	4.46	1.41	1.17
1967	2.16	6.08	8.18	2.80	4.79	4.55	3.82	4.17	1.40	1.15
1968	1.78	4.19	4.91	2.23	3.31	3.43	3.05	3.23	1.34	1.14
1969	2.13	3.20	3.34	1.85	2.48	2.78	2.54	2.66	1.25	1.12
1970	2.17	2.43	2.36	1.51	1.89	2.30	2.17	2.23	1.20	1.10
1971	1.56	1.63	1.64	1.24	1.42	1.43	1.42	1.43	1.07	1.05
1972	1.00	1.00	1.00	1.00	1.00	1.00	1.00	1.00	1.00	1.00
1973	0.91	0.79	0.76	0.98	0.86	0.70	0.74	0.72	0.94	0.92
1974	0.91	0.64	0.54	0.95	0.72	0.52	0.58	0.55	0.91	0.83
1975	0.99	0.56	0.41	0.87	0.60	0.41	0.48	0.44	0.87	0.80
1976	1.01	0.50	0.32	0.86	0.52	0.34	0.43	0.38	0.83	0.76
1977	1.03	0.38	0.25	0.82	0.46	0.33	0.45	0.38	0.79	0.76
1978	0.62	0.21	0.20	0.79	0.40	0.31	0.47	0.38	0.74	0.76

Source: Phister, *Data Processing Technology*, pp. 251, 256–62, 266, 335, 339, 367, 377, 384–85, 594, 600, 602–05, 607, 629, 631, 640.
a. A two-year lag on speed measures was used to reflect vintage effects in population for other than CPUs and printers. In all cases current-year average capacity numbers were used, since they are built up from disaggregated populations of component types.

MOPS. Unlike processors, where the total installed bandwidth (MOPS) was computed by Phister from disaggregated estimates of the stock of individual computer models and their respective processor speeds, and printers, where an estimate of average speed for the installed base was used, the performance indexes refer to representative technologies in their year of introduction. Because the stock of installed systems reflects older vintage technologies as well as the latest products, a two-year lag on the performance measures for speed is used in table A-3 as an alternative to the current speed of recently introduced products. The average unit storage capacity estimates refer to the current year, since they are built up from the underlying component population.

The results of these calculations appear in table A-3. The value of the stock of central processors is produced by subtracting the value of all peripheral equipment from the market value of all U.S. general purpose computer systems and then from this remainder subtracting the replacement cost of internal memory. (This assumes that computers are supplied under competitive conditions, that is, the cost of the system is the sum of the costs of its components.) The estimate of the value of the processor stock is divided by the estimate of total capacity in table A-2, and an average price per unit of processor bandwidth is then reported in the first column of table A-3.

As table A-4 shows, the six major components have historically accounted for almost the entire value of a computer system, and most of the major changes in the cost of the hardware are presumably accounted for by simple indices using this abbreviated list of components. Note the rather dramatic swings in the percentage of a system's value accounted for by these subsystems.

---

ration (founded by someone who had worked on the earlier censuses for the magazines). The installed-value figures price obsolete machines at the value at which they sold when still in production, and hence probably somewhat overestimate their true market value. However, because the computer stock was increasing rapidly over the entire 1957–78 period, and computer life was quite short, the value of very old computers was small relative to the value of the entire stock, and the net overestimation was probably relatively small.

Since all other system components use an independently estimated market value, and central processor value is calculated as a residual, the residual value of central processor units will exceed a true market value. The central processor installed value estimate also has a higher margin of error, since the sum of errors in all other estimates is subtracted from the error in the estimate of the installed value of computer systems. See Phister, *Data Processing Technology*, pp. 10, 246–52, for further methodological description of installed computer systems value.

Table A-4. *Value of Major Components as Share of Computer System Cost, 1955–78*

Year	Central processing unit	Internal memory	Moving-head files	Magnetic tape units	Punch card equipment	Line printers	Major as percent of all components
1955	0.83	0.07	0.00	0.01	0.03	0.07	98.33
1956	0.66	0.13	0.00	0.02	0.05	0.14	97.81
1957	0.56	0.16	0.03	0.03	0.06	0.16	96.85
1958	0.48	0.18	0.05	0.05	0.06	0.18	96.33
1959	0.42	0.20	0.07	0.06	0.07	0.19	97.46
1960	0.34	0.22	0.07	0.10	0.07	0.20	98.07
1961	0.35	0.21	0.05	0.14	0.07	0.18	98.58
1962	0.40	0.18	0.05	0.16	0.06	0.14	99.00
1963	0.33	0.23	0.07	0.18	0.07	0.13	99.30
1964	0.25	0.24	0.09	0.20	0.07	0.14	99.37
1965	0.25	0.23	0.10	0.21	0.07	0.14	99.51
1966	0.20	0.22	0.13	0.22	0.07	0.15	99.43
1967	0.27	0.22	0.12	0.19	0.07	0.13	99.28
1968	0.29	0.24	0.12	0.18	0.06	0.12	98.85
1969	0.34	0.22	0.13	0.16	0.06	0.10	98.21
1970	0.34	0.23	0.15	0.15	0.05	0.09	97.67
1971	0.33	0.23	0.16	0.14	0.05	0.10	97.47
1972	0.29	0.24	0.17	0.14	0.05	0.11	97.18
1973	0.29	0.22	0.20	0.12	0.05	0.13	97.08
1974	0.32	0.20	0.19	0.11	0.04	0.14	97.21
1975	0.38	0.18	0.18	0.10	0.03	0.13	97.35
1976	0.42	0.18	0.17	0.08	0.03	0.12	97.53
1977	0.47	0.16	0.16	0.08	0.02	0.11	97.75
1978	0.50	0.15	0.16	0.08	0.02	0.09	97.94

Source: Phister, *Data Processing Techniques,* pp. 251, 257, 259, 261, 266, 600, 602, 604–05, 607.

To calculate the cost of computing capacity, a price for a "box" (processor and main memory) was calculated first so that the results would be comparable to other hedonic studies of computer boxes. The index is tabulated in table A-5.[12] Also presented in this table are the more general indexes of computing capacity unit cost. The high, low, and mean estimates reflect differing assumptions about the cost of bandwidth for disk and tape storage devices.

These results provide a valuable check on existing hedonic studies, which vary considerably in their assessment of the rate of quality-

12. This index also was calculated without the two-year lag on measures of component speed. Using current, best-practice component speed little affects the general pattern of prices over time, although fluctuations around the original index do occur from year to year.

Table A-5. *Fisher ''Ideal'' Price Indexes for Computer Systems, 1957–78*
Current dollars; 1972 = 1.00

| | "Box" only[a] | | Complete systems[b] | | | | | | | |
| | | | Upper bound | | Lower bound | | Geometric mean of upper and lower bounds | | Index using geometric mean for components | |
Year	Index	Percent change	Index	Percent change	Index	Percent change	Index	Percent change	Index	Percent change
1957	190.37	. . .	79.09	. . .	53.97	. . .	65.33	. . .	64.21	. . .
1958	144.91	−23.88	61.01	−22.86	41.93	−22.30	50.58	−22.58	49.65	−22.30
1959	112.61	−22.29	48.94	−19.78	33.54	−20.01	40.52	−19.89	39.77	−20.01
1960	71.85	−36.19	33.92	−30.69	24.29	−27.60	28.70	−29.16	28.21	−27.60
1961	57.04	−20.61	25.28	−25.48	18.64	−23.23	21.71	−24.37	21.36	−23.23
1962	50.57	−11.35	18.78	−25.72	14.25	−23.56	16.36	−24.65	16.04	−23.56
1963	33.59	−33.58	13.16	−29.91	10.17	−28.65	11.57	−29.28	11.14	−28.65
1964	19.74	−41.23	9.50	−27.82	7.41	−27.08	8.39	−27.45	8.12	−27.08
1965	13.34	−32.39	7.50	−21.08	5.89	−20.60	6.64	−20.84	6.46	−20.60
1966	5.81	−56.46	4.97	−33.71	3.91	−33.61	4.41	−33.66	4.31	−33.61
1967	3.34	−42.59	3.45	−30.64	2.85	−27.13	3.13	−28.91	3.11	−27.13
1968	2.53	−24.08	2.64	−23.49	2.30	−19.40	2.46	−21.47	2.45	−19.40
1969	2.51	−1.05	2.38	−9.76	2.14	−6.63	2.26	−8.21	2.26	−6.63
1970	2.28	−9.19	2.07	−12.82	1.92	−10.52	1.99	−11.68	1.99	−10.52
1971	1.59	−30.02	1.48	−28.66	1.42	−26.18	1.45	−27.43	1.45	−26.18
1972	1.00	−37.21	1.00	−32.44	1.00	−29.37	1.00	−30.92	1.00	−29.37
1973	0.85	−14.66	0.83	−17.43	0.87	−13.14	0.85	−15.31	0.85	−13.14
1974	0.79	−7.87	0.71	−14.12	0.79	−8.91	0.75	−11.56	0.75	−8.91
1975	0.79	0.26	0.65	−7.70	0.76	−4.41	0.70	−6.07	0.71	−4.41
1976	0.78	−1.44	0.61	−7.33	0.73	−3.14	0.67	−5.26	0.67	−3.14
1977	0.73	−6.63	0.56	−7.63	0.70	−4.69	0.63	−6.17	0.63	−4.69
1978	0.43	−40.99	0.39	−31.22	0.50	−28.91	0.44	−30.07	0.44	−28.91

Source: Phister, *Data Processing Technology*, pp. 251, 256–62, 266, 335, 339, 367, 377, 384–85, 594, 600, 602, 604–05, 607, 629, 631, 640.
a. Central processing unit and memory.
b. Central processing unit, memory, disk, magnetic tape, printer, and card reader.

Table A-6. *Unweighted Average Rates of Change,*
Real Computer Price, 1958–85

Years	Computer "box"[a]				Computer system	
	IBM-BEA	Chow	Knight[b]	Flamm	IBM-BEA	Flamm
1958–65	n.a.	− 22.5	− 27.5	− 29.0	n.a.	− 26.2
1966–72	n.a.	n.a.	− 28.0	− 32.0	n.a.	− 26.7
1973–78	− 22.8	n.a.	− 16.6	− 18.2	− 19.6	− 18.6
1979–85	− 22.0	n.a.	n.a.	n.a.	− 19.6	n.a.

Sources: Author's calculations. Computer price series are taken as follows. IBM-BEA: Rosanne Cole and others, "Quality-Adjusted Price Indexes for Computer Processors and Selected Peripheral Equipment," *Survey of Current Business,* vol. 66 (January 1986), p. 49; David W. Cartwright, "Improved Deflation of Purchases of Computers," *Survey of Current Business,* vol. 66 (March 1986), p. 8; and unpublished data from U.S. Department of Commerce, Bureau of Economic Analysis. Chow: Gregory C. Chow, "Technological Change and the Demand for Computers," *American Economic Review,* vol. 57 (December 1967), p. 1124. Knight: Kenneth E. Knight, various sources, as reported in A. J. Alexander and B. M. Mitchell, "Measuring Technological Change of Heterogeneous Products," *Technological Forecasting and Social Change,* vol. 27 (1985), p. 191. Flamm: appendix A. To produce a real price series, computer prices have been divided by the GNP implicit price deflator from *Economic Report of the President,* January 1987, p. 248.

n.a. Not available.

a. Central processing unit and memory.

b. Where Knight gives price indexes for the end points of a two-year interval, a constant annual rate of change has been assumed. Although the Knight index of price-performance uses a price for a "box," the performance measure is calculated as a function of arguments that include the characteristics of other system components.

adjusted price decline in any given year and are sometimes based on a rather ad hoc collection of characteristics.[13] As table A-6 shows, the rates of change in the preceding tables are roughly in line with the magnitudes calculated by others.

---

13. The studies referred to are discussed in Jack E. Triplett, "Price and Technological Change in a Capital Good: A Survey of Research on Computers" (U.S. Department of Commerce, Bureau of Economic Analysis, 1986). Perhaps the best example of an improper choice of characteristic is Stoneman's use of size as a measure of processor power. Clearly, as sizes shrank with the advent of semiconductor technology in the late 1960s, statistical methods using size as a proxy for performance would behave poorly in modeling computer price. This, perhaps, explains Stoneman's uniquely low estimates of the rate of technological advance in computers. See Paul Stoneman, *Technological Diffusion and the Computer Revolution: The UK Experience* (Cambridge: Cambridge University Press, 1976).

Social and Private Rates of Return on Investment in Computer Technology

EQUATION 2-2, the starting point for calculations in this appendix, gives the annual increase in consumers' surplus attributable to one year's technological advance in computer hardware. When considering the benefit from any single year's round of innovation, however, it is important to remember that the benefit recurs every year after the innovation is made. Information processing (IP) costs continue to be cheaper year after year even if no further innovation occurs. To value these future benefits, they must be discounted to the present, using whatever the appropriate social discount rate happens to be.

Figure 2-7 assumes that the demand curve for IP capacity used in producing final goods and services is fixed. If total income is increasing, demand (see equation 2-1) will also be increasing as the output of goods and services grows. In addition, benefits will increase since the total input of computing services, cheaper in perpetuity as a result of one year's innovation, increases with output growth. Thus the demand curve in figure 2-2 ought to be interpreted as computing demand per unit of output, function i in equation 2-1. To estimate the benefits of innovation to consumers (CS), the benefit associated with one unit of output of goods and services should be multiplied by total output every year.

If income grows at rate g, and the discount rate is r, then the discounted benefit to consumers associated with one year's innovation, per dollar of computing demand at the pre-innovation cost of computing, C_O, can be expressed

$$\frac{CS}{C_O \cdot IP} = \sum_{j=1}^{\infty} \left(\frac{1 + g}{1 + r}\right)^j \cdot F(C_O, C_N)$$

(B-1)

$$= \left(\frac{1 + g}{r - g}\right) \cdot F(C_O, C_N).$$

In this equation F is the consumers' surplus as a fraction of the value of base IP consumption (see equation 2-2). Equation B-1 assumes an R&D expenditure in year zero results in a permanent cost decline in year one and every following year.

To calculate an average social rate of return on investments in computer technology, add up the social costs of R&D investments in computers (RD), deduct them from the social benefit given in equation B-1, and express this net benefit as a fraction of R&D costs: $(CS - RD)/RD$.

Choice of a particular discount rate will have a major effect on the outcome of these calculations. A discount rate r that sets the social rate of return to zero could be chosen. This internal rate of return can then be compared with a particular social discount rate. If it exceeds this discount rate, the research project will be judged worthwhile.

The internal rate of return is therefore a measure of the "break-even" discount rate at which a particular investment ceases to be attractive. It has the virtue of being independent of highly debatable judgments about the appropriate social discount rate and can be directly compared with the internal rate of return associated with alternative investments.[1]

To calculate any rate of return, some notion of the costs of computer research and development is needed. The American computer industry currently spends well under 10 percent of its global revenues on research and development (about 7 percent, in fact, in 1982).[2] If all IP capacity was leased to users, computer company revenues from rentals would equal the rental value of the stock of IP capacity. In recent years,

1. There are some difficulties in using internal rates of return to compare mutually exclusive investment projects (that is, where undertaking one project precludes another). But investing in computers presumably does not preclude alternative investments.

2. Foreign markets accounted for a sizable 40 percent of worldwide revenues in 1982, but only about 10 percent of worldwide R&D expenditure that year was in overseas projects. In 1982 global R&D expenditures by U.S. parent firms with majority-owned foreign affiliates represented 6.4 percent of sales, 7.2 percent including R&D performed by the foreign affiliates and 8.5 percent including federally funded research and development. See U.S. Department of Commerce, Bureau of Economic Analysis, *U.S. Direct Investment Abroad: 1982 Benchmark Survey Data* (Government Printing Office, 1985), tables III.H5, III.Q1, and table 1-4 in this book.

however, the balance has shifted toward outright sales to customers. Since sales of new hardware have been considerably smaller than the rental value of the stock of existing hardware, industrial R&D expenditure as a fraction of the rental value of IP capacity is certainly less than its fractional share of sales.[3] Using 8 percent of base-year IP sales worldwide as an estimate of industrial R&D expenditure associated with one year's technological advance probably greatly exceeds the correct figure and lends a marked downward bias to estimates of the rate of return.

Because foreign sales range from 40 to 50 percent of U.S. domestic sales, and because welfare calculations are calibrated using total, base-period domestic consumption of computing capacity as a numeraire, an estimate of industrial research and development expenditure as a fraction of IP consumption is needed. If about 8 percent of global sales is accounted for by research, this adds up to a considerably higher percentage of domestic sales. Assuming 80 cents of foreign income for every dollar of domestic revenue (that is, 44 percent of all revenues coming from abroad), industrial research and development expenses would have accounted for 14.3 percent of domestic revenues when equal to 8 percent of global income. A 15 percent figure will be used in order to err on the conservative side.

To compute a social rate of return, public funds invested in industrial research, as well as nonindustrial research, must be added to the private investment in computer R&D. When U.S. government-funded industrial R&D in the computer industry is added to company funds, under 8.5 percent of the worldwide sales of American computer firms were accounted for in 1982.[4] If all public funding accounts for about one-fifth of relevant research and development (as is shown in chapter 4), 8 percent for private R&D implies as much as 10 percent of worldwide sales may be accounted for by public and private R&D. In the interests of conservatism, a 12 percent figure will be used. Adjusting for foreign sales as described earlier, this would make the United States' total investment in the technology less than 22 percent of its base-year IP consumption. A conservative 25 percent will be used.

Advances in the price and performance of computers have largely been derived from advances in semiconductors. Much of the research

3. See chapter 2, note 22.
4. Department of Commerce, *U.S. Direct Investment Abroad*, tables III.H5, III.Q1, and table 1-4 in this book.

Table B-1. *Internal Social Rate of Return on Investment in Computer Technology*
Percent

Income growth rate	Cost decline	Return with elasticity of demand	
		1.5	1.0
0	30	147	138
0	20	92	88
4	30	157	148
4	20	100	96

a. The internal rate of return was calculated iteratively on a Supercalc 4 spreadsheet using the "regula falsi" algorithm, and assumes R&D in year zero leads to cost decline in year one and zero private rent on technology. (Foreign sales then produce no rental income and are irrelevant to social return.)

by computer companies has been on semiconductors, and this portion of R&D investment is accounted for in these calculations.

Furthermore, the estimates of the costs of research and development are clearly excessive. Using actual 1982 values, the correct figures would have been a 13 percent share of U.S. sales (and a still lower portion of rental income) invested in private R&D; a 17 percent share with government-funded expenditure added. The actual figures used were 15 and 25 percent, respectively.

Table B-1 shows the internal rate of return on investment in computer technology calculated in this manner. Two different growth rates, cost declines, and elasticities of demand have been used.

The social return is very high. An internal rate of return on this investment, with reasonable assumptions about demand and price-performance improvements, is between 90 and 150 percent in a no-growth economy, another 8 to 10 percent higher with brisk 4 percent growth. These results are fairly insensitive to choice of demand elasticity.[5] The magnitude of the cost decline is what is causing these extraordinarily high returns.

A More Realistic View

The very simple calculations made thus far ought to be regarded as upper bounds. Actual returns, both private and social, are likely to be considerably lower for two reasons.

5. Using the ultraconservative demand elasticity of 0.5 lowers the benefit calculations very slightly because the bulk of the benefit comes from reduced cost for the existing demand for information processing capacity.

First, to make private investments in research and development worthwhile, producers must be able to charge, at least for some period of time, a price that exceeds the new production cost for computing capacity. Although they are not pocketed by consumers, these rents must be added to the increase in consumer's surplus when calculating social return.

Second, critical lags delay the fruits of R&D investments. A *gestation lag* occurs before R&D investments can be translated into commercial products. Moreover, because of the ease with which competitors can generally imitate important computer innovations, there is only a short window of time during which the innovator can claim a rent from exclusive use of the innovation. After a *diffusion lag,* imitators can copy the innovation at low or no cost.[6]

The gestation lag essentially postpones the reaping of the benefits of innovation and reduces the discounted value of both social and private returns. The diffusion lag limits the time period in which a private firm can collect some return on investments in innovation, and it reduces private return as it grows shorter. Because a firm must charge a price exceeding its new production cost for IP capacity to recoup some return on its R&D investments, the benefit to consumers will fall short of that shown in figure 2-7. Even adding the resulting rents received by producers will not make up the difference. A higher price means that use of IP will not "widen" as much as if the full cost decline were passed on to consumers immediately, and the potential social benefit will not be entirely realized.

Figure B-1 illustrates the innovation implicit in this description. No benefit at all, private or social, is reaped until m years, corresponding to the gestation lag, have passed. Then, for the next n years, corresponding to the diffusion lag, only the innovating firm has access to the innovation. To recoup some return on R&D investments, a price greater than C_N must be charged. This price, P, retains for the innovator some fraction, s, of the resulting cost decline:

(B-2) $$P = C_N + s \cdot (C_O - C_N).$$

6. In real life, of course, there is no pulse of R&D investment resulting in innovation after some fixed gestation lag. Neither are innovations instantaneously adopted by "follower" firms after some fixed diffusion lag. Real R&D projects are associated with a time profile of investment (perhaps bell shaped) and a time profile of technological rents (also perhaps bell shaped). The discrete, gestation and diffusion lag approach used here essentially collapses those two distributions of costs and return over time into mean lag values. Although not entirely realistic, this approach captures the economics of the situation in a simple and useful way.

Figure B-1. *Benefits from Advances in Computer Technology*[a]

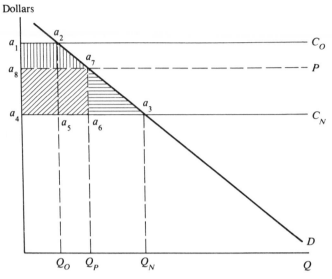

Dollars

D = demand; Q = quantity; P = price.
a. The capture rate equals $(a_8 - a_4)/(a_1 - a_4)$.

Parameter s is the "capture rate" or portion of cost improvement received by the innovating firm as rent during its temporary period of technological advantage. The rate will depend on the nature of competition in the industry. If the innovating firm had a monopoly on innovation, profit maximization would dictate that it set s equal to one.[7] If the innovation were immediately available to a large number of competing firms, s would equal zero, and no rent would be earned to recoup the costs of the necessary investment in R&D; such an investment could not be sustained in the long run.

The price charged to computer users will drop from C_O to level P after a gestation lag of m years has passed. Consumers will then reap a benefit equivalent to the standard benefit associated with a decline in price to level P, equal to trapezoid $a_1a_2a_7a_8$. Producers will receive rents equal to rectangle $a_8a_7a_6a_4$, and this "producer's surplus" must be added to the consumers' benefits in calculating the social benefits of the technological advance.[8] Triangle $a_3a_6a_7$ is the so-called "dead-weight loss,"

7. This assumes that the innovation is not a "major" one in the sense that the marginal revenue associated with demand curve D is less than C_N at the level of consumption corresponding to the old, "base" technology, Q_O.
8. This framework is an extension of the methods used by Zvi Griliches in 1958. See Edwin Mansfield and others, "Social and Private Rates of Return from Industrial Innovations," *Quarterly Journal of Economics*, vol. 91 (May 1977), pp. 221–40.

the potential benefit to consumers from lower prices in excess of the rents that would be forgone by producers.[9]

Finally, after another n years have passed, corresponding to the diffusion lag, the technology is assumed to spread to the public domain for costless use by all. The price charged to consumers of IP services then falls to C_N, and an augmented social benefit, equal to trapezoid $a_1a_2a_3a_4$, is received in perpetuity. Private rents drop to zero at this point.

In short, there are three basic phases during which the returns to innovation can be identified. First, an R&D investment is made in some base period. For the next m years, while this investment is gestating, no return is received either privately or socially. Second, after m years have passed a window of time opens during which a private firm investing in innovation can reap some rent on its new technology. Third, even after another n years have passed and the window has closed on private rents, a social return is received in perpetuity.

Foreign sales play a significant role in the income of U.S. computer firms. Assume that foreign income amounts to fraction f of domestic sales and that the technological rents earned on foreign sales during the window of profitability on technology investments are identical to those on U.S. sales.[10] Also assume that f is equal to 0.8 (that is, foreign markets account for roughly 44 percent of all sales and therefore of technological rents earned).

The gross private return as a fraction of original, base technology consumption of information processing per dollar of GNP, R_P, can be expressed

$$(\text{B-3}) \quad R_p = s \cdot \left(\frac{C_O - C_N}{C_O} \right) \cdot (1 + f) \cdot \frac{Q_P}{Q_O} \cdot \sum_{j=m+1}^{m+n} \cdot \left(\frac{1+g}{1+r} \right)^j,$$

where Q_P/Q_O is the ratio of consumption of IP per dollar of GNP at price

---

9. This can be expressed as follows:

$$F(C_O, C_N) > F(C_O, P) + \frac{(P - C_N)Q_P}{C_O Q_O}.$$

Profits on foreign sales would be added to the right-hand side; if large enough, they would alter the direction of inequality. Thus the net social impact of a price increase may be positive if foreign profits are sufficiently large to offset dead-weight loss at home.

10. The upper bound calculation of social return in table B-1 assumes that all returns are passed on to U.S. consumers in the form of price declines. Foreign sales are then irrelevant to social return since no technological rents are earned by firms.

P to the consumption of IP per dollar of GNP at the old cost. A first-order approximation, $1 + \left\{E \cdot (1 - s) \cdot [(C_O - C_N)/C_O]\right\}$, will be substituted for this ratio when the expression for R_P in B-3 is calculated.[11]

Social return (as a fraction of base-year IP consumption) during the window of profitability is equal to the private return, R_P (the producer's surplus), plus the consumers' surplus corresponding to a price decline to P, $F(C_O,P)$. (See equation 2-3 for a definition of F.) After the window has closed the social gain received into the indefinite future is $F(C_O,C_N)$. Thus the total social return can be expressed

$$(B\text{-}4) \qquad R_S = R_P + \left[F(C_O, P) \cdot \sum_{j=m+1}^{m+n} \left(\frac{1 + g}{1 + r}\right)^j \right]$$
$$+ \left[F(C_O,C_N) \cdot \sum_{j=m+n+1}^{\infty} \left(\frac{1 + g}{1 + r}\right)^j \right].$$

Market Structure and Return

Given this conception of the process of innovation, divergence between private and social returns depends on behavior during the window of profitability. The shorter it is, the lower the private returns in relation to the social returns. And the lower s, the fraction of the cost savings appropriated by the innovator as technological rent, the lower the technological returns received by innovators as a fraction of the potential social return—$F(C_O,C_N)$. After the diffusion lag the full potential consumer's surplus is realized into the indefinite future.

What portion of a cost reduction is passed on to consumers? And what fraction, s, is appropriated by an innovating firm during the window it has for technological rent collection? These are difficult questions. For the moment assume s to be a parameter reflecting market structure, varying between zero and one. Conditional on s, one can observe how

---

11. The elasticity of demand, E, can be defined as $(-dQ(P)/dP)(P/Q)$. The convention of defining E as a positive number is adopted here. The first-order approximation that yields this result is

$$Q_P = Q_O + (P - C_O) \cdot Q',$$

where Q' is the first derivative of IP demand Q_P with respect to price at price C_O. The virtue of this approximation is that it requires only knowledge of the elasticity of demand in addition to observed quantities.

private and social rates of return will vary with assumptions about gestation and diffusion lags.

In principle, total social returns must always exceed private returns (see equation B-4). However, because an internal rate of return is calculated after deducting R&D costs from the benefits (expressed in either equation B-3 or B-4), and because private R&D costs are considerably less than the total, it is possible for the private rate of return to exceed the social rate of return.

The effects of varying the parameters are fairly straightforward in the case of private return (equation B-3). Increasing the magnitude of technological advance (and the cost decline associated with it), foreign sales (f), the growth rate of the economy (g), and the diffusion lag or length of time over which technological monopoly is exercised (n) all increase private return. Increasing the gestation lag (m) decreases private return. A more elastic demand (greater E) increases return since at any price more of the good is sold after a technological advance has lowered cost. Normally, an increase in capture rate also increases private return.[12]

---

12. "Normal" conditions can be described as follows: Profits, π, are an increasing function of price ($\pi'(P) > 0$), for price in the range from C_O to C_N. To trace the impact of an increase in P (or s) on R_P, note that $R_P = \pi(P) K$, where $\pi(P) = (P - C_N) Q(P) = s(C_O - C_N) Q_P$ is profit (producer's surplus), the excess of total revenues over total cost exclusive of research and development) and

$$K = \frac{(1+f)}{C_O Q(C_O)} \sum_{j=m+1}^{m+n} \left(\frac{1+g}{1+r}\right)^j$$

is a positive constant that does not change as P (or s) is varied. Then

$$\frac{\partial R_P}{\partial s} = \frac{\partial R_P}{\partial P}\frac{\partial P}{\partial s} = \frac{\partial \pi}{\partial P} K \frac{\partial P}{\partial s} = \frac{\partial \pi}{\partial P} K (C_O - C_N)$$

will have the same sign as $\partial \pi / \partial P$.

The numerical simulation model used here employs a simple linear demand function as a first-order approximation to calculate R_P, that is,

$$Q_P = \left[1 + \left(\frac{C_O - P}{C_O}\right) E\right] Q_O,$$

which implies that

$$\pi = (P - C_N) Q_P = (P - C_N) Q_O \left[1 + \left(\frac{C_O - P}{C_O}\right) E\right]$$

and that

$$\frac{\partial \pi}{\partial P} = Q_O \left[1 + \left(1 + \frac{C_N}{C_O} - \frac{2P}{C_O}\right) E\right]$$

The situation is somewhat more complex when social return (equation B-4) is considered. The first term is private return. The second term is the benefit pocketed by consumers during the window of profitability. The third term is the gains to consumers after the window of profitability has closed and price declines to just cover cost of production. An increase in gestation lag will decrease all three; greater cost declines, demand elasticities, and economic growth will increase all three. But for other parameters, the effects on the second and third terms can offset increased private returns. A higher price (greater capture rate s) during the window of profitability increases profit but decreases the benefit received by U.S. consumers; the second term drops by more than the additional profit on U.S. sales added to the first term (because of dead-weight loss). With no foreign sales, the net effect on social return is negative. With foreign sales, however, additional foreign profits can offset the increase in dead-weight loss in the U.S. market and the net effect is ambiguous.

Similarly, an increase in the diffusion lag (n) extends the window of profitability and raises private return but at the cost of a shorter time period during which the full potential social benefit of innovations can be realized. With no foreign sales, a net dead-weight loss in the U.S. market reduces social return. Foreign profits, however, may offset the dead-weight loss.[13] The net effect is again ambiguous.

An increase in foreign sales affects social welfare only by raising private profits, and thus it has a uniformly positive effect on both social and private returns. Table B-2 summarizes these various effects.

Results

It is conservatively assumed that the more or less continuous technological progress in computers is the result of a private R&D investment

$$= Q_O \left\{ 1 + \left[\left(\frac{C_O - C_N}{C_O} \right) (1 - 2s) \right] E \right\}, \text{ using (B-2).}$$

For the range of parameter values considered here ($1 \le E \le 1.5$, $.2 \le (C_O - C_N)/C_O \le .3$, $0 < s < 1$), this will always be positive.

13. Increasing n by one period has a net impact on social return of

$$\left[(1 + f) \frac{(P - C_N)Q_P}{C_O Q_O} + F(C_O, P) - F(C_O, C_N) \right] \left(\frac{1 + g}{1 + r} \right)^{(m+n+1)}.$$

With no foreign sales, this is always negative because of dead-weight loss. With foreign sales, the net impact may be positive (see note 9).

Table B-2. *Impact of Key Parameters on Social and Private Return*

Parameters	Effects of an increase on	
	R_P (*equation B-3*)	R_S (*equation B-4*)
Capture rate (s)	+ [a]	− [b]
Cost-saving effect of innovation		
as fraction of pre-innovation cost [$(C_O - C_N)/C_O$]	+	+
Elasticity of demand for computers (E)	+	+
Foreign sales (f)	+	+
Growth rate for economy (g)	+	+
Gestation lag (m)	−	−
Diffusion lag (n)	+	− [b]

a. Positive under the normal conditions described in footnote 12.
b. Negative with no foreign sales; otherwise ambiguous and dependent on size of foreign markets.

of about 15 percent of the rental value of U.S. information processing capacity and a social investment of 25 percent of the value of computer use. Estimates of private and social rates of return can then be calculated (see table B-3). A demand elasticity of 1.5 and a real cost decline of 30 percent have been selected as the optimistic case, while a demand elasticity of 1.0 and a 20 percent real annual drop in computing cost have been used as a conservative lower bound on the benefits.

Recent studies indicate that the gestation lag between industrial R&D investment and the availability of new technology is quite short.[14] The pace of advance in computers and electronics has certainly been no slower than that for U.S. industry in general and, allowing for additional lags in product design and development, a two- to three-year lag seems conservative.

The diffusion lag also appears to be quite short. Competing firms often mimic successful innovation in computers within a year or two. For example, IBM announced its System 360 family of computers in the spring of 1964; by December RCA had announced its own family of machines compatible with the IBM hardware and by 1965 had begun

14. Griliches and his collaborators find little lag between R&D expenditure and patent applications by U.S. firms. See Bronwyn H. Hall, Zvi Griliches, and Jerry A. Hausman, "Patents and R and D: Is There a Lag?" *International Economic Review*, vol. 27 (June 1986), pp. 265–83. See also Ariel Pakes and Mark Schankerman, "The Rate of Obsolescence of Patents, Research Gestation Lags, and the Private Rate of Return to Research Resources," in Zvi Griliches, ed., *R&D, Patents, and Productivity* (University of Chicago Press, 1984), pp. 73–88. Pakes and Schankerman estimate a mean 1.17-year lag before R&D is embodied in products in the electronics industry and a 1.5- to 2.5-year lag for a broad sample of industries.

Table B-3. *Rates of Return on Computer R&D with Normal Foreign Sales*[a]

Percent growth rate for economy	Years of gestation lag, diffusion lag	Percent social return[b]		Percent private return[b]	
		(1.5,30)	(1,20)	(1.5,30)	(1,20)
		Capture rate = 70 percent			
0	2,3	69	52	76	54
	3,2	52	40	48	33
4	2,3	76	58	83	61
	3,2	58	46	54	38
		Capture rate = 20 percent			
0	2,3	63	46	32	14
	3,2	49	37	16	2.4
4	2,3	69	52	37	18
	3,2	55	42	21	6.5

a. Normal foreign sales are assumed to be 0.8.

b. The first numeral in parentheses is the elasticity of demand for computers. The second numeral is a percentage, the cost-saving effect of innovation as a fraction of pre-innovation cost $[(C_O - C_N)/C_O]$.

shipping.[15] The short time window for a new innovation is implicit in the very fast clip at which new products have been introduced in the industry. At IBM, for example, memory products usually have about a one-year life.[16] In the electrical equipment industry in the United States, 88 percent of the firms sampled by Edwin Mansfield knew about the nature and operation of a rival's new product or process in less than one year, 100 percent in less than eighteen months.[17]

Taken together, these observations suggest a lag of two to three years before significant returns are perceived from R&D investments, followed perhaps by another two- to three-year window in which significant technological rents are received. Although the pace of advance and the degree of competition are likely to be more accelerated in the computer industry than in other industries, these assumptions are roughly consistent with more general empirical studies of innovation.[18]

15. See Franklin M. Fisher, James W. McKie, and Richard B. Mancke, *IBM and the U.S. Data Processing Industry: An Economic History* (Praeger, 1983), p. 204.

16. William E. Harding, "Semiconductor Manufacturing in IBM, 1957 to the Present: A Perspective," *IBM Journal of Research and Development*, vol. 25 (September 1981), p. 653.

17. See Edwin Mansfield, "How Rapidly Does New Industrial Technology Leak Out?" *Journal of Industrial Economics*, vol. 34 (December 1985), pp. 217–23.

18. Pakes and Schankerman note that the average life span of applied R&D investments in all durable goods products—from start of research to virtual obsolescence

As table B-3 shows, growth assumptions for the economy include no real growth and fast-track 4 percent growth. The portion of cost decline assumed to be captured by the innovating firms as a technological rent ranges from 70 percent, a significant degree of monopoly control over the new technology, to a relatively competitive 20 percent.

Even short gestation lags cut the social returns to R&D investment tremendously. The exact structure of gestation and diffusion lags appears to be vital when calculating returns. With a short two-year gestation lag, and little private appropriation of technological benefits, the social rates of return presented in table B-1 are roughly halved.

The divergence between private and social returns varies depending on the parameters associated with market structure. With a relatively large portion of the benefits of advance captured as technological rent (s is high), the private rate of return can even exceed the social return because private R&D costs are less than the total social investment in technology development. With a smaller portion, however, private returns can run from one-half to one-quarter of social rates of return.

The most important parameter affecting social returns is the extent of cost declines; the second most important is lag structure. The effects of market structure and economic growth rates are relatively minor on social return but much greater on private return. Over the range of parameter values considered, social return increases with the capture rate—an argument for policies favoring greater private appropriation of the benefits of technological advance.

The Role of Foreign Sales

Access to foreign markets plays an important role in determining private and social returns. It increases social return by adding the private technological rents earned through foreign sales to the social benefits perceived in the national market. Thus as private appropriability of technology increases (through either a higher capture rate or a longer diffusion lag), the foreign component of returns to R&D investment

---

of the product—was just nine years. See "Rate of Obsolescence," table 4.2. Product lives are considerably shorter in electronics than in other areas. See also F. M. Scherer, "R&D and Declining Productivity Growth," *American Economic Review,* vol. 73 (May 1983), pp. 215–18. In his sample of American firms, peak profits occurred with a four- to six-year lag after R&D spending.

Table B-4. *Rates of Return on Computer R&D with No Foreign Sales*

Percent growth rate for economy	Years of gestation lag, diffusion lag	Percent social return[a]		Percent private return[a]	
		(1.5,30)	*(1,20)*	*(1.5,30)*	*(1,20)*
		Capture rate = 70 percent			
0	2,3	56	42	50	32
	3,2	45	35	30	16
4	2,3	63	48	56	37
	3,2	51	40	35	21
		Capture rate = 20 percent			
0	2,3	58	43	13	−1.8
	3,2	47	35	1.9	−10
4	2,3	65	49	18	2.1
	3,2	52	41	6	−6.5

a. The first numeral in parentheses is the elasticity of demand for computers. The second numeral is a percentage, the cost-saving effect of innovation as a fraction of pre-innovation cost $[(C_O - C_N)/C_O]$.

increases. The social and private benefits derived from sales abroad are identical and rise with increased appropriation.

Increased private capture of return on technology investment lowers that component of social return originating in domestic markets. Therefore, foreign markets tend to be a relatively more significant component of social return when private appropriation of returns on technological advance is greatest.

A comparison of table B-3 and table B-4 reveals three significant points. First, even with a relatively high degree of private appropriation of the benefits of new computer technology (a large s), the social benefit perceived in domestic markets by U.S. consumers over the long haul far outweighs the rents received from foreign sales. Foreign sales contribute a marginal component to social return; they are of greater importance when private appropriation of technology increases.

Second, foreign sales are of strikingly greater significance to private return than to social return. When capture rates are high, losing access to foreign markets lowers rates of return by one-third to one-half. With low capture rates, foreign markets grow even more important: rates of return are often lowered by one-half to three-quarters, and marginally positive returns turn negative.

Third, foreign markets are an important element in making the case for public policies to increase the extent to which innovations can be appropriated. Without foreign sales, a greater capture rate reduces social return. The opposite occurs with a large foreign market.

In reality, of course, investment in computer technology is a collection of small, diverse investments, not one big, economy-wide project. Many marginal R&D investments with low returns would not be sufficiently profitable for a private firm if foreign markets were unavailable. Although foreign markets play a minor role in affecting the social return on these investments, they play an absolutely central role in determining private profitability.

Market Structure with Sustainable Innovation

There is no generally accepted view of how firms in a technology-intensive industry enter or compete in product markets. Because a return on a fixed investment in technology must be earned to justify further R&D investment, some degree of monopoly power must be held by an innovating firm. If other firms were able to costlessly imitate the innovator, no private investment in new technology would occur.

Analyses of the behavior of firms in such a context generally treat the firms as participants in an oligopoly. Assumptions then are made about the extent to which firms collude or compete, the homogeneity or heterogeneity of competing firms, the reactions by other firms when any given firm decides how to set price or how much to produce, and the extent to which fixed costs of entry can be recovered if a firm liquidates its operations.

The nature of these assumptions will determine how much spending for research and development, in the aggregate, is associated with a given rate of technological advance and what price is charged by innovators before diffusion spreads the benefits into the public domain. In the context of the simple model used here, the capture rate is the main (unobserved) parameter affected by market structure. As noted earlier, it must lie between one (corresponding to a monopoly on the new technology) and zero (corresponding to costless imitation and entry). A capture rate of zero is clearly too low to be realistic since there would be no private return and no incentive for private investment in research and development.

Firms would be foolish to invest in R&D unless, over the long run, they were able to earn at least a "normal" rate of return on assets invested in these activities. One might then ask what price (and capture rate) must be set over the window of profitability to receive this normal return. If an industry is to sustain further innovation, the capture rate must be at or above this level over the long haul; firms earning less would eventually exit, and the actual return would rise to at least this level.

One increasingly popular and convenient assumption about market structure in an industry with significant fixed costs is that of a "contestable market."[19] As long as the fixed costs of entry can be fully recovered when a firm exits and liquidates its assets, there is no barrier to a firm entering such an industry when greater than normal returns are available. If such costless entry and exit into a research-intensive industry is possible, firms will have an incentive to enter the industry by investing in research as long as the technological rents they may expect to receive more than cover the normal return on their R&D investments.[20]

Firms will enter a perfectly contestable, technology-intensive industry, or threaten entry, and put downward pressure on prices for innovative products until technological rents are just sufficient to provide the normal rate of return on investments with the risk and return characteristics appropriate to that industry.[21]

To obtain the minimal capture rate necessary to produce a normal return (what can be called the "sustainable" capture rate), select the normal private rate of return from technology investments and choose some reasonable values for the gestation and diffusion lags. Then plug this rate of return into the left-hand side of equation B-3. After solving for the sustainable capture rates, the social rate of return can then be calculated using equation B-4.

The normal rate of return chosen should reflect the particular risk and return characteristics of computer investments. If capital markets are efficient, then the market return on investments in computer firms should

19. See William J. Baumol, John C. Panzar, and Robert D. Willig, *Contestable Markets and the Theory of Industry Structure* (Harcourt Brace Jovanovich, 1982).

20. Much of the research and development may duplicate investments by existing participants in the industry. Since R&D investment in one industry may have limited applicability to other activities, it is unclear who the customers for such liquidated, industry-specific investments will be.

21. The term *perfect contestability* means the total absence of sunk costs and free access to the same R&D technology used by an incumbent firm. Steven A. Morrison and Clifford Winston, "Empirical Implications and Tests of the Contestability Hypothesis," *Journal of Law and Economics,* vol. 30 (forthcoming), argue that a notion of *imperfect contestability* is needed to express the deviations from this ideal that occur in the real world.

Table B-5. *Social Rates of Return and Private Pricing Behavior with Minimum Sustainable Profits*[a]

Percent growth rate for economy	Years of gestation lag, diffusion lag	Normal foreign sales (f = 0.8)		No foreign sales (f = 0)	
		(1.5,30)[b]	(1,20)[b]	(1.5,30)[b]	(1,20)[b]
		Percent social return			
0	2,3	61	46	58	39
	3,2	49	38	46	35
4	2,3	67	51	65	49
	3,2	54	43	52	41
		Percent capture rate			
0	2,3	12	21	21	43
	3,2	19	34	36	66
4	2,3	10	18	18	33
	3,2	16	29	30	54

a. A private return of 15 percent is assumed to obtain the capture rate.

b. The first numeral in parentheses is the elasticity of demand for computers. The second numeral is a percentage, the cost-saving effect of innovation as a fraction of pre-innovation cost $[(C_O - C_N)/C_O]$.

be the rate at which firms discount their investment projects. To select this normal rate of return for computers, one can draw on historical data. The real rate of return on equity across the industry in prosperous years in the 1980s has been about 15 percent after inflation.[22]

In sum, hypothesized values for *m, n,* and *g,* and a normal rate of return on computer investments can be chosen. Given the assumption that innovation is sustained, a minimal capture rate *s* and a corresponding social rate of return can then be imputed.

Table B-5 shows the results of these calculations. With foreign markets available, the minimal *s* required for sustained R&D investment generally ranges from about 0.10 to about 0.35. Without foreign markets, the minimal capture rate would have almost doubled. Social rates of return are generally in the 50 to 70 percent range with more realistic assumptions.

22. The 15 percent real return is based on the 1984 computer industry average nominal rate of 18.1 percent on common equity. See *Business Week,* "Scoreboard Special Issue," March 22, 1985, p. 49.

U.S. Government Expenditure on Computer Research and Development

IN THE early 1950s the federal government spent an estimated $15 to $20 million annually on computer research and development. This estimate is based on the relatively well documented costs of the Whirlwind project at the Massachusetts Institute of Technology (MIT) and the magnitude of the computer effort at Engineering Research Associates (about three times the budget and staff of the MIT group). It is assumed that these two programs—the largest and most expensive at that time—accounted for one-third to one-half of military expenditure on computer R&D.[1]

Table C-1 presents private computer R&D expenditure in the early 1950s. These estimates are based on total R&D spending by IBM, Remington Rand, and NCR. The portion of research and development related to computers is assumed to equal one and one-third of the portion of sales accounted for by electronic data processing equipment. Privately funded computer R&D by other manufacturers in 1950 was probably minimal. It seems reasonable to conclude that all private spending was less than $5 million.

Industrial Computer R&D

Private expenditure on computer R&D by IBM, Remington Rand, and NCR may have climbed to the $13 million range by the mid-1950s,

---

1. Flamm, *Creating the Computer: Government, Industry, and High Technology* (Brookings, forthcoming), chap. 3.

Table C-1. *R&D Expenditure by Computer Producers in the Early 1950s*[a]

Millions of dollars unless otherwise specified

Expenditures	IBM		Remington Rand		Burroughs		NCR	
	1950	1954	1950	1954	1950	1954	1950	1954
Total R&D	5.3	14.6	2.9	5.9	3.6	8.3	2.1	5.3
Electronic data processing (EDP) R&D[b]	3.5	11.1	0.8	2.4	0.2	1.0	0.0	0.3
Percent of sales in EDP	50	57	20	30	5	9	0	4

Source: Alvin J. Harman, *The International Computer Industry: Innovation and Comparative Advantage* (Harvard University Press, 1971), pp. 108–11.

a. Company R&D figures exclude military funding, which accounted for most of the computer research and development at this time.

b. Estimated by multiplying 1.33 times percent of sales times R&D.

with about $10 million accounted for by IBM alone. If Burroughs, General Electric, and RCA are factored in, the total would be closer to $15 million.

In 1965 about half of all computer R&D and one-third of industrial R&D in the United States was funded by the federal government according to an Organization for Economic Cooperation and Development questionnaire.[2] The OECD estimates for universities and nonprofit institutions primarily reflect manufacturers' discounts on purchases of university computing equipment and probably do not include funding by the Defense Advanced Research Projects Agency. Some research by U.S. companies overseas, however, is included. Therefore, the federal share of American computer R&D is almost certainly underestimated.

Table C-2 presents National Science Foundation (NSF) data on company and federal funds for the performance of research and development within the office, computing, and accounting machines (OCAM) industry from 1972 to 1984. Only incomplete series are published: 1972 to 1980 for total industry R&D; 1975 to 1984 for company funds; and 1975 to 1979 for federal funds.

Based on the original published data for 1981 to 1984, a reasonable estimate can be constructed for federal- and company-funded R&D in the office, computing, and accounting machines industry (see table C-3). The basic method devised to estimate the missing data on total R&D

2. Organization for Economic Cooperation and Development, *Electronic Computers: Gaps in Technology,* Report presented at the Third Ministerial Meeting on Science of the OECD Countries, March 11 and 12, 1968 (Paris: OECD, 1969), p. 135.

Table C-2. *NSF Data on R&D Funds in the Office, Computing, and Accounting Machines Industry, 1972–84*
Millions of dollars

Year	All funds	Company funds	Federal funds
1972	1,456	n.a.	n.a.
1973	1,733	n.a.	n.a.
1974	2,103	n.a.	n.a.
1975	2,220	1,734	486
1976	2,402	1,893	509
1977	2,655	2,220	435
1978	2,883	2,556	327
1979	3,214	2,958	256
1980	3,962	3,436	n.a.
1981	n.a.	3,847	n.a.
1982	n.a.	4,722	n.a.
1983	n.a.	5,182	n.a.
1984	n.a.	6,176	n.a.

Sources: National Science Foundation, *Research and Development in Industry, 1984* (GPO, 1986), pp. 20, 23, 26.
n.a. Not available.

funding makes use of detailed data reported in the original NSF report for the relevant year. The distribution of both total and federal funding across firms, grouped by size of R&D program (four firms with largest R&D programs, next four, next twelve, and, by subtraction, the rest of the industry), is reported. A similar distribution of net sales, as well as the total for all size groups, is also reported. In addition, total R&D as a percentage of sales for each of these groups (except "rest of the industry") is given.

Total research and development for each size group is then calculated. An estimate of total R&D for the entire industry can be expressed as:

Total R&D = (total R&D, size group i) / (share R&D, size group i).

Because of its greater precision (two to three significant digits of R&D share are reported), the estimate of total R&D derived from data for the top four R&D performing firms is used. Company-funded R&D may be subtracted from total funds to estimate federally funded industrial R&D. Because the company-funded figures are retrospectively revised, the preliminary estimate of federal funds may be added to the latest figure on company-funded R&D to update the estimate of total funds. This

Table C-3. *Federal- and Company-Funded R&D in the Office,*
Computing, and Accounting Machines Industry, 1981–84

Year and companies	As reported by NSF				As estimated by author	
		Distribution across firms			Federal funds as percent of total R&D[a]	Federal R&D funds (millions of dollars)
	R&D as percent of sales	Percent of industry sales	Percent of industry R&D (all funds)	Percent of federal funds		
1981						
Top 4 companies	14.6	59	74	97	16.9	564
Next 4 companies	8.5	15	11	0	0.0	0
Next 12 companies	6.3	16	9	2	3.0	12
Rest of industry	n.a.	10	6	1	2.0	6
Industry total	n.a.	100	100	100	12.9	581
1982						
Top 4 companies	14.8	61	76	89	15.2	625
Next 4 companies	7.8	16	11	0	0.0	0
Next 12 companies	6.9	14	8	10	15.9	70
Rest of industry	n.a.	9	5	1	2.4	7
Industry total	n.a.	100	100	100	13.0	702
1983						
Top 4 companies	13.9	66	77	97	20.9	987
Next 4 companies	10.3	11	9	0	0.0	0
Next 12 companies	7.0	14	8	0	0.0	0
Rest of industry	n.a.	9	6	3	9.5	31
Industry total	n.a.	100	100	100	16.6	1017
1984						
Top 4 companies	14.0	65	76	99	19.8	1092
Next 4 companies	10.3	11	9	0	0.0	0
Next 12 companies	7.8	13	9	0	0.0	0
Rest of industry	n.a.	11	6	1	2.5	11
Industry total	n.a.	100	100	100	15.2	1104

Sources: NSF, *Research and Development in Industry, 1981,* NSF 83-325 (GPO, 1983), pp. 27, 30, 32; ibid., *1982,* NSF 84-325 (GPO, 1984), pp. 22, 25, 27; ibid., *1983,* NSF 85-325 (GPO, 1985), pp. 34, 37, 39; and ibid., *1984* (GPO, 1986), pp. 23, 32, 35, 37.
n.a. Not available.
a. Preliminary figure for total R&D is used.

procedure has been followed in constructing the estimates of total industrial R&D used in tables 4-3 and C-5 for the years 1981 to 1984.

Nonindustrial Computer R&D

Significant amounts of computer research are performed outside of industry in universities, government laboratories, and nonprofit institutions. Research by the Bell Telephone Laboratories, not classified as part of the OCAM industry in available statistics, has greatly influenced the computer industry. In recent years roughly half of the labs' resources has gone into computer hardware and software.

Unfortunately, data on R&D performed in laboratories within the government are not available by subject area. However, the Los Alamos National Laboratory and the Lawrence Livermore National Laboratory, which among federal labs played the most important role in leading-edge U.S. computing, are administered as university FFRDCs (federally funded research and development centers) and therefore counted in these statistics. The Johns Hopkins University Applied Physics Laboratory, once a university FFRDC and now incorporated into the school itself, has propelled Hopkins into first place among U.S. universities in the competition for federal R&D funding in math and computer science. Other FFRDCs run by industry are included in the industrial R&D statistics.

There are also no data available on privately funded computer R&D performed in nonprofit institutions outside of the academic sector (for example, the Charles Stark Draper Laboratories, in Cambridge, Massachusetts, formerly associated with MIT). Since there does not seem to be a large amount of computer research performed by nonprofit institutions, this is a negligible omission. The most important exception has probably been SRI International, of Menlo Park, California, which performs internally funded computer research, as well as research on government contracts. Today research on government contracts represents about one-half of its research and development in all areas.[3]

Since the research performed in federal labs probably exceeds privately funded research in nonprofit institutions, the estimate of the share of federal funding will be biased downward. The federal shares reported in tables 4-4 and 4-5 fall short of what their values would have been had these omitted R&D efforts been included.

Federal and nonfederal expenditures for research (but not development) in math and computer science, electrical engineering, and materials science are shown in table C-4. In all these areas federal support dropped in real terms in the early 1970s and recovered in the late 1970s. By far the largest expenditures have gone to electrical engineering but

---

3. Thomas J. Murray, "SRI Charts an Ambitious Course," *Dun's Business Month,* February 1985, p. 64.

Table C-4. *Support for Computer-Related Research, 1967–86*
Millions of 1982 dollars[a]

	Federal obligations						Nonfederally funded university R&D	
	Basic and applied research			Basic research only				
Year	Math and computer science	Electrical engineering	Materials science	Math and computer science	Electrical engineering	Materials science	Math and computer science	Electrical engineering
1967	356.55	735.38	337.05	178.27	69.64	130.92	n.a.	n.a.
1968	313.00	896.55	307.69	175.07	74.27	114.06	n.a.	n.a.
1969	271.36	668.34	314.07	135.68	62.81	108.04	n.a.	n.a.
1970	226.19	676.19	323.81	140.48	80.95	119.05	n.a.	n.a.
1971	240.99	626.13	353.60	123.87	78.83	130.63	n.a.	n.a.
1972	260.22	718.28	391.40	144.09	90.32	135.48	36.56	n.a.
1973	232.32	602.02	349.49	121.21	88.89	137.37	n.a.	n.a.
1974	211.11	498.15	353.70	98.15	70.37	138.89	n.a.	n.a.
1975	210.79	483.98	374.37	104.55	80.94	168.63	33.73	n.a.
1976	250.40	472.27	435.82	129.95	83.99	163.23	33.28	n.a.
1977	291.23	569.09	436.85	123.33	81.72	185.74	43.66	n.a.
1978	299.17	599.72	396.12	135.73	78.95	186.98	56.09	n.a.
1979	267.18	531.81	316.79	132.32	78.88	192.11	57.32	n.a.
1980	281.21	603.27	275.38	135.36	82.85	141.19	60.75	49.26
1981	296.81	592.55	272.34	148.94	84.04	146.81	62.31	48.92
1982	350.90	612.00	309.00	165.00	94.00	156.00	70.09	51.59
1983	403.66	592.49	320.81	200.39	92.49	176.30	77.51	66.58
1984	407.03	582.79	315.45	222.94	120.26	172.99	89.76	80.43
1985[b]	518.35	556.85	327.66	230.98	118.17	174.57	n.a.	n.a.
1986[b]	545.85	600.87	328.38	246.29	134.50	172.05	n.a.	n.a.

Sources: National Science Foundation, *Federal Funds for Research and Development: Federal Obligations for Research by Agency and Detailed Field of Science, Fiscal Years 1967–1986* (GPO, 1985), pp. 6, 31, 61, 87; NSF, *Academic Science/Engineering: 1972–83; R&D Funds, Federal Support, Scientists and Engineers, Graduate Enrollment and Support*, NSF 84-322 (GPO, 1984), pp. 43–44; and unpublished NSF data for 1977–84.

n.a. Not available.

a. Current dollars have been converted to 1982 dollars by using the GNP deflator found in *Economic Report of the President, January 1987*, p. 248.

b. Federal obligations are NSF estimates based on the president's 1986 budget.

were not primarily for basic research. Computers and materials research have been much more heavily weighted toward basic research.

Funding for Basic Research

Table C-5 combines basic research performed in the OCAM sector with basic research undertaken in the area of math and computer science in universities and government. After 1979 it is assumed that 1.6 percent of all industrial R&D is basic (as is indicated by NSF data for 1979, see table 4-3). It is also assumed that negligible amounts of privately funded

Table C-5. *Estimated Funding and Performance of Basic Computer Research, 1979, 1981, 1983*[a]

Millions of dollars unless otherwise specified

Year and source of funds	Companies	Universities	University FFRDCs	Federal government	Other	Total
1979						
Federal	} 51	69		35		>104
Company		} 25	0	0	0	n.a.
Other	0		0	0	0	n.a.
Total	51	94		35		<180
Percent of						
federal funds	n.a.	73	100	100	100	>58
1981						
Federal	} 71	103		37		>140
Company		} 39	0	0	0	n.a.
Other	0		0	0	0	n.a.
Total	71[b]	142		37		<250
Percent of						
federal funds	n.a.	73	100	100	100	>56
1983						
Federal	} 99	147		61		>208
Company		} 53	0	0	0	n.a.
Other	0		0	0	0	n.a.
Total	99[b]	200		61		<360
Percent of						
federal funds	n.a.	74	100	100	100	>58

Sources: NSF, *Academic Science/Engineering: R&D Funds Fiscal Year 1983*, pp. 14–16; NSF, *Academic Science/Engineering, 1972–83*, pp. 43–44; NSF, *Federal Funds for Research and Development: Federal Obligations for Research to Universities and Colleges by Agency and Field of Science, Fiscal Years 1973–1986* (GPO, 1985), pp. 43, 61; and NSF, *Federal Funds for Research and Development: Detailed Historical Tables, Fiscal Years 1955–1986* (GPO, 1985), p. 287.

n.a. Not available.

a. Basic research refers to all basic research in companies in the OCAM sector and all nonindustrial basic research in the field of math and computer science. Basic research performed in companies is an estimated 1.6 percent of total company R&D expenditure. It is not possible to distinguish between federal and internal funding. Expenditures in FFRDCs administered by industry are counted in these figures. University basic research is taken from NSF, *Academic Science/Engineering: R&D Funds*, various years. These fiscal year expenditures are divided into federal and "other" sources of funds.

Federal funds for basic research carried out in university-administered FFRDCs, federal agencies, and other nonindustrial, nonuniversity labs are estimated by subtracting federally funded basic research expenditure in universities from all federal obligations for basic math and computer science research. Nonfederally funded basic research in this group of institutions is assumed to be practically nil.

In calculating the federal share, all basic research in companies is treated as if coming from company funds. Thus the total for the "federal" row is a lower bound; because some of these company funds may have been drawn from federal funds assigned in this table to the university FFRDCs, federal government, and other sectors, the sum of items in the "total" row overestimates total basic research expenditure. Because the numerator is underestimated, and the denominator is overestimated, the percent of total basic research funded by the federal government is underestimated.

b. Estimated.

basic computer research are performed outside of industry and the universities.

To produce a conservative estimate of the share paid for by the federal government, all basic research performed in industry is treated as if paid for out of company funds. Since the numerator (federal obligations) undercounts federal support for industry, and the denominator over-counts all basic research (by doublecounting some federal obligations going to industrial basic research), the federal share is underestimated.

Information Technology R&D in Japan

INFORMATION technology is defined as a social objective in Japanese statistics on R&D spending, and includes both computer hardware and software.[1] Table D-1 shows such expenditure over the 1970–84 period. The figures presented are for intramural R&D expenditure on information technology; spending for R&D performed outside of the various sectors listed shows up in the sector where it is performed. Nippon Telephone and Telegraph (NTT) accounts for the bulk of the R&D spending in the transportation and communications sector. Funds covered by procurement from NTT's outside contractors are not counted within this sector. Also not counted as information technology is much of NTT's R&D spending on electronic components, though it may be directly related to computer systems.

Table D-2 lists by program MITI funding of computer-related R&D from 1970 to 1985. Not all of the money was given to industry or to the cooperative research associations formed by industry. A portion of the funding for the national R&D projects finances research at MITI's own Electrotechnical Laboratory (ETL). About one-third of the funding for the PIPS (pattern information processing system) program, for example, went to the ETL between 1970 and 1978.[2] Industry, however, received the bulk of this funding.

Table D-3 shows available figures on production and deliveries of computers in Japan, as well as purchases by the Japan Electronic

1. See Statistics Bureau, Management and Coordination Agency, *Report on the Survey of Research and Development* (Tokyo: Japan Statistics Association, various years).

2. See Electrotechnical Laboratory, *Pattern Information Processing System: National Research and Development Program* (Tokyo: ETL, 1978), p. 5.

Table D-1. *Expenditures on Information Technology R&D in Japan, 1970–84*
Millions of yen

Performer	1970	1971	1972	1973	1974	1975	1976	1977	1978	1979	1980	1981	1982	1983	1984
All companies	29,710	40,221	33,035	45,070	37,738	52,788	65,333	81,903	88,589	118,008	140,783	168,607	199,998	241,500	343,641
Manufacturing	24,644	27,396	18,885	33,425	28,143	39,142	53,590	67,065	72,739	99,804	122,953	143,427	182,731	222,279	319,985
Nonelectrical machinery	0	48	714	2,339	1,016	2,701	1,958	2,462	2,839	3,579	7,309	13,131	11,893	6,870	8,864
Electrical machinery	8,392	7,970	9,465	18,555	12,487	19,167	25,820	35,243	35,344	45,914	51,251	56,970	74,417	84,707	136,086
Communications equipment	15,040	17,990	5,916	8,572	9,761	11,389	16,379	18,655	27,074	32,635	44,946	58,051	75,462	104,097	148,590
Transport and communications	4,839	12,551	14,019	11,460	9,144	13,169	11,504	13,420	14,864	15,927	16,346	23,365	13,782	14,580	18,756
Research institutes	n.a.	923	17,902	36,664	48,920	45,028	47,357	30,151	36,487	29,475	16,083	38,330	42,114	38,408	34,361
Central government	n.a.	608	1,857	2,230	2,378	2,655	2,847	2,316	3,489	5,628	2,679	3,048	6,067	6,519	5,644
Local government	n.a.	129	40	128	72	447	296	398	210	231	352	640	681	1,104	836
Private	n.a.	150	291	390	46,358	41,722	43,970	27,071	32,341	23,406	12,522	33,978	34,816	30,268	27,629
Public corporation	n.a.	37	15,715	33,916	111	204	244	366	446	210	531	664	550	517	252
Universities & colleges	n.a.	n.a.	n.a.	n.a.	5,018	5,590	5,249	5,448	6,646	11,339	7,727	8,820	10,391	12,232	12,638
National	n.a.	n.a.	n.a.	n.a.	4,330	4,410	3,466	3,494	4,545	8,119	5,522	6,468	6,945	8,518	8,583
Public	n.a.	n.a.	n.a.	n.a.	33	12	114	118	129	173	173	202	195	109	179
Private	n.a.	n.a.	n.a.	n.a.	655	1,168	1,641	1,864	1,972	3,046	2,033	2,149	3,251	3,606	3,877
All performers	29,710	41,144	50,937	81,734	91,676	103,406	117,939	117,502	131,722	158,822	164,593	215,757	252,503	292,140	390,640
Addendum:															
NTT R&D (all fields)	19,800	28,300	34,400	36,700	39,300	45,100	45,800	57,900	62,000	69,200	75,500	80,200	89,000	94,000	127,000

Sources: Statistics Bureau, Management and Coordination Agency [Prime Minister's office prior to 1983], *Report on the Survey of Research and Development, 1985* (Tokyo: Japan Statistical Association, 1986), pp. 133, 153, 165; *1984*, pp. 129, 149, 161; *1983*, pp. 127, 147, 159; *1982*, pp. 117, 137, 149; *1981*, pp. 117, 137, 149; *1980*, pp. 103, 123, 135; *1979*, pp. 99, 119, 131; *1978*, pp. 99, 119, 131; *1977*, pp. 109, 129, 141; *1976*, pp. 103, 123, 135; *1975*, pp. 105, 125, 137; *1974*, pp. 107, 127; *1973*, pp. 137, 163; *1972*, pp. 133, 157; *1971*, p. 135; JECC [Japan Electronic Computer Corporation], *Konputa Noto, 1983* [Computer notes, 1983] (Tokyo: JECC, 1983), p. 194; and Nippon Telephone and Telegraph Corporation, *Annual Report 1985*, p. 33.
n.a. Not available.

Table D-2. Selected MITI Support for Computer Technology, 1970–85
Billions of yen

Item	1970	1971	1972	1973	1974	1975	1976	1977	1978	1979	1980	1981	1982	1983	1984	1985
National R&D projects																
Super high performance electronic computer (SHPEC)	2.00	1.50	...	...	...	...	...	...	...	...	...	...	...	...	...	...
Pattern information processing system (PIPS)	...	0.20	1.07	1.63	2.18	3.37	3.39	2.92	2.51	2.80	1.85	...	...	...	...	...
Optical measurement and control system	...	...	...	...	...	...	...	...	...	0.05	0.93	2.40	3.24	3.39	2.33	3.44
High-speed computer for scientific and technological uses	...	...	...	...	...	...	...	...	...	...	...	0.03	0.81	1.57	2.25	2.77
New function elements	...	...	...	...	...	...	...	...	...	...	...	0.67	1.13	1.45	1.48	1.59
Fifth Generation program	...	...	...	...	...	...	...	...	...	...	...	0.02	0.42	2.72	5.12	4.78
Interoperable database system	...	...	...	...	...	...	...	...	...	...	...	...	...	...	...	0.02
Industrial research support																
New computer types	...	...	4.51	14.41	15.25	12.48	10.83	...	...	...	...	...	...	...	...	...
Computer peripheral equipment development	...	...	0.70	1.03	1.40	0.90	0.60	...	...	...	...	...	...	...	...	...
Software promotion measures	...	...	...	0.60	1.20	0.90	...	...	...	...	...	...	...	...	...	...
IC development program	...	...	...	1.70	1.80	...	...	...	...	...	...	...	...	...	...	...
VLSI program	...	...	...	...	...	...	3.50	8.64	10.05	6.91	...	...	...	...	...	...

Next-generation computer basic technology	⋯	⋯	⋯	⋯	⋯	⋯	⋯	⋯	⋯	⋯	1.70	5.79	6.20	5.62	2.86	⋯
Small research projects	⋯	⋯	⋯	⋯	⋯	⋯	⋯	⋯	⋯	⋯	⋯	⋯	⋯	⋯	⋯	⋯
Automobile traffic control system	⋯	⋯	⋯	0.20	0.84	2.01	2.15	1.37	0.58	0.15	⋯	⋯	⋯	⋯	⋯	⋯
Medical information system	⋯	⋯	⋯	0.11	0.21	0.31	0.46	⋯	⋯	⋯	⋯	⋯	⋯	⋯	⋯	⋯
Video visual information system	⋯	⋯	⋯	⋯	0.03	0.22	0.55	0.80	0.55	0.58	0.04	0.03	0.04	0.05	0.03	0.03
Trade information system	⋯	⋯	⋯	⋯	⋯	⋯	⋯	0.11	0.04	0.03	0.03	⋯	⋯	⋯	⋯	⋯
Alternative urban energy system	⋯	⋯	⋯	⋯	⋯	⋯	⋯	⋯	⋯	0.01	0.04	0.05	0.03	0.03	0.03	⋯
Health care network system	⋯	⋯	⋯	⋯	⋯	⋯	⋯	⋯	0.19	0.19	0.22	0.22	0.19	0.17	0.12	0.11
Support for Information-Technology Promotion Agency (IPA)																
Initial capitalization of IPA	0.20	0.40	0.43	⋯	⋯	⋯	⋯	⋯	⋯	⋯	⋯	⋯	⋯	⋯	⋯	⋯
Annual subsidy to IPA	0.30	0.40	0.37	0.79	1.00	1.32	1.73	2.05	2.28	2.58	2.78	2.66	2.62	2.08	2.48	2.35
Miscellaneous "informatization" measures	⋯	⋯	⋯	⋯	⋯	⋯	⋯	⋯	⋯	0.22	0.30	0.64	0.57	1.21	0.38	0.39
All	2.50	7.13	20.69	24.43	22.09	23.32	15.60	15.69	14.67	14.67	11.94	12.89	14.63	14.15	15.47	15.44
All (millions of dollars)	6.98	7.18	23.53	76.07	83.66	74.38	78.52	57.99	74.71	66.99	52.60	58.30	58.77	65.00	59.47	64.56

Sources: JECC, Konpūta Nōto, 1986, pp. 90, 147; 1985, p. 75; 1983, pp. 70, 72, 106; Japanese Information Processing Development Center [JIPDEC], Computer White Paper, 1981 (Tokyo: JIPDEC, 1982), pp. 4–5; 1980, pp. 6, 7, 35–36, 39, 40; 1976, pp. 30, 33–34; 1974, pp. 19, 20, 22–23, 26; 1972, p. 35; Agency of Industrial Science and Technology and Ministry of International Trade and Industry, National Research and Development Program (Large-Scale Project): 1985 (Tokyo: Japan Industrial Technology Association, 1985), p. 15; H. J. Welke, Data Processing in Japan, Information Research and Resource Reports, vol. 1 (Amsterdam: North-Holland, 1982), pp. 31–32; and author's estimates for SHPEC. Exchange rates used to calculate dollar equivalents are from International Monetary Fund, International Financial Statistics: Yearbook 1986 (Washington: IMF, 1986), pp. 418–19, line af.

Table D-3. Role of Japan Electronic Computer Corporation in Japanese Computer Demand, 1960–81

Year	Billions of yen[a]			JECC purchase as percent of production	JECC purchase as percent of delivery	Foreign machines as percent of delivery	JECC as percent of delivery less foreign share	Foreign companies as percent of sales by major Japanese computer producers[b]	Estimate of JECC purchase as percent of total production less foreign share	Foreign machines as percent of value of installed computers
	Deliveries of computers, Japan	Production of computers, Japan	Purchase by JECC							
1960	6	2	n.a.	n.a.	n.a.	n.a.	n.a.	n.a.	n.a.	n.a.
1961	13	4	1	28	8	73	31	n.a.	n.a.	n.a.
1962	23	8	3	40	14	82	78	n.a.	n.a.	n.a.
1963	39	17	6	35	15	67	46	n.a.	n.a.	n.a.
1964	50	22	12	52	24	70	79	n.a.	n.a.	n.a.
1965	52	32	21	66	40	57	94	n.a.	n.a.	63
1966	67	49	27	55	40	48	77	n.a.	n.a.	55
1967	109	87	37	42	34	46	63	n.a.	n.a.	52
1968	161	141	67	47	41	44	74	n.a.	n.a.	49
1969	212	171	83	48	39	n.a.	n.a.	n.a.	n.a.	47

Year									
1970	331	270	92	34	28	n.a.	n.a.	n.a.	45
1971	350	311	87	28	25	n.a.	n.a.	n.a.	45
1972	419	382	89	23	21	n.a.	n.a.	n.a.	47
1973	528	428	101	24	19	n.a.	n.a.	n.a.	46
1974	641	536	124	23	19	n.a.	n.a.	n.a.	45
1975	614	497	126	25	21	n.a.	36	40	43
1976	732	575	134	23	18	n.a.	35	36	n.a.
1977	790	659	134	20	17	n.a.	34	31	n.a.
1978	798	820	131	16	16	n.a.	33	24	n.a.
1979	834	1,006	144	14	17	n.a.	30	21	n.a.
1980	970	1,137	178	16	18	n.a.	28	22	n.a.
1981	1,010	1,315	184	14	18	n.a.	29	20	n.a.

Sources: National Academy of Sciences, National Academy of Engineering, National Research Council, Computer Technology/Resources Panel of the Computer Science and Engineering Board, "The Computer Industry in Japan and Its Meaning for the United States" (Washington, 1973), p. 76; JIPDEC, Computer White Paper, 1982, pp. 15, 17; Fujitsu Limited, Fujitsu and the Computer Industry in Japan (Tokyo: Fujitsu Limited, 1983), p. 11; G. B. Levine, "Computers in Japan," Datamation, vol. 13 (December 1967), p. 23; James K. Imai, "Computers in Japan—1969," ibid., vol. 16 (January 1970), p. 149; JECC, Konputa Noto, 1983, pp. 12, 27; Noburō Minamisawa, Nihon Konpūtā Hattatsushi [History of the development of Japanese computers] (Tokyo: Nihon Keizai Shimbunsha, 1978), pp. 212–13; and Welke, Data Processing in Japan, p. 68.

n.a. Not available.

a. For 1960–70, deliveries and production figures from NAS, "Computer Industry," have been converted to yen at 360 yen per dollar.

b. Foreign companies are IBM and UNIVAC; estimates of JECC share of production assume foreign companies' share of Japanese sales is the same as their share of Japanese production.

Table D-4. *Liberalization of the Japanese Computer Industry*

Measures	Year of liberalization						
	Hardware				Integrated circuits		
	Central processing units	Peripherals	Parts	Software	Less than 100 elements	100–200 elements	More than 200 elements
Foreign investment liberalized							
50 percent share	1974	1974	1974	1974	1971[a]	1971[a]	1971[a]
100 percent share	1975	1975	1975	1976	1974	1974	1974
Quotas removed	1975	1972[b]	1975	[c]	1970	1973	1974
Technology transfer and licensing unrestricted	1974	1974	1974	1974	1968	1968	1968

Sources: Welke, *Data Processing in Japan*, p. 40.
a. Except for computer integrated circuits, which were liberalized in 1974.
b. Except for memory and terminals; those quotas were removed in 1975.
c. None applied.

Computer Corporation (JECC), over the 1960–81 period. JECC purchases are also shown as a fraction of production in Japan and of total deliveries. Because production includes the output of foreign computer companies' Japanese affiliates and deliveries include foreign imports as well, neither ratio captures JECC's true role in providing a market for "Japanese" machines (since only computers with a minimum Japanese content were eligible for JECC purchase). To assess JECC's importance to national producers, figures on the portion of deliveries accounted for by foreign computers (for the period 1961–68) as well as sales (for 1975–81) have been used to estimate the portion of "national" output purchased by JECC.

Tables D-4 and D-5 depict the formal process through which trade and investment in the Japanese computer industry were liberalized. Table D-4 gives the years in which direct controls on trade and investment were lifted; table D-5 depicts the gradual reduction in tariff rates. Recent U.S. and European tariff rates are included by way of comparison.

Table D-5. *Japan's Tariff Rates on Computer Hardware and Integrated Circuits*

| Year and type of rate[a] | Hardware | | Integrated circuits |
	Central processing unit	Peripherals	
1965	15.0	15.0[b]	n.a.
1972	13.5	15.0	n.a.
1977			
Actual	13.5	22.5	12.0
Statutory	15.0	n.a.	15.0
1978			
Actual	10.5	17.5	12.0
Statutory	15.0	n.a.	15.0
1980			
Actual	9.8	16.1	10.1
Statutory	12.5	20.3	12.3
1983			
Actual	4.9	6.0	4.2
Statutory	10.0	15.5	9.6
1984			
Actual	4.9	6.0	4.2
Statutory	8.7	13.1	8.3
Addenda:			
U.S. rate (1984)	3.9	3.9	4.2
European Community rate (1984)	4.9	4.9	17.0

Sources: JECC, *Konputa Noto, 1983*, p. 100; U.S. Department of Commerce, Domestic and International Business Administration, *Global Market Survey: Computers and Related Equipment* (GPO, 1973), p. 72; and U.S. General Accounting Office, International Division, *Industrial Policy: Case Studies in the Japanese Experience*, GAO ID-83-11 (Washington: GAO, 1982), p. 8.

n.a. Not available.

a. The actual rates are those that were used; the statutory rates are the maximum rates allowed by law and treaty.

b. Rate for disks; rate for other peripherals was 25 percent.

Index

Ackley, Gardner, 149n
ACME system, HIH, 90
Ada language, 75, 76
Advanced computer architecture, 65;
  clustered computer systems, 67;
  multiprocessor computer, 65–66;
  parallel computation, 67, 68, 77
AD-X2 scandal, 44
AEC. *See* Atomic Energy Commission
AEG Telefunken, 157
Alchian, A. A., 8n
Alic, J. A., 198n
ALOHA Net, 60, 61
Alvey program, U.K., 143, 165, 171
Ammer, Karen A., 120n
Anders, George, 166n
Anderson, John W., 118n
Arden, Bruce W., 48n, 61n, 207n
Argonne National Laboratory, 79, 82
ARPANET system, 59n, 60, 61, 70, 123
Arrow, Kenneth J., 8n, 13n, 186n
Artificial intelligence: DARPA funding
  for, 63; defined, 61; Lisp language,
  63n, 65; SUR projects, 64
Atomic Energy Commission (AEC), 78,
  94; computer for nuclear research
  laboratories, 79; funding for computer
  and math research, 82–83; support for
  industry supercomputer development,
  79–81. *See also* Energy, Department
  of
Augarten, Stan, 66n
AVIDAC, 79
Ayres, Robert U., 70n

Bacon, Glen, 63n, 100n
Baily, Martin Neil, 112n
Bambrick, Richard, 117n, 197n
Bandwidths: defined, 24; effective, 208;
  measurement, 208, 211–12, 214;
  utilized system, 208
Baran, Paul, 59n

Bard, Yonathan, 207n
Barney, Clifford, 63n, 77n
Barr, Avron, 64n, 85n
Basic research: European, 170; Japanese,
  128–29, 136, 141–42; military services,
  46; purpose, 183; total U.S. funding
  for, 245, 247; university-based, 46;
  U.S., 100–03, 104, 181, 183
Bass, Brad, 76n
Baum, Claude, 56n, 58n, 76n, 122n
Baumol, William J., 28, 29n, 238n
Baxter, James Phinney, III, 7n
Baxter, William F., 114n
BBN. *See* Bolt, Beranek, and Newman
Behr, Peter, 117n
Bell, C. Gordon, 22n, 58n, 61n, 67n, 81n,
  84n, 179n, 207n
Bell Telephone Laboratories, 6n;
  artificial intelligence research, 63n;
  computer-related research, 103, 243–
  44; research expenditures, 137; and
  SAGE system, 49
Belzer, Jack, 56n
Benda, Miroslav, 142n
Beranek, Leo, 51
Berger, Mike, 130n, 141n
Bergsten, C. Fred, 12n
Berston, Joseph C., 143n
Bethel, Howard Emery, 94n
Betts, Paul, 166n
Blackman, Anne Batey, 29n
Bolt, Beranek, and Newman (BBN), 51,
  59n, 60n, 67, 96; artificial intelligence
  research, 63, 64; timesharing computer
  system, 55
Bolt, Richard, 51
Borrus, Michael, 78n, 110n, 194n
Bowker, Albert, 86n
Brandin, D., 77n, 141n, 142n
Brannon, Phillip R., 78n
Bresnahan, Timothy F., 34n, 35n
Brooks, Harvey, 197n

256

Brown, Robert L., 57n
Bruce, Peter, 159n
Brueckner, Leslie, 78n, 194n
Buchanan, Bruce G., 85n, 90n
Burgan, John U., 4n
Burroughs, 95, 98n, 99
Bush, Vannevar, 195

California Institute of Technology, 67;
  Jet Propulsion Laboratory, 77, 84
Capron, W. M., 8n
Capture rate, of technology rents, 37–39,
  41, 228, 238
Carlton, Dennis W., 34n
Carnegie-Mellon University, 55; artificial
  intelligence research, 63; Software
  Engineering Institute, 76, 117; SUR
  project, 64
Carrington, Tim, 190n
Caruso, Denise, 70n
CASNET system, 91
Caves, Richard E., 1n
Census Bureau, 9
Central processor, 19; improvements in,
  21; operations, 20; price, 24, 25, 26;
  speed, 208–09. See also Information
  processing capacity
Cerveny, R. P., 22n
Chira, Susan, 120n
Chow, Gregory C., 27, 32
Chu, J. C., 79n
CII. See Compagnie International pour
  l'Informatique
Clark, David D., 61n
Coakley, Judith, 45n
Cobol language, 76, 119
Cochrane, Rexmond C., 44n
Cody, W. J., 82n
Cohen, Charles L., 66n, 130n, 142n, 202n
Cohler, Geoffrey L., 67n
Cole, Rosanne, 28n
Collins, Eileen L., 111n, 112n
Commerce, Department of, 44, 198
Communications equipment, 1, 4, 5
Compagnie International pour
  l'Informatique (CII), 154, 156
Competition, 3, 13; dynamics of, 14;
  international, 14, 17, 179; among
  Japanese producers, 151–52, 153; U.S.
  federal standards influencing, 118–19
Computer-assisted design (CAD), 119,
  164
Computer components: cost, 21, 22, 25,
  26, 209–10, 215; measuring bandwidths
  of, 208, 211–12, 214; output capacity,
  23

Computers, Japan: competitive-
  cooperative market structure for, 151–
  52; copyright protection for, 120; early
  development, 126–27; factors
  contributing to success, 170–71;
  financing leases of, 145–46;
  government procurement of, 143–46,
  167; information processing, 129;
  market for, 129, 141, 175–76, 181;
  supercomputers, 128, 129. See also
  Research and development, computer-
  related Japanese
Computers, U.S.: basic design, 19–21;
  copyright protection for, 120–21;
  declining cost, 43; demand price
  elasticity, 29–31; design technology,
  69; domestic versus foreign sales, 36–
  37, 235–37; federal standards for, 118–
  19; Generations, 27; integration with
  communications and electronics, 6; as
  key input to industrial production, 16;
  performance measurement, 21–24; size
  classes, 109; technological expansion
  in, 8–9; wartime uses, 7. See also
  Market, computer; Prices, computer;
  Research and development, computer-
  related U.S.
Connolly, Ray, 78n
Control Data Corporation, 99, 107;
  federal support for computer research
  at, 95; and Microelectronics and
  Computer Technology Corporation,
  114; supercomputers, 80–81, 109
Conway, Lynn, 74n
Cooper, Robert, 73
Cooperative research ventures: Japan,
  127, 128, 131, 134–36, 151–52; U.S.,
  114–18
Coran, Carl Louis, 131n
Corbató, F., 52n, 56n
Corcoran, Elizabeth, 73n, 91n
Corporation for Open Systems, 120n
Corrigan, Richard, 112n
Cowan, Alison Leigh, 152n
Cowell, Wayne R., 82n
Cragun, Donald W., 123n
Cray, Seymour, 81
Cray-1 computer, 81, 82, 109
Curtis, Kent, 80n, 87n, 88n

DARPA. See Defense Advanced
  Research Projects Agency
David, Edward E., Jr., 45n, 88n
Davies, Donald, 59n
Davis, Dwight B., 115n
Davis, Randall, 90n, 91n

DEC. *See* Digital Equipment Corporation
Defense, Department of, 43–44, 91;
   academic research funding, 46–47;
   IR&D funding, 94; math and computer
   science budget, 45. *See also* Defense
   Advanced Research Projects Agency;
   National Security Agency; Office of
   the Secretary of Defense
Defense Advanced Research Projects
   Agency (DARPA): advanced
   microelectronics research, 70–72;
   artificial intelligence research, 63–65;
   basic research, 54; computer networks
   involvement, 59–61; design aids
   research, 69; graphics, design, and
   productivity technology research, 68,
   69–70; Information Processing
   Techniques Office, 51, 52; intelligent
   sensor systems, 70; military research
   funding, 52–53, 96; semiconductors
   research, 71; and software
   development, 121, 123; Strategic
   Computing Initiative, 55, 64, 72–75,
   91, 105; timesharing projects, 55–58;
   university research funding, 55
Defense Communications Agency, 60
De Janvry, Alain, 40n
Demand, computer price elasticity, 29–31
DENDRAL system, NIH, 90
Denicoff, Marvin, 63n
Denning, Peter J., 57n
Dertouzos, Michael L., 63n
Dethier, Jean-Jacques, 40n
Dickson, David, 168n
Diewert, W. E., 213n
Digital Equipment Corporation (DEC),
   52; artificial intelligence research, 63n;
   timesharing system, 58; VAXcluster
   system, 67
DOE. *See* Energy, Department of
Dorn, Fred W., 82n
Dorn, Philip H., 113n
Dornheim, Michael A., 68n
Dosi, Giovanni, 156n
Draheim, Kirk, 107n
Dunning, John H., 1n

EC. *See* European Community
Economies of scale, 13, 15, 37
EDP. *See* Electronics data processing
   program
Eisner, Robert, 112n
Electronic Computer Technology
   Research Association, Japan, 127
Electronic data processing (EDP)
   program, West Germany, 154,157–59

Electronics equipment, 1; data standards
   for design information, 119; integration
   with computer and communications
   equipment, 6
Electronics Industry Act of *1957*, Japan,
   129
Electrotechnical Laboratory (ETL),
   Japan, 126, 130, 248; high-performance
   components, 127; internal research
   activity, 137
Elson, Benjamin M., 68n, 123n
Energy, Department of (DOE), 79, 81, 82
Engineering Research Associates (ERA),
   82, 95, 107
ENIAC, 48, 78
Erman, Lee D., 64n
Esprit program, EC, 143, 164
ETHERNET system, 60, 61n, 63n
ETL. *See* Electrotechnical Laboratory
Eureka program, EC, 165
Europe: competition among computer
   producers, 153–54; government ·
   funding for computer R&D, 160–63;
   trade in technology-intensive products,
   1. *See also* France; United Kingdom;
   West Germany
European Community (EC): cooperative
   projects among computer producers,
   166; Esprit program, 143, 164; Eureka
   program, 165; and IBM, 113–14, 168;
   RACE program, 164; tax policies
   favoring computer producers, 167–68
Evanczuk, Stephen, 65n
Evans, Bob O., 57n, 113n
Everett, Robert R., 69n

FACOM projects, Japan, 127
Falk, Howard, 66n
Fano, Robert M., 52n, 56n, 57n, 58n
Federal government: computer
   standards, 118–19; fiscal assistance to
   computer firms, 110–12; funding for
   basic computer-related research, 100–
   03; funding for computer R&D, 18, 43,
   95–100, 105, 179, 182; funding for
   mathematics and computer science
   research, 44–45; military research
   funding, 6–7, 43–44, 46, 97; patents for
   computer products, 120–21; purchases
   of computers by, 107–09; role in
   software development, 121–22; support
   for academic research, 46–47
Federally funded research and
   development centers (FFRDCs), 45n,
   101, 244
Feigenbaum, Edward A., 64n, 85n, 90n

Fennell, Joseph, 86n, 87n
Fernbach, Sidney, 65n, 80n, 81n
FFRDCs. *See* Federally funded research and development centers
Fifth Generation program, Japan, 72, 114, 152, 176; described, 142–43; foreign reaction to, 180
Filière Electronique R&D program, France, 165
Fischetti, Mark A., 68n
Fisher, Franklin M., 50n, 57n, 80n, 234n
Flamm, Kenneth, 7n, 10n, 18n, 48n, 113n, 135n, 194n, 209n, 240n
Flanagan, Patrick James, 120n
Floud, Roderick, 9n
Flynn, Michael J., 21n
Fong, Glen R., 78n, 194n
FONTAC project, Japan, 127, 130
Foy, Nancy, 166n
France: computer market, 174–75, 181; government computer procurement, 167; government funding for computer R&D, 160, 162, 163, 165, 176–77; government subsidies, 156–57; Plan Calcul, 154, 156; tax policies favoring R&D, 168
Franken, Peter, 56n
Fraser, A., 61n
Freiherr, Gregory, 90n, 91n
Frenkel, Karen A., 65n
Fuchi, Kazuhiro, 143, 152
Fujitsu, 127, 131; leasing operations, 146; R&D expenditures, 141
Fullerton, Don, 111n
Fuss, Dieter, 82n
Future Electron Device Research Association, Japan, 152

Gage, John, 123n
Gallagher, Robert T., 114n, 166n
Gallium arsenide (GaAs), technology, 71–72, 77
General Agreement on Tariffs and Trade (GATT), Government Procurement Code, 144, 167
General Electric, 57, 131
Gibson, Richard, 179n
Glauthier, T. James, 58n
Goldstine, Herman H., 79n
Gordon, Theodore J., 22n
Gosch, John, 159n, 164n, 166n
Graham, Daniel A., 17n
Graphics technology, 68, 69
Gray, Martha Mulford, 108n
Greenwood, Joen E., 50n
Gresser, Julian, 143n

Griliches, Zvi, 34n, 40n, 184n, 228n, 233n
Gross national product (GNP): benefits from computers as percent of, 34–35; computer rental value as percent of, 34; implicit price deflator, 24, 28n; information processing capacity per dollar of, 30
Grunwald, Joseph, 194n
Gullo, Karen, 179n

Hall, Bronwyn H., 233n
Halloran, Richard, 77n
Hamblen, John, 88n
Hard disk moving-head file, 25–26, 214
Harding, William E., 234n
Hausman, Jerry A., 233n
Hecker, Daniel E., 4n
Helm, Leslie Donald, 146n, 152n
Henry, David K., 108n
Heron, S. D., 8n
High technology: defined, 4; economic arguments in support of, 15–17; international market for, 17–18. *See also* Technology policy, national
Hills, Jill, 204n
Hilton, Barry, 142n
Hitachi, 129, 131; leasing operations, 146; R&D expenditures, 141
Hitch, Charles J., 8n
Hockney, R. W., 21n, 66n, 71n, 81n
Holzman, Albert G., 56n
Honda, T., 137n
Honeywell-Bull, 75, 96, 97, 98n, 179n; merger with CII, 156; military research, 99n
Hord, R. Michael, 66n
Horst, Thomas, 12n
Houston Area Research Consortium, 179n
Hout, Thomas M., 146n, 152n
Howell, Richard P., 107n
Howlett, J., 69n, 79n
Hudson, Richard L., 166n
Hughes, Kirsty S., 12n
Hulten, Charles R., 111n

IBM, 50n, 84; agreement with EC, 113–14; agreement with MITI, 152; antitrust action against, 113; artificial intelligence research, 63n; computer manufacturing base in Japan, 126; EC action against, 168; foreign market, 175, 176; government funding for, 95; R&D investment, 105–06, 240–41; and SAGE System, 49; share of federal

computer market, 108; Stretch supercomputer, 49, 80; System *360*, 10, 27, 50n, 95, 127; System *370*, 131
Ichbiah, Jean, 75n
ICL. *See* International Computers Limited
ICOT. *See* Institute for New Generation Computer Technology
ILLIAC I, 79
ILLIAC IV supercomputer, 45, 48, 64, 66, 83, 84
Imada, Ken, 143n
Imai, James K., 144n
Independent research and development (IR&D), 94
Information processing (IP) capacity: bandwidth to measure speed of, 207–08; implicit quantity index for total U.S., 30; cost, 23, 223; Kuck model of, 208–09; price elasticity of demand for, 31–32; rental value, 224–25; social benefits from declining cost of, 32–35
Information Processing Techniques Office, 51, 52. *See also* Defense Advanced Research Projects Agency
Information Technology Promotion Agency, Japan, 130, 136
Innovation: applied research projects for, 183; capture rate, 37–39, 41; consumer benefits from, 33–34, 223; government support for, 181; market structure with sustainable, 237–39; models of, 15; monopoly power through, 12–13, 228; rents to finance, 13, 17. *See also* Research and development
Input-output peripheral equipment, 19; prices, 25–26. *See also* Hard disk moving-head file; Line printer; Magnetic tape storage; Punched card equipment
Institute for Defense Analysis, 50
Institute for New Generation Computer Technology (ICOT), Japan, 142–43, 152
Institute for Advanced Studies, 48, 79
Integrated circuit development: Europe, 164, 171–72; Japan, 128, 171; U.S., 6, 77–78, 119, 172
International Computers Limited (ICL), United Kingdom, 154,159–60
INTERNIST system, NIH, 91
Investment, computer-related R&D: for basic research versus innovation, 183–84; effective tax rate on, 110–11; private versus social returns on, 35–39, 41, 180; returns from domestic

versus foreign sales, 36–37, 39, 41, 235–37; tax credits on, 112; and technological progress, 36
IPTO. *See* Information Processing Techniques Office
IR&D. *See* Independent research and development
Ishi, Hiromitsu, 149n
Ishii, Osamu, 127n, 129n
Iverson, Wesley R., 115n

Jackey, Jonathan, 72n
Jacobsen, Stephen E., 34n
Janow, Merit E., 130n
Japan, 1, 2; cooperative research ventures, 114, 127, 128, 131, 134–36, 151–52, 179; efforts to obtain U.S. computer technology, 175–76; and Multics development, 57; private industrial research associations, 130; software industry, 77n, 130–31; synchrotron research, 202, 205; trade policy, 126, 152–53. *See also* Computers, Japan; Research and development, computer-related Japanese
Japan Development Bank, 147, 149
Japan Electronic Computer Corporation (JECC), 144, 248, 254; financing of computer leases, 145–46, 147
Japan Robot Leasing Corporation, 146
JECC. *See* Japan Electronic Computer Corporation
Jécquier, Nicholas, 158n, 166n
Jesshope, C. R., 21n, 66n, 71n, 81n
Johnson, Chalmers, 145n
Johnson, George, 85n
Johnson, Howard, 56n
Johnson, Jan, 72n
Johnson, Lyndon B., 87
Joint Research and Development Act, *1984*, 114
Joint Software Development Corporation, Japan, 136
Jovial language, 76
Jublin, Jacques, 157n

Kahn, Robert E., 52n, 60n
Kaplan, Eugene J., 130n
Katz, Michael L., 114n
Kelley, Clint, 73
Kennedy, John F., 51, 52
Kent, Allen, 56n
Kerrebrock, Jack L., 84n
Keyes, Robert W., 71n
Kimura, Tosaku, 126n

Kirchner, Jake, 73n
Klass, Philip J., 73n
Klein, Burton H., 8n
Kleinrock, Leonard, 22n
Knight, Kenneth E., 22n, 28
Kuck, David J., 207n; computer model, 208–09
Kurushima, Morihiro, 129n

Lampson, B. W., 58n
Landau, Ralph, 197n
Landis, Carolyn, 88n
Languages, computer, 63n, 65, 75–76
LANs. *See* Local area networks
LARC computer, 80
Lau, Lawrence J., 213n
Lawrence, Robert Z., 112n
Lawrence Livermore Laboratory, 48n, 80, 81, 83, 244
Le Boucher, Eric, 156n
Lederberg, Joshua, 90
Leopold, George, 76n, 190n
Lerner, Eric J., 51n
Levy, David M., 184n
Lichtenberg, Frank R., 184n, 191, 192n
Lichtenberger, W. W., 58n
Licklider, J. C. R., 51, 52n, 55, 63n, 64n, 69
Lightning, Project, 49–50
Lincoln, Edward J., 135n
Lincoln labs, 64, 68
Lindamood, George E., 128n, 130n
Lindgren, Nilo A., 49n, 52n, 69n
Lineback, J. Robert, 67n, 115n
Line printer: price, 26; speed, 212, 219
Lisp language, 63n, 65, 67n
Lloyd, Andrew, 166n
Local area networks (LANs), 60, 81
Lorenzi, Jean-Hervé, 156
Los Alamos National Laboratory, 79, 80, 82, 83, 244
Lubeck, Olaf, 178n
LUNAR system, 85
Lynn, Leonard, 70n, 135n
Lyon, Andrew B., 111n

McCarthy, John, 52n, 56n
McCloskey, Donald N., 9n
McCormick, B. H., 80n
McGowan, John J., 50n
McKean, Roland N., 8n
McKie, James W., 50n, 57n, 80n, 234n
McNamara, John E., 22n, 58n, 67n, 207n
MacNeal, Richard H., 85n
Machine tool industries, computer-controlled, 48–49

MAC Project, 56–58, 69, 117
Magaziner, Ira C., 146n, 152n
Magnetic tapes, testing and standards for, 118–19
Magnetic tape storage: bandwidth, 212; price, 26
Mancke, Richard B., 50n, 57n, 80n, 234n
MANIAC computer, 79
Mansfield, Edwin, 12n, 16n, 39, 40n, 111n, 112n, 184n, 192n, 228n, 234n
Mansfield Amendment, 88
Manuel, Tom, 63n, 65n, 66n
Manufacturing Automation Protocol (MAP), 120n
Marcom, John, Jr., 113n
Market, computer: cooperative research undertakings, 114–18; entry, 37–38, 42–43; foreign, 10–11, 17; government policies regulating, 113–14; growth, 9–10, 181; international competition for, 174, 178, 179; R&D investment return from sales, 36–37; returns from domestic versus foreign, 225, 235–37; social return and structure of, 230–32; sustainable innovation and, 237–39
Markoff, John, 70n
Marsh, Alton K., 72n, 85n
Marshall, A. W., 8n
Martin, Edith W., 76n
Massachusetts Institute of Technology (MIT): DARPA funds for, 55, 62; government-supported computer research projects, 95; robotics research, 70; and SAGE system, 49; timesharing system, 56–58; Whirlwind computer, 49
Maugh, Thomas H., II, 118n
MCC. *See* Microelectronics and Computer Technology Corporation
Meckling, W. H., 8n
Memory, computer internal: cache, 211; function, 20; improvements in, 21; prices, 22, 25, 26; speed, 209, 211–12, 214; technology, 25–26
Mendez, Raul, 178n
Meyers, Edith, 65n
Metcalfe, R., 61n
Metropolis, N., 69n, 79n
Microelectronics, advanced, 70–72
Microelectronics and Computer Technology Corporation (MCC), 114–16
Military sector: commercial spinoffs from funding by, 192; computer development funding by, 43–44, 173, 176, 177; political pressure for

technology development support by, 189–90; R&D expenditures, 6; technological origins from, 7, 14–15, 203

Miller, Steve, 70n

Millstein, James, 110n

Minasian, Jora R., 8n

Minc, Alain, 156n

Ministry of Education, Japan, 126, 141

Ministry of Trade and Industry (MITI), Japan, 248; agreement with IBM, 152; basic research, 141–42; and cooperative international research, 175–76; early role in computer production, 126–27; R&D subsidies, 129–30, 139–40; research funding, early 1970s, 131, 134–36; SHPEC project, 128, 129; synchrontron project, 202

MIT. See Massachusetts Institute of Technology

MITI. See Ministry of Trade and Industry

Mitterrand, François, 156

Monopoly power, innovation and, 12–13, 228

Monroe, Linda, 67n

Moon, Donald L., 74n

Moore, James, 178n

Moran, Theodore H., 12n

Morrison, Steven A., 238n

Moses, Joel, 63n

MOSIS system, 70, 71

Mudge, J. Craig, 22n, 58n, 67n, 207n

Multics system, 57

Munson, T. R., 22n

Murray, Thomas J., 244n

MYCIN system, NIH, 90

Nadiri, M. Ishaq, 40n, 192n

Naegele, Tobias, 68n, 194n

Nagel, Laurence W., 70n

NASA. See National Aeronautics and Space Administration

National Advanced Scientific Computing Centers, 89

National Aeronautics and Space Administration (NASA), 92; computer research funding, 45–46; IR&D funding, 94; software development, 84–85

National Bureau of Standards (NBS), 44, 48, 86n; applied research, 200; magnetic tape testing, 119

National Institutes of Health (NIH), computer applications and software, 90–91

National laboratories, 244; computers for nuclear research, 79; software development, 82; supercomputers, 81

National Science Foundation (NSF), 44, 45, 56, 85; academic research funding, 46–47, 86–87; applied R&D expenditures, 101; computer research support, 88, 92; data on R&D funding, 241; joint industry-government-university program, 118; role in national technology policy, 195–96; supercomputing centers, 179

National Security Agency (NSA): computer development program, 49–51; magnetic tape testing and standards, 118–19

National Technology Office (NTO), proposed: function, 199; personnel for, 199–200; potential role in synchrotron research, 201–02; purpose, 198

NBS. See National Bureau of Standards

Neff, Robert, 141n

Nelson, Richard R., 8n, 14n, 197n

Networks: circuit-switched, 58n; described, 58; local area, 60, 81; packet-switched, 59

Nevins, J., 203n

Newell, Allen, 22n, 67n, 81n, 84n, 86n, 207n

Newman, Robert, 51

Newton, A. R., 119n

New York University, Ultracomputer research project, 68

NIH. See National Institutes of Health

Nilsson, Nils J., 64n, 85n

Nippon Electric Corporation, 127, 128, 129

Nippon Telephone and Telegraph (NTT), 126, 175, 248; basic research, 141–42; DIPS project, 129, 131; research expenditures, 137, 139, 169

Nisenoff, N., 10n

Nixdorf, 158

Noble, David F., 49n

Nora, Simon, 156n

Norris, William C., 83n, 115n

NSA. See National Security Agency

NSF. See National Science Foundation

NTO. See National Technology Office

NTT. See Nippon Telephone and Telegraph

OCTOPUS system, 81

OECD. See Organization for Economic Cooperation and Development

Office of Management and Budget, 87

Office of Naval Research, 47–48, 86n
Office of the Secretary of Defense (OSD), 52; silicon semiconductor technology, 77–78; software programs, 75–77
Olmos, David, 71n
O'Neill, R. W., 96n
Open system interconnection (OSI) standard, 166
Oppenheimer, Alan, 56n
Organization for Economic Cooperation and Development (OECD), 103, 241
OSD. *See* Office of the Secretary of Defense
Osgood, Donna, 70n

Pakes, Ariel, 233n, 234n
Pantages, Angeline, 166n
Panzar, John C., 238n
Pasztor, Andy, 113n
Patents, computer products, 120–21
Patrick, Hugh, 149n
Peacock, Alan, 167n
Peck, Merton J., 8n, 115n
Penick, James L., Jr., 14n
Pepper, Thomas, 130n
Perlis, Alan J., 86n
Perry, Tekla, 63n
Peterson, Victor L., 84n
Philco, 49, 50n
Philips, 159, 164
Phister, Montgomery, Jr., 34n, 210n, 214n, 219
Pinkston, John T., 115n
Pirtle, M. W., 58n
Plan Calcul, France, 154, 156, 160
Poe, Robert, 179n
Pogran, Kenneth T., 61n
Pollack, Andrew, 114n, 116n
Prendergast, Karen A., 61n, 91n
President's Commission on Industrial Competitiveness, 200
Prices, computer: box, 27–28, 220; computer characteristics and, 22–23, 222; computer component costs and, 22, 23–24, 214–15; decline, 25–29; and demand, 29–32; social benefits from declining, 33–35; technological progress and, 21, 27, 32; total price index relation to, 24
Prince, M. David, 69n
Procurement, government computer: European, 166–68; Japanese, 143–46; as policy instrument, 178; U.S., 107–09, 179
PUFF system, NIH, 90

Pugh, Emerson W., 25n, 50n
Punched card equipment, 26, 210
Pyatt, Rudolph A., Jr., 51n

Quatrepoint, Jean-Michel, 157n

RACE program, EC, 164
Ralston, Anthony, 22n
Rand, Michael B., 63n
Rand Corporation, 69, 121
Rand, Project, 79
Raun, Laura, 159n
RCA, 50n, 96, 131, 158
Reddy, Raj, 63n, 64n
Reed, David P., 61n
Rees, Mina, 47n
Reinganum, Jennifer, 13n
Rents, technological, 1, 3; capture rate, 37–39, 41, 228; to finance innovations, 13, 17; to finance R&D, 36–37; value of computer stocks, 34
Research and development (R&D): basic versus applied, 183–84; case study versus statistical analysis of, 191; fixed "sunk cost" nature of, 13; government support for military applications, 6–7; high-technology products, 4–5; market power through expenditures for, 15–16; percentage of expenditures for research, 100; tax credit for, 187–88. *See also* Research and development, computer-related Japanese; Research and development, computer-related U.S.
Research and development, computer-related Japanese: cooperative ventures for, 114, 127, 128, 131, 134–36; government funding for, 128–29, 130–31, 135–36, 139, 177; information-processing, 134, 139, 141; by private companies, 134, 140–41; by public sector, 136–37, 139; tax benefits for, 147, 151, 171, 177–78
Research and development, computer-related U.S., 19; computer cost decline and, 32–33; consumer benefits from, 33–34, 36, 223; defined, 101; federal funding to industry for, 18, 43, 95–100, 105, 179–80, 182, 241; in government laboratories, 79, 81, 82, 244; international aspects of, 12; nonindustrial, 243–44; as percent of sales, 4–5; privately funded, 95, 100, 103, 240–41; tax treatment, 110–12; total expenditures on, 242. *See also* Investment, computer-related

Riche, Richard W., 4n
Roberts, Lawrence G., 59n, 60
Robertson, James E., 79n, 80n
Robertson, James W., 111n
Robinson, Arthur L., 71n
Robinson, Phillip, 70n
Robotics, 49, 63, 70, 146
Romeo, Anthony, 12n
Rose, Craig D., 68n
Rose, Peter, 201n
Rosenberg, Nathan, 197n
Rosenberg, Robert, 64n, 68n
Rosovsky, Henry, 149n
Rota, Gian-Carlo, 69n, 79n
Rugman, Alan M., 1n
Ruina, Jack, 54n

SAGE air defense system, 48, 49, 68,
    177; funding for, 174; role in software
    development, 121–22
Sammet, Jean E., 76n
Sanger, David E., 77n, 114n, 115n, 116n,
    118n
Sangiovanni-Vincentelli, A. L., 119n
Sauer, Charles H., 207n
Schankerman, Mark, 233n, 234n
Schatz, Willie, 72n, 73n, 113n, 178n
Scherer, Frederic M., 8n, 235
Schlaifer, Robert, 8n
Schmalensee, Richard, 34n
Schneck, Paul B., 68n
Schneiderman, Ron, 123n
Schrage, Michael, 51n, 72n, 74n, 116n
Schumpeter, Joseph A., 12–13
SCOOP Project, 48
SDI. See Strategic Defense Initiative
Seaberry, Jane, 21n
Seifert, William E., 61n
Semiconductor Industry Association, 117
Semiconductor Research Corporation,
    116, 117
Semiconductors: cooperative research
    for, 116; cost, 25; DOD support for
    research on, 71; French, 156;
    Japanese, 128–29; silicon, 77–78
Serial design, computer. See Von
    Neumann design
Shapero, Albert, 107n
Sharpe, William F., 28n
SHPEC project, Japan, 128, 129
Siemens, West Germany, 154; funds for
    EDP program, 157–59
Siewiorek, Daniel P., 22n, 67n, 81n, 84n,
    207n
Simon, Herbert A., 86n
Single instruction stream, single data

stream (SISD) computer. See Von
    Neumann design
Slotnick, Daniel, 65–66
Slutz, Ralph J., 79n
Smith, Kevin, 160n
Smith, R. Jeffrey, 77n
Snyder, Samuel S., 50n, 119n
Softech, 69
Software: federal role in, U.S., 121–23;
    Japanese, 77n, 130–31; NASA
    development program, 84, 85; OSD
    development, 75–76; patent protection,
    120–21
Software Productivity Consortium, 116
SOLOMON computer, 48n, 66
Spence, Michael, 114n
Sperry Rand, 49, 80, 97, 98n, 99
Spinrad, Robert, 58n, 63n, 80n
SRI International, 55, 69; artificial
    language research, 63; SUR projects,
    64
Stanford University, 55, 63, 90
STAR computer, 84
Stefik, Mark, 74n
Stein, Kenneth J., 74n
Stevenson-Wydler Technology
    Innovation Act of 1980, 198
Stipp, David, 116
Stone, Harold S., 207n, 213n
Stoneman, Paul, 29, 167n, 222n
Stowsky, Jay, 194n
Strategic Computing Initiative, DARPA,
    55, 64, 91; application, 73–74;
    objective, 72–73; industry funding for,
    75
Strategic Defense Initiative (SDI), 77, 91
Stretch supercomputer, 49, 80
Subsidies, computer industry, 154, 178;
    British, 159–60, 168; French, 156–57;
    Japanese, 129–30, 136, 139–40, 141;
    U.S., 111, 141; West German, 157–59,
    168
SUMEX facility, NIH, 90, 91
Supercomputers, 65n, 92; AEC program
    for development, 80; Control Data
    Corporation, 80–82; federal
    government purchases of, 109; gallium
    arsenide technology for, 71–72;
    Japanese, 128, 129, 178–79
Supercomputing Research Center, NSA,
    50
SUR projects, 64
Sutherland, I., 68–69
Suzuki, Kazuyuki, 40n, 137n
Suzuki, Yoshio, 149n
Swardson, Anne, 112n

Swarztrauber, Paul N., 87n
Switzer, Lorne, 112n
Synchrotron research, 201–02, 205
Systems Development Corporation, 55;
    timesharing systems, 56, 58

Tagliabue, John, 165n
Targeting policies, computer: competitive
    advantage from, 168; cycles in, 170;
    European, 164–66; international
    comparison, 169–70; Japanese, 125,
    169; U.S., 125
Tariffs, 152, 153, 167
Tarui, Yasuo, 128n
Tate, Paul, 114n
Tax policies, to encourage computer
    development: European, 167–68;
    Japanese, 147, 151, 171, 177–78
Tax system, U.S.: to encourage
    computer-related investment, 110–11;
    to encourage proposed national
    technology policy, 197; tax credits for
    R&D, 112
Taylor, Robert, 63n
Technological progress, computer:
    computer R&D investments and, 35–
    36; computing power costs and, 21, 27,
    32; protection of, 12; social benefits
    from, 33–35
Technology-intensive manufactures: firm
    size and, 13–14; international
    comparison, 1–2; proposed incentives
    for, 3; tax policy to encourage, 111.
    See also High technology
Technology policy, national: arguments
    for public support for, 186–88; civilian
    versus military support for, 189–94;
    combined cooperation and competition
    in, 188; diversity in funding for, 188–
    89; NSF role in, 195–96; proposed,
    196–98; proposed National Technology
    Office to monitor, 198–201; proposed
    reciprocity in research and markets,
    204–06
Terleckyj, Nestor E., 184n
Texas Instruments, 66n, 185–86
Thornton, James, 81n
3.5 Generation computer, Japan, 27, 135
Tilton, John E., 110n, 128n
Timesharing computer systems, 51;
    compatible, 56; Cray system, 82;
    described, 55; multiple access, 56–58;
    networks as extension of, 58–59;
    precondition for artificial intelligence
    research, 63
Tojo, Akio, 128n

Trade: high technology and conflicts in,
    17; Japanese barriers, 126; and tariffs,
    152, 153, 167; in technology-intensive
    products, 1
Triplett, Jack E., 23n, 222n
Tull, Carol G., 82n
Turin, G., 203n

Unidata, 159
United Kingdom: Alvey program, 143,
    165, 171; computer market, 174–75;
    government computer procurement,
    167; government funding for computer
    R&D, 159–60, 162; ICL, 154; tax
    policies favoring R&D, 168
UNIVAC, 48, 79
University-based research, 46–47, 55,
    191
University of California, Berkeley, 55
University of Michigan, 55
University of Tokyo, 126
University of Utah, 55
UNIX system, 57, 123, 166
U.S. Air Force: Project Rand, 79; SAGE
    air defense system, 48–49, 68, 121–22,
    174, 177
U.S. Army: Ballistic Research
    Laboratories Electronic Scientific
    Computer, 48
U.S. International Trade Commission, 17
Uyehara, Cecil H., 70n

Verity, John W., 72n, 73n, 113n, 114n
Vernon, John M., 17n
VHSIC (very high speed integrated
    circuit) program, 77–78, 119, 172
Vickers, John, 13n
Vizachero, Rick, 123n
VLSI (very large scale integrated
    circuits), 151, 164
Von Neumann design, 20–21, 25, 211
Von Tunzelmann, G. N., 9n

Wagner, Samuel, 12n
Waldrop, M. Mitchell, 63n, 65n, 72n,
    74n, 75n
Wallace, Bob, 120n
Waller, Larry, 72n
Wallich, Paul, 63n, 70n
Walsh, John, 117n
Waxman, Ron, 119n
Webber, Bonnie Lynn, 64n, 85n
Weik, Martin H., 48n, 80n
Welke, H. J., 139n
Wells, John Varick, 107n
Wengler, John, 78n

West Germany: computer market, 174–75; EDP program, 154, 157–59; government computer procurement, 167; government funding for computer R&D, 162–63, 165, 177; government subsidies for computer technology, 157–59; tax policy favoring R&D, 168

Wheeler, Jimmy W., 130n

Whirlwind computer, 49, 68

White, Lawrence J., 114n

Wieder, H., 203n

Wildes, Karl L., 49n, 52n, 69n

Williamson, David L., 87n

Willig, Robert D., 33n, 238n

Winston, Clifford, 238n

Winston, Patrick H., 61n, 90n

Wolff, Edward N., 29n, 40n, 192n

Wood, Lowell, 84n

Wynter, Leon E., 69n

Xerox, 61n, 63, 131

X/Open group, for international UNIX system standard, 166

Yasaki, Edward K., 142n

Yoder, Stephen Kreider, 120n

Zschau, Ed, 72n

Zue, Victor, 63n, 64n

Zysman, John, 157n